A Call to the Nations

Warning Signals for the Coming Russian Exodus

Lilli Myss, MA

Prov 24, 11-12

Lilli Myss

New Wine Press

New Wine Press　　　　　Christian Friends of Israel (UK)
PO Box 17　　　　　　　PO Box 2687
Chichester　　　　　　　Eastbourne
England PO20 6YB　　　　England BN22 7LZ

The Scripture quotations in this book are taken from The New
International Version (NIV) Study Bible by Zondervan Publishers (1985),
unless otherwise specified.

ISBN: 1 874367 92 2

Statistics
I am grateful to the Israeli Government Statistics Office for their valuable
help in providing statistical material. However, it should be understood
that statistics given in this book, particularly from the 1930s, are from
various sources and reflect the incomplete information available. The
refugees' country of origin (the Reich) seldom recorded all cases of
emigration, particularly after *Kristallnacht*, and the forced expulsion in
November 1938, as it was impossible to keep track of such data.
Furthermore, there was no specific record-keeping by either governments
or refugee organisations of the actual number of refugees, in either
Germany, Great Britain or other European countries.

Typeset by CRB Associates, Reepham, Norfolk.
Printed in England by Clays Ltd, St Ives plc.

*This book is dedicated to my Jewish friends
who have taught me so much about Israel and her people.*

*I would like to extend my grateful thanks
to all who have helped me prepare the manuscript:
Valerie Lockhart, Patricia Russell and particularly
Alison Marchant for her valuable support and
many, many hours of work. Also to Derek White of
Christian Friends of Israel (UK) for making this book a reality.*

Contents

Foreword   11

Chapter 1   How It All Began For Me   13

Prelude to the Holocaust   19

Chapter 2   The Abandonment of German Jewry in the
1930s   22

Setting the Scene   22
German Jews and Nazism

Persecution of the Jews Begins in Germany   25
Antisemitic Laws of 1933
Second Phase: the Nuremberg Laws of 1935
The Difficult Task of the High Commissioner
The Olympic Games in Berlin – the Silent Consent
Germany's Assault on Austria – 1938
The Nations' Gamble over German Jewry at Evian
What was Accomplished at Evian?
Annexation of the Sudentenland – 1938
Czechs to London
Increased Nazi Actions Against the Jews – the
    Horror of *Kristallnacht*, 1938
London's Response to the Stepped-up Persecution
Final Annexation of Czechoslovakia – Spring 1939
A Last Attempt to Save Jewish Lives
In Search of a Homeland

**Responses in the British Empire to Jewish
Immigration**   49
The British Colonies – Jews Not Wanted!
Jews to Africa?
The Dominions

The Mandate of Palestine   53
The Struggle for a 'Jewish Homeland'
The Balfour Declaration

The 'Jewish Homeland' Sliced
Arab Attempt to Cut Jewish Immigration
The Hardship of European Jewry Increases
Illegal Arab Immigration to Palestine
Arab Rebellion Erupts Again

Palestine – Jews Not Wanted!   60
The Peel Commission – 1937
The Woodhead Commission – 1938
Britain Makes Her Own Decision
The Catastrophic White Paper – 1939
Illegal Immigration
The Last Hope Quenched
Summary: Britain's Response to the Plight of
    German Jewish Refugees

*Other Nations' Response to the German
Jewish Refugee Problem*   67
France
Belgium and the Netherlands
Switzerland

The United States   76
The Shortcomings of American Jewry

Scandinavian Responses   79
The Jewish Rescue in 1943
Wallenberg's Unique Rescue
Finland Also Gives Protection

Italy and the Vatican   83
The Vatican

The Soviet Union   86
The Tragedy of Babi Yar
Summary: the Staggering Loss

What Might the Western Allies Have Done?   91

Chapter 3   Antisemitism and the Persecution of
              Russian Jewry   94

Ancient Antisemitism in Europe   94
Antisemitism in Europe During the Middle Ages

Tsarist Persecution and Pogroms Against Jews   98
In the Middle Ages
Hardship in Poland
Russia Re-opened for Jews in the Eighteenth
    Century
Phase I: 1791–1881
The 'Classification' Plan

Two Ways of Jewish Life
  1. The Hasidism
  2. The Haskalah
The Jew in Tsarist Literature
Intensification of the Persecution
Phase II: 1881–1917
May Laws and Pogroms
The Growing Workers' Union
Pogroms Climaxing
The Tsar Forced to Yield – the First Duma

The Depravity of the Tsarist Government   108
The Infamous Forgery: the Protocols of the Elders
    of Zion
The Beilis Trial
Winds of Freedom Blow over Russia – Jewish
    Philosophers of Russia
Propagation of Zionism
Herzl and the Jewish State
Fleeing from Russia
Russian Emigrants to Zion
World War I

*The Revolution and Persecution of Jews under
Communism*   114
Lenin at the Top
Jewish Communists Forsake Their Own Heritage
The New Economic Period
Killing Russian Landowners
The 'Golden Period' for Jewish Culture
Jews to Colonise Birobidzan in East Siberia?
Stalin's Purges
More Antisemitism under Stalin
World War II
Communist Attitudes Towards its Own People
Communist Attitudes Towards the Jews
The Last Years of Stalin
Kruschev – a Softening of the Political Climate
Jewish Emigration to the West under Brezhnev
'Let My People Go' Movement
The Right to Leave the Country
The Battle of Human Rights Activists
Refusenik Life in the 1970s
The Notorious Leningrad Trial
Soviet Agrees Not to Violate Human Rights – 1975
Emigration Resumed after 1975
Emigration of Other Ethnic Groups
'Prisoners of Zion'
The Cooling of the Emigration Climate

Oppressive Communism in the 1980s – Andropov
Antisemitism Crops up Again
Oppression of its Own People
Refusenik Life During the 1980s
The State-Secret Clause
Hebrew Language Learning Forbidden
Increasing Emigration Difficulties
Chemenko
The Growing, 'Drop-Out' Problem in the 1980s

The First Reformer: Gorbachev and Glasnost   141
Dark Clouds Spread – Glasnost
Sakharov the Human Rights Advocate
Amnesty Declared
Antisemitism from the 'Pamyat' Group
Emigration Policy – Intervention from the West
Western Human Rights Activists to Moscow

The Big Emigration Wave of the 1990s   147
The Attempted Revolt Against Glasnost

The Second Reformer: Boris Yeltsin   149
Russia's Shortcomings in Human Rights
The Political Battle over Russia's Future
Russian Roulette
The Last Two Emigration Waves In Retrospect
Two Views on Russian Emigration

**Russia and Human Rights – the Reverse Side
of Communism**   158

Chapter 4   The Biblical Aspect of the Exodus to Israel,
the Jewish Homeland   162

The Scattering of the Jewish People   162

Restoration of the Land   166
Key Prophecies Fulfilled
The Regathering of the Jews

The Pattern of a Biblical Exodus   174
The Return of the Jews in Our Time
From the East...
From the West...
   Europe and North America
   Morocco
   Algeria
From the South...
To the North...

The Major Exodus to Come   184
The Timing of the Exodus

Previous Emigration Waves from 'the North Country'
How Many Jews Will Come?

God Calls for Involvement of the Nations 188
'My People' *versus* 'the Nations'
The Abrahamic Blessing

Christian Response to the Exodus 192

Opposition to a Jewish Return (Islam) 193

What Might Lie Ahead for Russian Jews 199
Why Don't the Jews Flee the Country?
Is a Significant Emigration of Russians on the Way?

Early Warning Signals of a New Emigration Wave 202
Anticipation in Scandinavian Countries
Anticipating the Coming Emigration Wave

The Last Wars – the End in Sight! 209
The Gog-Magog War
Other Invaders in the Trail of Gog-Magog
The Final Battle of This Age
God's Judgement Expressed

The Hope of Israel – and for the Nations 219
The Only Hope for the Nations

Epilogue 222

Lessons from the Holocaust 222
The Rescuers

Organisations Involved in Supporting the Exodus Movement 225

A Personal Postscript –
My Auschwitz Experience 229

Appendices

I Statistics 231

II Jewish Population in Europe and Other Countries Around 1933 232

III Countries Invited to the Evian Refugee Conference 1938 234

IV Jewish Emigration and Immigration   235
    Table 1: Jewish Emigration from Central Europe
    1933–1939
    Table 2: Jewish Immigration to Palestine 1930–
    1939

 V Estimated Number of Jews Killed in the
    Final Solution   236

VI The Nations Vote in the UN for the
    Establishment of Israel in 1947   238

VII The Six Wars Against Israel from 1948   239

VIII The World Jewish Population   242

IX Jewish Emigration from the Former USSR
    1954–1998   243

    Notes and Bibliography   244

Foreword

I have known Lilli Myss since 1981. Those were the days of almost zero emigration from the USSR, of oppression of Soviet Jews and of refuseniks. They were the days of long-term imprisonment of Jewish activists, and of world-wide lobbying both by Jews and Christians for their release; and of the ceaseless efforts of the Women's Campaign for Soviet Jewry (The 35s) and of other groups.

I remember participating in demonstrations outside the Soviet Embassy in London, and carrying banners in Hyde Park, lobbying for the release of such outstanding figures as Ida Nudel and Anatoli Sharansky.

Lilli Myss was then living in Jerusalem, where I met her on my frequent visits, and where she produced a regular information letter concerning the situation of Jews in the USSR and of particular 'Prisoners of Zion'. Countless thousands of these letters went around the world to inform, and stimulate prayer and action.

Since the time of President Gorbachev the situation has changed, and there has been a period of unrestricted emigration from what is now Russia since the collapse of the Soviet Union. Dark clouds however are gathering on the horizon, and Lilli has known an increasing concern to 'sound a warning' about the future of the Jewish people in Russia. Her concern is crystallised in this book. It is more than an emotional appeal to become involved, it is a detailed history of the experience of the Jewish people in Europe and Russia, and is a sobering record of the shameful way the West has treated God's special people. The account of the free nations' refusal, at the Evian Conference in 1938, to help the German

Jewish refugees, is a sufficient example in which Britain amongst other free nations, stands guilty before God.

Unless we understand and learn from history we risk repeating the errors of the past. This book will require time and energy, but it is important if we are to act responsibly towards the Jewish people in this day of need, particularly as we see an increasing number of Jews coming out of Russia.

Derek White
Director
Christian Friends of Israel (UK)

Chapter 1

How It All Began For Me

On a sunny day in 1981, I was standing with other tourists in the Diaspora Museum in Tel Aviv. As with so many other visitors who come to Israel I was very moved by its unique history, its biblical background proved by archaeology, the huge diversity of nature displayed in this tiny country; and I admired the diligent pioneering spirit of the Jewish people in overcoming geographical obstacles.

Although I had grown up in Denmark under German army occupation during the Second World War, we were partly protected from the general disaster which overtook the European continent. As with many other young people at that time, I subsequently shunned the subject of war, and put it all behind me.

Now, as I stood in the Diaspora Museum in front of the memorial plaque for the Holocaust* victims, my eyes ran quickly across the inscription and I was stunned. I stopped in the middle of the sentence and reread it carefully. It said:

'In the year of 1933 of the *Christian era*,
Adolf Hitler came to power in Germany.
In his time Germans and their accomplices murdered
6 million Jews, among them $1\frac{1}{2}$ million children.
Imprisoned in ghettos, the victims fought desperately
for their lives, *while the world stood in silence.*'

Was it possible that the Allies and the people of so-called Christian Europe could have been apathetic to the German

---

* The meaning of the Hebrew word for holocaust indicates a 'burnt offering' or a complete destruction by fire of a person or animal.

Holocaust? Could such a thing take place again? If it did what would the response of Christians be in our generation? Would we still stand by in silence or would we act to support and protect the persecuted Jews?

Confronted by these thoughts, I started on a long, painful, mental journey to find out the truth. The thought took hold of me that even if history does not repeat itself precisely, there are still certain phenomena, which reappear with unswerving certainty – although disguised in new clothing, and using a different vocabulary. Would we recognise them and how would we react?

In retrospect, I began to understand how the Jews, who consider all Christians to be alike, could not in their great horror comprehend how such a genocide could take place in the heart of so-called Christian Europe, where they had lived for centuries. Moreover, a considerable number of the SS elite troops and many top-ranking Nazi leaders were at least nominal Christians. In his article *Who shall bear guilt for the Holocaust?* H. Feingold [1] states that over 42% of the SS elite troops and many of the leaders, including Hitler and Himmler, were at least nominal Catholics. Adolf Hitler died a Catholic, and a yearly mass is celebrated in his memory in Madrid; Hermann Goering was a Lutheran. [2]

A number of well-known post-war theologians, such as Karl Barth, R. Niebuhr, Fr Littell and Michael Ryan, have pointed out that the murder of European Jewry by baptised Christians places a critical question mark over the credibility of Christianity.

As we look back over the twentieth century, a number of historians would agree with the Jewish writer, Yehudi Bauer, that one of the major events in this century was the Holocaust. [3] It became a watershed for Western culture. With its dehumanisation of man by other men, who themselves had lost their humanity, not only was it a disaster for the Jews of Europe, but it became a tragedy for modern civilisation. With human depravity displayed, the whole world lost its confidence in the dignity of the West. This, possibly, is a most crucial warning signal for us today.

Now, more than fifty years later, we again see a number of issues in our society which remind us of the 1930s and conditions that led to World War II. In summary, the most significant are:

1. The instability of the money market. Even if the world gives evidence of much affluence, under the surface the money market is very shaky and may quickly crash, as we have seen in the late 1990s. This has been accompanied by sky-rocketing unemployment, giving rise to strikes and unrest. At the turn of the year 1996–97, over 20 million workers in Europe were without employment and without prospect of improvement in the near future.

2. Greater dependence upon the Arab world, not only for strategic purposes as in the late 1930s, but more so for politico-economic reasons to secure a continuous oil-supply to the major Western countries. A significant shift took place after the oil crisis in 1976, and in 1991 the fear of shortage of industrial oil in the West led the United States and Europe to enter the Gulf War against the Iraqi invasion of Kuwait, in order to ensure their oil supplies from Kuwait. The increasing Arab and Islamic influence in the Western world has indirectly led to a trade boycott of Israel.

3. Politically, there is a return to a stronger nationalism involving the danger of creating totalitarian regimes similar to the strong dictatorships in Europe in the 1930s. Since the war, we have seen dictatorial regimes develop in the new states: in East Germany under Eric Honecker and in Rumania under Nikolae Ceaucescu. After the fall of the Tito regime in former Yugoslavia, the Serbian President, Slobodan Milosevic, is trying to regain dictatorial power. Most recently, President Alexander Lukashenko has established himself autocratically in White Russia.

    The potential for the development of extreme nationalism in Russia is considerable due to continued economic crises and tensions between the many ethnic groups. If the government in the Kremlin were overturned, the main goal for a nationalist government would be to restore the image of Mother Russia, returning to the glory of Tsarist times by re-conquering the lost territories where the Slavic people once ruled. This might easily lead to a suppression of other minority groups, such as Jews.

4. Furthermore, nationalist movements or ultra-nationalism often bring heavy antisemitism. This too, is on the increase. Thus, the Institute of Soviet Jewish Affairs in London, declared that by 1991 antisemitism had already reached a post-World War II peak. A document covering sixty countries, pointed out that Russia, Poland, Hungary and Rumania were the most dangerous ones, as both members of mainstream parties, as well as the policies of many parties themselves, were antisemitic.

    Another worrying trend is Islam's rising power in North America and Europe through Moslem immigration and the increasing Arab influence on the economic market. These are factors that promote an 'Islamization of antisemitism' not only in the Arab and Moslem world, but also in countries where they gain influence.

5. In the religious world, the German higher biblical criticism of the 1930s which led to a questioning of scripture and the general discarding of the Old Testament, caused a lack of understanding of Israel and its significance for the Church. It blinded the main part of the German church and prevented them from acting before and during World War II to live up to their Christian responsibility in the face of political, human injustice.

    Today, Replacement theology (i.e. that the Church has replaced Israel in God's purposes) is taught in many parts of the Church, particularly in some traditional orthodox circles, but also in certain charismatic groups. Christians are said to be the sole inheritors of divine blessings and considered to replace Israel and the Jewish people in God's plan. This misguided view will prevent a correct understanding of the Bible, and hinder Christian countries from taking up their responsibility to act if injustices are committed against the Jewish people.

6. A new peace policy is again prevalent. During the 1930s, the British Minister, Neville Chamberlain, became spokesman for the policy of 'peace at any price', which paved the way for Hitler's occupation of one territory

after the other. These were ceded to him after only weak protests from the Allies, and without any military interference.

Today, in their endeavours to secure an international peace and a One-world Government, leading countries in the West are mainly pursuing the same policy. We have seen it spearheaded by the USA and the European Union (EU) in Bosnia. Most recently, it is being displayed in the Middle East, where it seems most Western and Arab powers would prefer, in the name of peace, to see a truncated Israel, submerged in a sea of Arab countries.

7. A resurgence of humanist influence with its overemphasis on the welfare of society at the expense of the individual could encourage disrespect for human life. In the 1930s, Hitler's New World Order began. It only lasted twelve years, but in it euthanasia became an accepted way to deal with unwanted population groups such as invalids, the insane, homosexuals, gypsies and latterly Jews. Hitler termed them 'useless eaters' and they were eliminated in order to 'purify' the Aryan race in Germany.

Today the strong emphasis on the welfare of society and the maintenance of a high living standard is already leading to disrespect for human life. In the 1990s with genetic engineering experimenting to obtain an 'improvement' of the human species, the prospect of Huxley's *Brave New World* becomes more real. Euthanasia is also coming to the fore once again.

This humanist ideology can blur a society's vision from what is just, to what is expedient, particularly in its right to decide over life and death. Thus, it becomes easier to cut off life at both ends by sanctioning unnecessary abortions and by precipitating the deaths of the elderly, the handicapped or an unacceptable people group.

One day our comparatively comfortable world may abruptly awaken from its slumber and we will realise, after some economic or political shakings, that we have not advanced much from the way people responded in the 1930s.

With nearly two thousand years of antisemitism continuing to be a feature of our modern society, we need to recall that one of the most tragic episodes of World War II was the Holocaust. Not only were six million Jews killed during the Holocaust, which meant that out of every three European Jews two would be dead by the end of the war; but two million of these were murdered in the German-occupied territories of the former Soviet Union. Since the hatred of minority groups, and Jews in particular, is still very strong there, this makes it potentially a very dangerous country for them to live in.[4]

Russia has the second largest Jewish population outside Israel, and many factors point to the danger that Russia may, even in our modern age, become fertile ground for the most severe pogrom (persecution) of the Jews – unless the tidal wave of the coming Exodus sweeps them out beforehand.

In order to throw light upon the current situation, I have chosen to look at it from three different angles. The first of three sections will focus on European history during the 1930s, when Jewish emigrants tried to leave Nazi Germany before they were trapped there during World War II. At that time it was still possible for the surrounding world to prevent the severe antisemitic persecution from developing. While focusing on Europe's leading country, Great Britain, we will also look briefly at the involvement of other countries such as France, Belgium and the Netherlands, and at the reason why other countries like Switzerland and Scandinavia did not become involved in the matter at that time.

We will seek to discover why Jewish history later pronounced the verdict over Europe that the nations mainly *'stood by in silence'* – **What went wrong?**

The second section takes a closer look at the Jews in Russia, a country that from Tsarist times has harboured severe antisemitism, right through the Communist period until today. In times of internal turmoil, the regime has used persecution and pogroms against Jews as a way to gain the upper hand over the society politically. Being justified through the teachings of the Russian Orthodox Church, the largest 'pogrom' ever took place during World War II. Regardless of international summits, political coalitions and economic trade agreements, considering Russia's past history and her steadily rising antisemitism, there is once again a strong possibility that Russian Jewry might be in danger.

In the last section, we will look at the matter from a biblical perspective. It is a very interesting time we live in because a number of prophecies are being fulfilled before our eyes. Both the formation of the State of Israel in 1948 and the return of five million Jews from the various countries of the diaspora are key issues for a vital understanding of the present days. One of the recent and most important signs is that during the 1990s over 750,000 Russian Jews arrived in Israel, the largest number of immigrants in her history. Yet the Bible predicts an even greater exodus in days to come from 'the land of the north', now understood to be the Russian Federation.

Even with our world in turmoil and the threat of wars, the Bible speaks of the welfare and future of Israel; of the Jewish people; and of those from the nations who have caught the vision of coming events, understand the situation from a biblical perspective and are taking initiatives to prevent a coming disaster.

It is my hope that some of the early warning signals that have previously been ignored will now be seen more clearly. May these pages stir the reader to a new understanding so we will be ready to stand in the gap and help to rescue the Jews in the diaspora. Thus as we put our faith into practice in difficult circumstances, its reality will be seen and its credibility acknowledged by Jew and Gentile alike.

Although I realise that people seldom learn from history, the question still remains – would our generation respond differently today? To a certain extent the answer lies with us.

Prelude to the Holocaust

Down through the centuries, there have been several examples of 'ethnic cleansing' – a systematic killing of a whole people or nation – and unfortunately such things do still take place. For example, let us look at the murder of the Armenian people which Hitler is said to have used as a model for the 'eradication' of his undesired population group, the Jews.

The Armenian genocide (systematic killing of other members of the human race), took place in the early 1900s. At that time, the Armenian people lived mainly in Turkey where they have had their roots for centuries. First, they were exposed to a severe slaughter by the Sultan in the 1890s, when about 100,000 were killed; but the second genocide, committed by the Young Turks from 1915–17, is the most well-known.

Before World War I, approximately 2 million Armenians were registered in Turkey. The trouble began in April 1915, when the government feared that this ethnic group might turn against them, so about 250 Armenian leaders were deported from Istanbul. At the same time, loyal Armenian officers and soldiers in the Turkish army were demoted to a special work force under the leadership of their ally Germany. They were then sent to improve Turkey's infra-structure, building roads and railways for military purposes. The slaughter began that summer, as a result of the govern-ment's vilification of the Armenians, accusing them of being traitors and inhuman, and its consequent radical policy of exterminating its victims.

It is estimated that around 1–1.5 million innocent men, women and children were brutally murdered. By October of 1915, Viscount Bryan reported in the House of Lords that the number of Armenian victims was 800,000.[5] It is possible that as many as 400,000 Armenians could have fled, mainly to Russia, but after the war only 100,000 of the approximately 2 million were left in the country. Later, in the 1920s, the Kemal Turks substituted the physical genocide with a cultural one, and the Armenian community was driven from its 3,000-year-old homeland. When these previously unheard-of atrocities did not provoke strong protests from leading, mainly indifferent, Western countries, Hitler counted on exactly the same response when, in a crisis situation, he turned against another unwanted population group, the Jews. And Hitler was right – they *'stood by in silence'*.

It must be added that the Nazis also directed their actions against the handicapped and certain religious and ethnic groups such as the gypsies and other 'undesired' people in their society. However, while it is correct that 200,000 out of

Germany's 700,000 gypsies were killed in a deliberate attempt to get rid of this population group, it needs to be understood that the action was specifically directed against their nomadic life style. When the gypsies settled down in local communities, the persecution of them ceased.

A further example of genocide unwound during the 1970s in Cambodia. After 5 years of Viet Cong incursions, the country had been more or less ruined, and the Cambodian population had suffered much. Then the extremely repressive Communist Khmer Rouge regime took power, and the country was closed to the outside world. In late 1978, when the Vietnamese overturned the former government, the country was on the verge of a severe famine. By then 1–2 million of Cambodia's population of 7 million had already been killed. Some historians conclude that there is a connecting line between the genocides, and that the Auschwitz tragedy is re-echoed in Cambodia.[6]

In the same way the ethnic cleansing, hardly 10 years ago, by Ceaucesco's horror regime in Rumania reflects the same attitude. In order to speed up the process of a gigantic agricultural project to reduce the country's 17,000 farming villages to a quarter of their number, the 'Red Tzar' and his Communist guard killed 64,000 of their own people. Lives are still cheap even in our time. We are living in an age where genocide is possible, but it is not unavoidable!

It is, however, clear that if we compare these examples of genocide, the Holocaust is unique in that never before has such a mass destruction been both aimed against a specific people, the Jews, and directed on a world-wide scale.

Chapter 2

The Abandonment of German Jewry in the 1930s

Setting the Scene

I n the early 1930s, a war-torn Europe was still shivering from the devastating after-effects of the First World War. One of the most serious blows to stability was the whirlwind of an economic crisis, which in 1929, went through the whole financial world, leaving a deep depression with financial crashes and high unemployment. In the big cities people were starving. In Britain in 1933, for example, one-fifth of its work force (2.5 million) was unemployed and without government assistance. Everyone was longing for peace and prosperity.

Added to this, during the 1920s there had been much instability caused by the uprooting of various population groups. There were mass movements of refugees who, because of political, racial and religious persecution, fled their countries in search of a new homeland. They included citizens of the devastated countries of Eastern Europe, those escaping from the 1917 Russian Revolution, Greeks, Armenians, Assyrians and others. By 1926, an estimated 10 million refugees constituted a serious international problem in Europe.

By 1930 most Western countries, including Great Britain, had effectively shut their borders to would-be immigrants by imposing protectionist laws, mainly in order to prevent a deterioration of their economy and an increase of unemployment. In 1933, when refugees from Hitler's Third Reich* came on the international scene, they were less of a novelty, much more of a nuisance.

In response to this need, the League of Nations[1] established a High Commission for Refugees in 1921 known as 'Nansen's International Office' (named after the Norwegian polar explorer, directing the work). Previously, these efforts had been carried out mainly by private agencies in Eastern Europe and the USA. The High Commission dealt with the status of these mainly stateless people, providing them with identity cards and settling them in Europe or elsewhere. It was anticipated that the office dealing with East-European refugees would finish the task by the end of 1938. But the peace did not last that long. Over the years the influence of the League of Nations diminished, and large numbers of German fugitives who so seriously influenced the whole picture after 1933, remained outside its domain.

German Jews and Nazism

For hundreds of years Jews had lived in Germany, where they had become a well-integrated, middle-class group. Therefore, it became the irony of destiny that it was Germany – where the Jews of Europe had probably reached their highest level of assimilation – who sought to rid itself of them. By 1933, there were approximately 522,000 Jews in Germany, of whom 80% were German citizens. The remaining 20% were more recent immigrants from Eastern Europe, mainly Poland. The Jewish minority group was less than 1% of the total German population. (See Appendix II.)

When Hitler took power on 30 January, 1933, the country was still suffering severely from the economic depression. Historians agree that if Germany had not been economically paralysed and its citizens driven to desperation, Hitler would not have been able to take advantage of the following years of economic improvement and would never have succeeded.

---

* *First Reich*: Holy Roman Catholic Empire of Germany 962–1806; *Second Reich*: German Empire 1871–1918; *Third Reich*: Hitler's Third Reich 1933–45.

Hitler wrote his ideological literary work *Mein Kampf* (My Struggle) in 1923 during a period when he was imprisoned after an attempted coup to seize power in München. His writings contained strong statements about his future expansionist politics, trimmed with vicious antisemitic statements, and often, incoherent talk.

In order to support his political views Hitler needed a scapegoat. Back in 1919, when the leaders of the Weimar Republic had wanted a plausible explanation for the defeat of the Great German Reich, the blame was very conveniently placed on an enemy of international character, namely the Jews. In its hour of need, they claimed, the Jews had forsaken the Vaterland and stabbed them in the back. This so-called 'Dolchstoss Legende' became a favourite theme in Nazi propaganda and contained the ideological motivation for the coming world war. In many countries, and particularly in Russia, the idea was promoted that the Jewish people were a treacherous force conspiring against the government.

It was the desire of Hitler's new regime to create a 'New World Order', an ideal Aryan state. In reality, the 'creeds' for The Third Reich propagated a post-Christian, pagan and tribal religion. The Nazis began to 'cleanse' the country by persecuting citizens with any convictions deviating from the new ideology. The undesirable categories were divergent groups within the socialist block: Communists, pacifists, certain Christian churches and gypsies. While the Slavs were considered 'subhuman', Hitler never had plans to annihilate any Slavic nation completely, only the leadership. He also sought to destroy the mentally ill, handicapped and others he termed 'useless eaters'. The most objectionable group, however, was the Jews, whom they categorised as 'non-human'. They were regarded by the Nazi regime as the ideological and biological enemy of the German people, an evil, parasitic and destructive race.

While the medieval church had hoped to save Jewish souls through baptism, national socialism put its effort into making the German soil *judenrein* (cleansed of Jews). The Nazi ideology had taken over the concept of the 'satanic Jew' from the Church Fathers, stating that only a people possessed by Satan could have killed the Messiah.

Two ideas in Nazi ideology are particularly important to understand:

1. The ideological concept that, not only Germany, but the whole world needed to be cleansed from the influence of Russian Bolshevic efforts to achieve world dominion, as well as from 'international Jewry', who were considered a demonic force conspiring to control Western 'pluto-cracies'.

2. The expansionist idea: after World War I, and the defeat of Germany 'caused' by Jewish conspiracy, Germany lost its colonies. Therefore, it was said that German citizens needed more living space, *Lebensraum*, particularly towards the east.

Even though Western politicians were well-acquainted with Hitler's ideology and plans for his regime when he took power, his plans were usually laughed at – or at best ignored.

When the Nazis issued antisemitic laws or invaded neigh-bouring countries, it resulted in new refugee waves. Six consecutive waves can be counted, beginning with the first Nazi antisemitic law in March 1933 through to Germany's annexation, six years later, of the Czech Rump State in March 1939. Not only in Europe could these waves be traced, but are also seen even more clearly in the Jewish attempts to escape to the British Mandate of Palestine.

Persecution of the Jews Begins in Germany

Antisemitic Laws of 1933

Already in March of 1933, a few months after becoming chancellor, Hitler began to issue antisemitic laws. They were aimed at excluding 'non-Aryans' from civic and economic life, but in practice only applied to Jews. Jewish businesses were vandalised. In the streets German 'storm-troopers' (the SA) began to persecute and terrorize Jews. Through their example, the Nazis encouraged the people to do the same, but interestingly, since such actions did not get the expected response from local Germans, Hitler had to postpone his antisemitic plans until later.

Even though there was international condemnation as well as a boycott of German goods, this did not change the

German Government's attitude to the Jews. During the 1930s, the Western boycott hurt Germany considerably but did not deter them from their plans.

As an immediate result of the antisemitic laws about 60,000 refugees fled Germany and streamed into the neighbouring countries. More than 53,000 of these were Jews, who fled to France, Holland and Belgium. Their arrival threatened to disrupt the labour markets there. When these countries complained to the League of Nations in October 1933, it led to 12 European governments appointing a High Commissioner for Refugees from Germany to co-ordinate the international efforts. The League had wanted Britain to take the lead in the Commission, but fearing it would put too much pressure on the issue of immigration to Palestine, they refused. Instead an American, James McDonald, was chosen as High Commissioner. In protest, Germany withdrew from the League, and it then became very difficult to impose sanctions on her.

Second phase: the Nuremberg Laws of 1935

After a couple of years of quiet, during which confidence agreements were made with England and France, and Britain had given Germany permission to build up their fleet to equal 35% of the British tonnage, Hitler decided that the time was ripe for another antisemitic move. In September 1935, the far-reaching Nuremberg Laws were introduced. Through these the Nazi regime began to force the assimilated Jews out of the national life. Later the *Law for protection of German blood and honour* was added.

According to Nazi ideology, race was determined by religion. Their theory was that race was hidden in the blood and visible through certain physiological features such as the size and form of the human skull. These factors then determined who would be Aryan or Jewish. In a decree of November 1935, the Germans defined a Jew as a person with at least two Jewish grandparents; or an individual who belonged to the Jewish religion or was married to a Jew. Also the group called *Mischlinge* (children of mixed marriage with Aryan Germans).

The Nazis had several schemes to get rid of German Jews by emigration. One was a 5-year plan from 1935 for a continuous emigration of 20,000 per year. But it was soon felt that a much larger exodus was needed.

In order to combat the heavy post-war economic depression a flight-tax *Reichfluchtsteur* had been introduced to preserve the German foreign reserve. The Nazis retained the tax and from 1934 a fee of 25% was levied on everyone who, since 1931, had had an income of more than RM20,000 (£1,680) in any one year, or on the property of any emigrant who possessed capital of more than RM50,000 (£4,200). The remainder of the emigrant's capital was retained in Germany and paid into a special Reich Mark account to be paid when the emigrant reached their new country. The loss on transfer varied from 20–50% in the case of emigration to Palestine, while to other countries the loss was from 20–95%. The flight tax revenue from 1933–34 amounted to RM50 million (£4.2 million).[2]

Another way of extracting Jewish funds was the 'aryanisation' process, which had begun in the autumn of 1935 after the Nuremberg Laws. It was partly a voluntary process, whereby Jewish property was sold for only a very insignificant amount of its worth, but was returned to the owner. In 1933 the value of Jewish property was estimated at RM10 billion (£840 million). The official Nazi view was that the Jewish wealth really belonged to the Reich. It was felt that the Jews, having arrived poor, had become wealthy by their exploitation of the German people; therefore the appropriation of Jewish property was justified in their eyes.

In spite of these measures, the Jews were not pushed out of Germany sufficiently quickly for the Nazis. In fact the Jews who fled in 1933 were, though faced with the prospect of humiliation and suffering, still returning at a rate of 5% per year. However, after the Nuremberg Laws, when the German authorities felt that the returning flow was too large, they decided to place the returnees in 'training camps', i.e. forced labour camps. This measure finally stopped the flow.

✛ ✛ ✛

During the first German refugee wave in 1933, Great Britain, in its position as the leading country in Europe, tried to stay aloof from the refugee issue. With its 66 million people and high unemployment rate Britain was not an ideal immigrant country, at most a transit place. So Britain was generally by-passed, and only a few hundred Jewish 'visitors' with good connections were admitted each month. They could only prolong their stay if they were able to guarantee that they would not become a charge on the British public. The so-called LPC (Liability on the Public Charge) clause of the Immigration Act of 1917 was still in force. It became, there-fore, necessary to establish a Central British Fund for German Jewry and through Jewish gifts facilitate transfer to other countries.

With the second wave in 1935, a few thousand, carefully screened refugees received asylum in Britain. Particularly welcomed were people from the middle class, who were able to start small industrial plants with their capital, as well as leading scientists and researchers. Medical workers and lawyers were quickly weeded out because their British colleagues soon feared their competition. Although about four-fifths of those given asylum were Jews, they came under the general category of 'Germans'. This was an anti-ethnic approach adopted by Jewish leaders. During this period, about 10,000 German refugees were issued work permits annually, more than half of them in domestic service.

The Difficult Task of the High Commissioner

Appointed to his office in 1933, James McDonald tried to fight for the cause of German Refugees by raising the issue with the Nazi government of the need to transfer enough of an emigrant's capital to prevent them being a liability. In spite of warm-hearted support from Jewish refugee agencies, he was fighting against the unequal odds of being rebuffed by the Germans, lack of political support from the League countries, and not enough funds delegated for his office. In frustration he resigned in December 1935. Faced with the prospect of having to absorb a growing number of German refugees landing on her shores, England was prompted to take the lead in the Commission.

For the new High Commissioner in January 1936, the League chose a retired Major General from Malaysia, Sir Neill

Malcolm. He was considered to be less conspicuous than his predecessor. The British succeeded in limiting his sphere of work to programmes of settlement and legal bureaucracy on behalf of German refugees. International German policy was declared out of bounds, and the principle was laid down that he could only deal with Jews after they had left Germany. His term of office was to be two years only, as the refugee work was expected to be complete by 1938.

The Olympic Games in Berlin – the Silent Consent

1936 was the year of the well-known Berlin Olympic games. In spite of the fact that the Nuremberg Laws were issued the previous year, the Reich wanted to use the games as propaganda for the Nazi regime, and the racial issue was kept low key. While Jewish athletes from foreign countries were allowed to participate in the games, German Jews were excluded. The German workers' organisations, felt to be under Communist influence, were also denied permission to take part. In spite of some protest, the nations mainly kept silent, pouring in to participate in the festival.

Germany's Assault on Austria – 1938

With the *Anschluss*, the German annexation of Austria on 13 March, 1938, the anti-Jewish campaign was speeded up considerably as the Nuremberg Laws were extended to Austria with a total population of 6.8 million. The Nazi invasion gave rise to a new refugee wave with mass panic and flight, far exceeding the emigration that occurred when Hitler took power 5 years previously. As a result of the German attempt to obtain more *lebensraum* (living space) by annexing Austria, 180,000 Austrian Jews were suddenly brought under his power.

The 165,000 Jews living in Vienna were particularly exposed to severe attacks. They were beaten, sent away to concentration camps or imprisoned. Dozens of Austrian Jews committed suicide. Storm troopers rounded them up and simply thrust them across the border without identity papers or money. Now 20,000 Polish Jews, who had previously fled to Austria, became refugees for the second time. Hungary and Yugoslavia kept their borders shut, France and Italy only

offered doubtful prospect for rescue, and Switzerland tightened her frontiers.

Within 2–3 months after the German annexation of
Austria, the Nazis managed to drive the Jews out of the
Austrian national economy and life, a process that had taken
years in Germany. Further decrees issued throughout the
Reich in April 1938, greatly speeded up the forced sale
of Jewish property to the government. In comparison
the 'aryanization' process, which began in Germany in the
autumn of 1935, was not completed there before December
1938.

In order to get rid of the Austrian Jews quickly, the Gestapo
organised a Central Office of Jewish Emigration in Vienna.
Before long, the bureau chief, Adolf Eichmann, and his men
just took the Jews and dumped them across the border into
the woods of Czechoslovakia, the only country which had
not sealed its frontiers with Austria.

The third German refugee wave of 1938 quickly became an
international problem. When a greater influx of the more
wealthy Austrian Jews began to arrive in Britain, it caused
consternation in the British Home Office because they feared
that the Austrian passport would soon be declared invalid. It
would then be impossible to deport them. Between April and
November 1938, 50,000 Jews fled from Austria, over 30,000
more than left Germany in the same period.

The Austrian Aid Committee in London considered that
they were unable to accept the financial responsibility,
except for certain Jews selected after consultation. The British
Foreign Office, therefore, fearing the social and labour problems such an influx would cause, introduced a visa system for
all aliens holding German and Austrian passports. When
Germany was informed about the British visa system they,
in return, expelled a number of British tourists visiting
Germany. The Foreign Office was rather upset over the
inconvenience the expulsion caused to their tourists. The
more severe implications for the Austrian Jews were not
mentioned.[3] However, if a person could prove that he was
in danger and represented an exceptional case, he might be
granted political asylum.

During the following months, the Austrian situation went

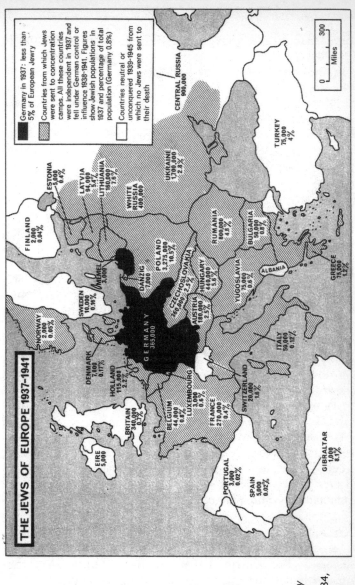

THE JEWS OF EUROPE 1937-1941

- ■ Germany in 1937: less than 5% of European Jewry
- ▨ Countries from which Jews were sent to concentration camps. All these countries were independent in 1937 and fell under German control or influence 1938-1941. Figures show Jewish populations in 1937 and percentage of total population (Germany 0.8%)
- □ Countries neutral or unconquered 1939-1945 from which no Jews were sent to their death

0 ——— 300
Miles

FINLAND
2,000
0.04%

NORWAY
2,000
0.05%

SWEDEN
10,000
0.16%

ESTONIA
5,000
0.4%

LATVIA
95,000
5.4%

LITHUANIA
160,000
7.6%

CENTRAL RUSSIA
900,000

WHITE RUSSIA
400,000

UKRAINE
1,700,000
2.8%

DENMARK
7,000
0.17%

MEMEL
3,000

DANZIG
7,000

POLAND
3,275,000
10.5%

HOLLAND
115,000
2.2%

G E R M A N Y
365,000

CZECHOSLOVAKIA
360,000
2.5%

RUMANIA
800,000
4.5%

BULGARIA
50,000
0.8%

BRITAIN
340,000
0.7%

BELGIUM
44,000
0.5%

LUXEMBOURG
3,000
0.6%

AUSTRIA
60,000
2.2%

HUNGARY
400,000
5.5%

YUGOSLAVIA
75,000
0.5%

ALBANIA

GREECE
70,000
1.2%

TURKEY
75,000
4%

EIRE
5,000

FRANCE
270,000
0.7%

SWITZERLAND
20,000
1.6%

ITALY
50,000
0.12%

PORTUGAL
3,000
0.02%

SPAIN
5,000
0.02%

GIBRALTAR
1,000
8.1%

Map 1
The Jewish History Atlas, Sir Martin Gilbert, CBE, 1984, Routledge. Used with permission.

from bad to worse. In May 1938, there was virtually no possibility for Jews to obtain even a short-term exit visa for Britain from Vienna. The condition for being granted one was to sign a declaration never to return to Austria again, as well as handing over all their property to the state. Mass arrests continued.

In the meantime, the voluntary refugee organisations were able to convince the Home Office in London of the need to establish a Co-ordinating Committee for Refugees to avoid overlapping the work. It represented the collective interests of the British government as well as their own organisations, particularly regarding training facilities and official approaches to the Dominions, and Colonial and Foreign governments, on emigration matters.

Coinciding with the German annexation of Austria, a Polish law of 31 March, 1938 suddenly cancelled citizenship for Poles who had spent more than five years outside their country. This was Warsaw's attempt to prevent a possible repatriation of the 20,000 Polish Jews who had settled in Austria. By this action thousands of Jews living elsewhere in Europe became stateless, which added to the growing burden of refugees. Moreover, with the anti-Jewish riots in Poland, many Jews still living there had lost their property.

Despite the tremendous turmoil it caused in Europe, the annexation did not seem to produce much reaction from the British government apart from them trying to stop entry to Britain of the new wave of refugees by visa restrictions and making the conditions for admission more stringent.

The Nations' Gamble over German Jewry at Evian

Sadly the European response to the needs of the German Jews was generally very weak. The nations wanted Britain to take the lead in the High Commission for Refugees from Germany. However, during the 1930s the British government had pursued a policy of disarmament and non-intervention. They felt the approach of the humanitarian organisations would harm British politics and economic interests.[4] They feared too, that more pressure would be put on them to admit Jewish refugees into Palestine. Furthermore, it was the hope of the British organisations, particularly the Anglo-Jewish

Association who sponsored the Commission, to use it to put pressure on Germany to stop 'creating refugees'. The British government declined to intervene, fearing that an irritated German government would be more difficult to negotiate with.

In reality, the German government was fleecing the emigrants. As already mentioned, Germany demanded high taxes of Jews who wanted to emigrate, as well as the special flight tax of 25% of capital and property. By 1938–39 this tax had grown to approximately RM342 million (£28.7 million). Consequently German Jews, deprived of capital, were not wanted anywhere.

Spurred on by the growing number of refugees in Europe – swollen by fugitives from the Spanish Civil War of 1936–39 and the recent Nazi annexation of Austria – more countries began placing extra restrictions on admission. President Roosevelt took the initiative to call a conference to discuss the problem. There was much speculation as to why the US would want to be involved with the issue, but the upcoming election probably played an important role in the President's initiative. The former High Commissioner for Refugees from Germany, James McDonald, was his advisor.

Since the League of Nations was situated in Geneva, Switzerland was suggested as the host country; but not wanting to become involved in the matter, they declined. Instead France accepted the responsibility, and the well-known conference in Evian-les-Baines convened on 6 July, 1938.

Thirty governments (see Appendix III) from all over the world, who were able to settle refugees, were invited to discuss the acute problem and the possibility of emigration for 'political refugees' from Germany and Austria. But from the onset the attitude was one of non-commitment. This was the first time that the concept of 'political refugees' was used in international debate with reference to people who desired to emigrate because of some form of persecution, either for political, racial or religious reasons.

Before the conference, the German government had secretly contacted Lord Winterton, chairman of the British delegation, and secured for themselves the agreement that if

Britain would try to prevent anti-German feelings at Evian, they would, in return, permit the refugees to bring out some of their property. However, the British were well aware that the German policy of despoiling and expelling the Jewish population was not only a British issue, but was creating a world-wide problem, and that the German government itself should make some contribution to its solution.[5]

In his opening address the American chairman, Myron C. Taylor, an industrial magnate, announced that his government had taken steps to make the German and former Austrian emigration quotas fully available for a total of 27,370 immigrants annually to the United States. From 1933–38, the US could have admitted 130,000, but only 27,000 had immigrated. For economic reasons quotas had been cut since 1930.[6]

Lord Winterton, keeping to his instructions from Germany, spoke about Britain's traditional policy of offering asylum, but stated that with the present socio-economic difficulties this hospitality could be extended only with narrow limitations.

In spite of a significant pro-refugee lobby in the British Parliament who wanted to place the immigrants in their vast, unpopulated overseas territories, the British government disregarded their wishes, stating that most of their colonies were either already overcrowded or unsuited for European settlement. (Albeit Canada's population of less than 10 million lived in an area larger than USA, which had 130 million inhabitants.) The delegates from the British Commonwealth: Australia, Canada and New Zealand, did not offer any solutions either. South Africa, not wanting to receive refugees, did not participate at all. They all had carefully established barriers to keep out immigrants, and Britain had no authority over their policy, so there was no empire-wide policy on refugees.

Because of the danger of stirring up Arab rebellion in Palestine, Britain had made her participation dependent upon the condition that the question of settlement in the Mandate of Palestine would not be debated. Only on the last day was it mentioned; referred to as 'territories where local politics hindered admission'.[7]

Of the contributions from other participating delegates it should be mentioned that the European countries bordering Germany made elaborate speeches but regretted that, because of their dense population and economic situation, they could only offer visas for short periods. The two representatives from Poland and Rumania requested to have solutions to their Jewish refugee problem discussed as well, but it was absolutely refused. The German and Austrian issue in itself was enough.

For Latin American countries unemployment was the main reason given for restricting immigration. Most of them were basically agricultural countries with little need for intellectuals and traders. Behind their unwillingness to admit Jewish immigrants was also the fear of endangering their trade agreements with Germany.

The only exception was the Dominican Republic, little bigger than the size of Palestine, which indicated the possibility of large scale settlement of 100,000 colonists who were willing to become farmers, on the condition that expenses for land purchase and equipment would be covered. The country was, however, only able, practically, to absorb a very small number of immigrants.

One of the disheartening aspects of the conference was the private session of representatives from 39 refugee organisations, which showed the Jews' own unpreparedness. Despite strenuous efforts to co-ordinate their endeavours, rivalries between Zionist and non-Zionist groups blocked the attempt to form a unified representation under the leadership of Dr Chaim Weizmann and submit a joint plan for a practical solution to the problem, so this opportunity was lost.

During Evian, the Swiss delegate and chief of the Swiss Justice Department informed the German delegation that, in order to protect the Swiss interests from the immense influx of the Viennese Jews, his government had ruled that all holders of Austrian passports would require a visa to enter Switzerland. After leaving the conference, Switzerland persuaded the German government to mark passports issued to Jews with a big 'J', in order to prevent their country 'from being swamped with Jews'. Slowly the roads out of Germany were being closed for the Jews. Soon other countries also followed the same practice, looking with disfavour upon bearers of passports stamped in this way.[8]

What was Accomplished at Evian?

Very little! With the US government's pre-set goal not to commit themselves, and their vague phraseology – which hardly mentioned either the Jews or the German government by name – not much could be expected. The American government had wanted a resolution condemning the German government's actions, but the British delegation had prevented this.[9]

Evian underlined the unwillingness of the nations, primarily for political and economic reasons, to rescue despoiled and impoverished Jewish refugees. As a spokesman from the Wilhelmstrasse (the German 'Downing Street') gleefully reported back to his government in Berlin: the Western countries wanted the Jews no more than the Germans did themselves.[10] It was a terrible disappointment to the Jewish representatives of the refugee organisations.

A diplomatic endeavour, however, did result from the conference: the establishment of the Intergovernmental Committee on Refugees (the IGC). But the initiative came in so late, when the possibilities of new settlement places were closing, and it gave little hope. However, the IGC had the advantage over the League's High Commission for Refugees, of receiving American support and also being able to negotiate with the German government regarding the economic side of the refugee issue. This authority could easily have been bestowed upon the League's High Commission; and in fact, from January 1939, the posts of director of the IGC and the High Commissioner for Refugees were merged into one and given to retired British Governor, Sir Herbert Emerson.

Annexation of the Sudetenland – 1938

In the spring and summer of 1938, war clouds were looming on the horizon. Both Great Britain and France feared an Italian invasion of Egypt, which might endanger their positions in the Mediterranean; not least at the Suez Canal. For the Allies it was important to avoid a confrontation on two fronts at once with both Italy and Germany. Therefore, they chose to appease Hitler.

In Europe, the existence of the Czechoslovakian Republic with a population of almost 15 million, composed of many nationalities, was at stake. In the northern section, known as the Sudetenland, lived a minority group of about 2.5 million residents of German background. Pro-German extremists now tried to push for these to be incorporated into the Reich. The steady breakdown of resistance in Britain and France against the idea of German annexation of the Sudetenland culminated in a conference on 29 September, 1938 in Munich between Hitler, Mussolini (Italy), Chamberlain (UK), and Daladier (France). The meeting was conducted without agenda or minutes, and the terms were agreed upon in an atmosphere of haste, surrendering Sudetenland to German occupation within the first ten days of October. The border was to be decided by an International Commission composed of representatives of the governments involved. Plebiscites were to decide the allegiance of the German speaking areas and concessions were also to be made to Poles and Hungarians.

After intense pressure on the Czechs by the British and French representations, the Czech government surrendered to the German demands. Having sacrificed Czech sovereignty to German demands, Chamberlain returned victoriously to London, for he had also persuaded Hitler to sign a significant Anglo-German friendship agreement. Waving a piece of paper at the waiting crowds, he enthusiastically announced he had secured 'Peace in our time'.

During October and early November, Czechoslovakia was forced to surrender the Mayar areas in Slovakia and Ruthenia to Hungary, while Poland took the Teschen region with valuable industrial plants and coal fields. Even if the strategic economic loss caused by the division of Czechoslovakia might vaguely have been understood at the Munich Conference, the possibility of a huge number of refugees fleeing the territories did not trouble them.

When a military regime took charge of the Czech State in December 1938, the whole refugee situation broke down

because of the regime's collaboration with the German
government. With the signing away of the Sudetenland to
Germany many thousands of potential refugees came within
the expanded border of the Reich. Those in most danger were
the approximately 5,000 refugees from Germany and Austria
who had been resident in Czechoslovakia since 1933. Some
of these were well-known Social Democrats or members of
the left-wing groups, appearing on the Gestapo's wanted list.
Absorption into German territory would send them into
concentration camps or worse. Some of the Jews and other
'non-Aryans' came into this category. Flight over German
controlled highways was unthinkable; and the Polish government was very hostile.

Czechs to London

One of the Czech socialist leaders, Wenzel Jaksch, came to
Britain pleading for help for the 15,000–20,000 refugees of
his party who were in danger. As the British government felt
somewhat responsible for their plight, a departure was made
from their usual refugee policy, and 350 visas were issued for
a 3-month period to individuals in demonstrable danger.
Also a £10 million loan was granted for settling refugees in
other parts of Czechoslovakia – basically a payment to keep
refugees away from the British Isles. For the same reason
France gave a similar grant. However, when the British
Foreign Office tried to settle some of the refugees in the
dominions, the whole idea met with much opposition there.
When it later turned out that 20 Communist deputies and
senators were among the sponsored admissions, the whole
idea was abandoned.

In London, the Home Office and the major refugee organisations attempting to cope with the added burden from
Czechoslovakia, were on the verge of a collapse. In October,
the German Aid Society was way behind in trying to deal
with 1,500 applications, some of which dated back to June.
The German Jewish Aid Committee alone had 3,000 Austrian
refugees on its relief rolls and of these, only 10 % had been
sponsored before admission into Britain. With the already
widespread unemployment and economic distress, the
government feared that the presence of a large number of

refugees might cause an outburst of anti-alien and antisemitic elements in the country.

By the end of October, the German Aid Office had been registering several hundred new cases daily. Many were in such a deprived condition that they could not find employment in Britain, nor would they be able to emigrate overseas. The Committee had been paying about £4,000 for relief and emigration work per week and was getting close to the end of their physical and financial resources. In exasperation the German Aid Office refused to cope with the added burden, so the Home Office were forced to introduce a visa requirement for people with Czech passports, as they had previously done for people from Germany and Austria.

Increased Nazi Actions against the Jews – The Horror of Kristallnacht, 1938

Back in Germany things were building up to *Kristallnacht,* the watershed for the debilitated Jewish community in the Reich in November 1938. Several of the Eastern European states such as Austria, Hungary and Rumania imitated the Nazis by intensifying the discrimination against their own Jews. Nobody wanted what was regarded as a surplus Jewish population. In October 1938 when Germany cancelled Polish passports, 15,000 Polish Jews who had been living as residents in Germany, were immediately expelled. At the same time, a German diplomat was killed in Paris by a young exiled Polish Jew, Herschel Grünspan. His parents had been among the expelled victims. This started a well-orchestrated and furious nation-wide pogrom against Jews in Germany on the night of 9–10 November, *'the night of broken glass'.*

The German persecution which followed, could only be compared to the first days of the *Anschluss* in Vienna. 177 synagogues were set on fire, 7,500 Jewish shops looted and at least 20,000 Jews arrested and sent to concentration camps. The despoiling at *Kristallnacht* was a luxury Germany really could not afford: therefore, the German insurance companies were excused from any responsibility to pay for the losses. Instead, the whole Jewish community was given a totally unreasonable 'fine' of RM1 billion – equivalent to approximately £84 million.

The murder of the German diplomat in France provided Marshall Goering with the excuse to exclude the remaining 'non-Aryans' and Jews from the country's economic life. While the 'aryanisation' of Jewish property had been accelerated during 1938, the final compulsory take-over occurred in December. The effect of *Kristallnacht* was twofold:

1. The assimilated, Germanised Jews were forced to think in terms of emigration since there was no future for them in the Reich.
2. The world was made aware of the drastic measures taken against the German Jews.

It shook the refugee organisations who began to prepare for emergency emigration, but almost all doors were closed. While the public reaction in Britain unanimously condemned the German persecution, the Foreign Office warned that any intervention would only make matters worse, both for German Jews and British interests in the Reich. The Foreign Office realised that poor, despoiled German refugees would now be even less acceptable either for temporary refuge or for settlement projects overseas.

The worsening crisis in the Reich caused a straining of Anglo-American relations. At a British Cabinet meeting Viscount Halifax reported that the US Ambassador, J.F. Kennedy, had told him of American outrage over the *Kristallnacht*, and that the American opinion 'was tending to conclude that the policy of working for peace with Germany was a mistake.' In order to improve relations, the British Foreign Office suggested the possibility that part of the unused British immigration quota to the US could be made available for Jewish refugees from Germany. During 1938 only 4,000 Britons emigrated to the United States. However, this greatly upset the US government, who declared that quotas granted by the Congress were not free property of the nations to relinquish to others. The British Ambassador then revealed that the British proposal 'would be distasteful to the Jewish leaders in America, who feared any open and avowed increase of Jewish immigration, because it would have the effect of increasing antisemitic feelings in America.'[11] Basically, the US did not want the German Jews either!

London's Response to the Stepped-up Persecution

In view of the critical situation in Germany, Jewish organisations in Britain felt that some emergency action needed to be taken. Their spokesman, Viscount Samuel, urged the government to permit the admission of 10,000 children and young people under the age of 17. Jewish organisations would give a collective guarantee that no public funds would be used for these children. At the same time Weizmann made a plea for admission into Palestine of 6,000 young men, then in concentration camps, together with 1,500 children. Since the total emigration would cost a minimum of £30 million, Viscount Bearsted asked whether the government could not give some assistance in raising a settlement loan. While the Home Office consented to dispense with passports and visas to facilitate entry for the children, the Prime Minister was still undecided because of the financing problem.

Later, a combination of refugee organisations, the Movement for the Care of Children from Germany, guaranteed that the children would not become a public charge. Local committees in Britain arranged to place them in hostels pending their placement with families. The whole programme, known as the *Kindertransport*, was set up within a few weeks, ready to receive the first children arriving in December. It was a measure of the desperation of German Jewish parents to let their children go, knowing they might never see them again. Well over 9,000 children came to Britain before the door to safety finally closed in September 1939.

In mid-November, 1938, the Foreign Office received information from their Berlin Embassy that 30,000 male Jews, most of them prominent in Jewish society, had been arrested by the Gestapo. Since about half of them were in danger of being expelled or exterminated there was urgent need to set up British transit camps. (France, the Netherlands and Belgium had done this much earlier.) An unused army camp in Kent was made ready for 3,500 male refugees under 35 years with re-emigration in view.

The raising of funds had by then become too much for the private agencies. In the period from 1933 through to

November 1938, almost £5 million had been collected by Jewish organisations, the Quakers and other groups, but the need for a government grant was urgent. In December former Prime Minister Baldwin, supported by well-known figures such as the Archbishop of Canterbury and the Mayor of London, launched the 'Lord Baldwin Fund for Refugees'. When *The Times* opened their own subscription for the fund on 9 December, it pointedly wrote that 'private charity cannot take, and must not take the responsibility which belongs to the government'.

Since the Treasury did not want to commit itself to financial assistance, they invited other governments represented at Evian to help. In December, the League of Nations sent a memorandum to the British Foreign Office absolutely rejecting the idea that voluntary organisations should be responsible for the total financial burden of the British refugee programme or the surveys of areas for settlement in the Colonies and Empire. Instead, the League suggested that the governments co-operate in raising the sum of £75 million that should finance a loan guaranteed by the central banks of the Evian governments. But Britain reacted sharply to the loan because the German government would then have succeeded in despoiling its Jews and having the other governments foot the bill. While the British government rejected the League's suggestion, they did agree to grant loans for the settlement of refugees in such colonies as Rhodesia (now Zimbabwe), since 'such projects would increase the prosperity of the Empire'.[12]

It was not easy for the Home Office to find the middle road in the refugee issue. Since the Anschluss, pro-refugee groups had pressed the government for increased immigration, while labour groups voiced protests, indicating rising anti-alien and antisemitic feelings. The possibility of introducing a quota system for refugees was also discussed. In answer to the critics the Home Secretary, Sir Samuel Hoare, explained the remarkable facts that the 11,000 German refugees, who had so far settled in Britain, had started new enterprises, in which 15,000 British workers had found employment. Between April and July 1938, 181 factories had been established.

By 1939, in order to cope with the growing need, Britain began to move slowly towards a more flexible policy. The Home Office granted admission to children as well as trans-migrants, and refugees over 60 years of age were granted visas immediately. However, for all these categories the refugee organisations still had to guarantee their support.

Final Annexation of Czechoslovakia – Spring 1939

As could be expected, it did not take long before the next tragedy befell the Czech Rump State whose destiny had already been sealed by the fateful Munich Agreement. On 15 March, 1939, Hitler used the smouldering quarrel between Czechs and Slovaks as a pretext for occupying the whole country, and German troops invaded Bohemia and Moravia in order to take Prague. Refugees of all categories – Czech political figures, Jews and Poles – were in severe danger. Even the members of the local refugee committee in Prague were arrested. The borders were closed and emigration ceased. Although a very small number of the most prominent refugees were given asylum in foreign embassies, thousands of others had to go underground. By this increase of *Lebens-raum* for Germany yet more Jews, 117,000 in all, came under the Reich. Thousands had already fled but a number, even if they were in possession of entry visas for other countries, had tragically not left in time.

At first Prime Minister Chamberlain could not bring himself to condemn Germany, although this second invasion of Czechoslovakia clearly showed the failure of his appease-ment efforts. However, after much debate in the House of Commons he gave in. On 12 March, 1939, Chamberlain warned Hitler that Britain would resist his further territorial endeavours in Europe.

The British Minister in Prague was instructed to help all the refugees who had visas for the UK, and the British Ambassador in Berlin was asked to request the German government to remove the barriers to emigration from Czechoslovakia. Instead, the German authorities imposed the requirement of an exit visa, without which it would be illegal to leave the new protectorate. The Gestapo continued to arrest people, and those who had exit permits were often shuttled around the German railways, re-arrested, and robbed, before they were allowed out of the Reich. The Swiss government closed its borders, and the Dutch government threatened to do the same. At the Polish frontier all Jews among the refugees were turned away.

Furthermore, the destruction of the Czech State automatically made refugees of the thousands of Czechs living outside the country. Many had previously fled to France.

Needless to say there were many concerns in the British government, and strong criticism voiced in the newspapers. In the House of Commons the members blamed the government for lack of awareness of the time factor in the refugee problem. While settlement schemes were being investigated, thousands of refugees were in serious danger.

In the acute emergency situation of the spring of 1939 British policy basically remained the same. Although some favours were granted to a few categories whose stay – as before – was sponsored by the Jewish refugee organisations, immigration into Britain continued to be rather limited due to unemployment and rising antisemitism. In all, only 6,000 refugees from Czechoslovakia found asylum in Britain. Most arrived on the eve of World War II. In the first six months of 1939, the number of Germans with British work permits rose to 18,450.

The Czech refugees soon caused the refugee stream in Europe to become a flood. Outside greater Germany the number of Jewish refugees had doubled to around 100,000. Many countries bordering the Reich were already 'saturated', and new admissions would only be possible if countries overseas would accept more refugees for permanent settlement.

By 1939 any hope of 'an orderly exodus' or the export of Jewish capital was unrealistic. Each had to take his chance. In his book *The Unwanted*, Marrus[13] points out that after the Anschluss and following each of the Nazi persecutions in 1938, streams of German Jews came to Shanghai, the only international port, which required no entry documents. In spite of the British and American representatives' severe admonitions to Germany about not permitting Jews to emigrate to Shanghai, as they feared their own delicate trade balance with the Japanese might be upset, the Germans refused to comply. Their main goal was to get rid of their Jews. By August 1939, 14,000 German and Austrian Jews had settled in the city. This example shows how Western governments sometimes did more to hinder than help the desperate flight of German refugees.

In the first eight months of 1939 about 122,500 Jews left the Reich. From 1933 to October 1939, the total number of German refugees admitted to Great Britain was 49,500, including over 9,000 unaccompanied children who came during 1939.

A Last Attempt to Save Jewish Lives

After the Evian Conference in 1938 most South American countries tightened their immigration restrictions severely.* After *Kristallnacht* it was almost impossible for the IGC to find settlement places because of the tightening refugee policy. The most important task was to urge the British government to take a lead in finding a solution to the emergency situation and, raising an international settlement loan.

Several proposals were under discussion; one interesting one came from President Schacht of the German Reichbank. He suggested a plan under which an 'orderly emigration' would be arranged. An international Jewish trust fund should finance 150,000 German Jews of working age to emigrate, over a 3-year period, followed by up to 250,000 of their dependants. The remaining 200,000 elderly Jews who could not emigrate, would be allowed to live peaceably in Germany. However, the British government and the Jewish communities in Britain as well as the United States were very opposed to what they called 'an undisguised ransom scheme'. Even though the proposal was strongly criticised, Rabbi S. Wise, President of the American Jewish Congress, admonished the Jewish community to give careful consideration to any plan holding the last hope of saving hundreds of

* Hope Simpson: *The Refugee Problem*, 1939. From 1933–1937 (previous to the Evian Conference) over 18,000 German refugees entered South America. The major recipients were Argentine (7,000), Brazil (8,000) and Chile (2,000). Sources vary a lot. (pp. 479–485).

thousands of lives.[14] Acknowledging the seriousness of the situation the Congress consented to support the idea.

Realising the US interest in the matter, Britain declared herself willing to participate. At last Western governments were acknowledging the need to financially aid settlement plans for German Jewry. By the summer of 1939 there were two interesting plans. Tragically, however, the suggestions for rescue materialised on paper only, and came too late to relieve the desperate situation.

By the outbreak of World War II in September 1939, about half the Jews of Germany and Austria had left. While the Nazis tried to enforce emigration, there were still about 400,000 German Jews trapped in the expanded Reich, in addition to two million in the latest German acquisition, Poland. All were facing Hitler's *Final solution*.

In Search of a Homeland

The tragic events surrounding the SS St Louis of the Hamburg-American Line graphically illustrate the desperate situation of the German Jewish Refugees. At the same time they are typical of a number of similarly unfortunate attempts to escape.

On 13 May, 1939, the vessel sailed from Hamburg bound for Cuba with 936 passengers, of whom 930 were Jewish. Tickets had been bought very expensively for $262 each plus $81 as a guarantee for a return trip, in case entry should be denied. Inscribed in each passport was a red 'J' for Jude as a reminder of the ever-increasing antisemitism they were leaving. They anticipated immigrating to the United States from 3 months to 3 years after their arrival in Cuba. More than 700 of them had already obtained US visas, and a number of them had landing certificates at $150 apiece. Few of them were left with more than the $4 in cash they were allowed to bring out of Germany.

Upon arrival in Cuba two weeks later, they found that their landing permits were deemed to be illegal by the Cuban government in Havana. Only 28 refugees were allowed to leave the ship. Sceptical of the landing certificates, these had hired lawyers in Europe to obtain more complete documentation for a further payment of $500. The Jewish Joint

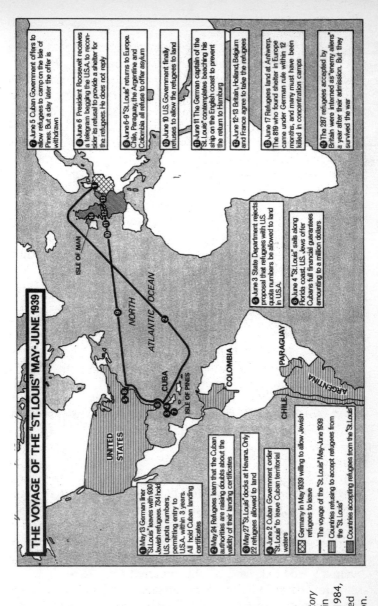

THE VOYAGE OF THE "ST. LOUIS" MAY-JUNE 1939

❼ June 5 Cuban Government offers to allow refugees to camp on the Isle of Pines. But a day later the offer is withdrawn

❽ June 6 President Roosevelt receives a telegram begging the USA. to reconsider its refusal to provide a shelter for the refugees. He does not reply

❾ June 6-9 "St. Louis" returns to Europe. Chile, Paraguay, the Argentine and Colombia all refuse to offer asylum

❿ June 10 U.S. Government finally refuses to allow the refugees to land

⓫ June 11 The German captain of the "St. Louis" contemplates beaching his ship on the English coast to prevent the return to Hamburg

⓬ June 12-13 Britain, Holland, Belgium and France agree to take the refugees

⓭ June 17 Refugees land at Antwerp. The 619 who found shelter in Europe came under German rule within 12 months, and many must have been killed in concentration camps

⓮ The 287 refugees accepted by Britain were interned as "enemy aliens" a year after their admission. But they survived the war

❶ May 13 German liner "St.Louis" leaves with 930 Jewish refugees. 734 hold US. quota numbers, permitting entry to U.S.A. within 3 years. All hold Cuban landing certificates

❷ May 24 Refugees learn that the Cuban authorities are raising doubts about the validity of their landing certificates

❸ May 27 "St.Louis" docks at Havana. Only 22 refugees allowed to land

❹ June 2 Cuban Government order "St.Louis" to leave Cuban territorial waters

❺ June 3 State Department rejects proposal that refugees with US. quota numbers be allowed to land in USA.

❻ June 4 "St.Louis" sails along Florida coast. US. Jews offer Cubans full financial guarantees amounting to a million dollars

ISLE OF MAN

NORTH ATLANTIC OCEAN

UNITED STATES

CUBA

ISLE OF PINES

COLOMBIA

PARAGUAY

CHILE

ARGENTINA

▨ Germany in May 1939 willing to allow Jewish refugees to leave

— The voyage of the "St.Louis" May-June 1939

▥ Countries refusing to accept refugees from the "St.Louis"

▦ Countries accepting refugees from the "St.Louis"

Map 2

The Jewish History Atlas. Sir Martin Gilbert, CBE, 1984, Routledge. Used with permission.

Distribution Committee (JDC) sent two representatives to Havana to work out a solution. Even though they offered to pay up to $125,000 to ensure the passengers would not become a burden to the Cuban government whilst waiting re-emigration, they were refused. The ship was ordered to leave immediately. Sailing along the coastline of Florida in order to gain time, further negative responses were obtained from Latin American countries in spite of the JDC's offer to become a guarantor for the refugees. Attempts to land at a Caribbean port or in the United States were also to no avail.

The hardship of the Jews soon made headlines in the US, but apparently even this did not move the government. A cable to President D. Roosevelt asking refuge for the 908 passengers, of whom more than 400 were women and children, received no reply.

On 9 June the fragile ship containing the refugees had no other option but to return to Germany towards an unknown fate. The *New York Times* wrote in an editorial:

'It is hard to imagine the bitterness of exile, when it takes place over a faraway frontier. Helpless families driven from their homes, to a barren island in the Danube, thrust over the Polish frontier, escaping in terror of their lives to Switzerland or France, are hard for us in a free country to vizualize. But these exiles floated by our shores. Some of them are on the American quota list and can later be admitted here. What is to happen to them in the interval has remained uncertain from hour to hour. We can only hope that some hearts will soften somewhere and some refuge be found. The cruise of the St Louis cries to heaven of man's inhumanity to man.'[15]

On 11 June a desperate cable was sent to the British Prime Minister begging for asylum before the vessel reached Hamburg. At a conference of refugee organisation representatives and government officials, it was agreed that since the Belgian, Dutch and French governments had jointly offered to receive two-thirds of the St Louis passengers, the British government would admit the remainder for whose maintenance the American Jewish Refugee Committee agreed to undertake responsibility. However, other similar refugee ships were not so fortunate. When the Parliamentary Under-Secretary at the Home Office announced the decision, he stressed strongly that the 'special arrangement in this case can not be regarded as a precedent for the reception in future of refugees who may leave Germany before definite arrangements have been made for their admission elsewhere'.[16]

As it turned out, with the German invasion of Poland on 1 September, World War II began, and only the Jewish refugees admitted to England found a safe refuge. The ones who went to Belgium, Holland and France were soon in danger yet again. When the Nazis invaded these countries the refugees salvaged from the St Louis most probably ended up in German concentration camps.

The United States' refusal to receive the St Louis passengers was not lost on the Nazi propagandists. To Hitler it was just another indication that his treatment of the Jews would not arouse much indignation in the US. Thus, the August 1939 issue of *Der Weltkampf* commented on democratic pretence and reality:

> 'We are saying openly that we do not want the Jews, while the democracies keep on claiming that they are willing to receive them – and then leave the guests out in the cold! Aren't we savages better men after all?'[17]

Responses in the British Empire to Jewish Immigration

The British Colonies – Jews not Wanted!

In the British colonial dependencies, the immigration policy varied according to the level of constitutional development each territory had attained. Generally, the restrictions were more stringent than in Britain itself. Besides proof of a definite prospect of employment, evidence of the possession of a minimum sum of money was generally required before the immigrants could enter the colony. Although the government in London could, in principle, overrule the governor's decision, they usually preferred not to do so. It needs also to be taken into consideration that a number of the colonies, due to tropical climate, dangerous diseases, lack of cultivable soil, or lack of a functioning communication system, did not offer ideal living conditions for a European population.

Another considerable obstacle to the resettlement of German refugees in British colonies was that, while the refugees had fitted reasonably well into Britain's economy, this was not the case in the colonies. About one third of the refugees were over 50 years of age and, being mainly businessmen and academics, were not in demand in the often underdeveloped countries where agriculturalists, technicians and craftsmen were needed. For these vocations only the younger refugees could be trained. Another crucial factor was that the German Jews, deprived of funds, were generally not welcome as prospective candidates for settlement anywhere because of lack of capital.

Back in December 1933, before the first High Commission's meeting in Lausanne, the British government had informed their representative, Lord Cecil, that there would generally be 'very little scope for the immigration of persons of a white race into the majority of colonies'.[18] The same restrictive line was followed after the Austrian *Anschluss* in March 1938, when the Colonial Office advised the British passport control officer in Vienna that he should strongly discourage Jewish refugees from attempting to go to any of the colonial dependencies unless they had definite offers of employment. During the five years from 1933 to 1938 Britain, with its vast empire, helped only 400 Jewish refugees to settle in their colonies.

Not until the preliminary debate in London, before the Evian Conference in July 1938, was the possibility of settlement in the colonies discussed in Parliament, and then largely because the British government wanted to avoid the controversial subject of immigration into Palestine. Alternative possibilities were then under investigation in East Africa.

At the Evian Conference, the participants agreed to the unfortunate principle that 'no government funds should be used for large scale settlement projects,' and that the 'country of origin' alone was responsible for securing 'an orderly emigration' by permitting refugees to bring out some capital. As true as this assertion was, such an unrealistic attitude from the countries involved would not help to solve the refugee problem. On the other hand, Britain feared that if exceptions were made for Jews, other groups like the Czechs for example, might try to press the issue.

Great Britain, for its part, did not really want to become involved. Even though Britain was the leading member of the League of Nations it refrained from putting pressure on Germany regarding the economic issues, and moreover, it did not seek to provide settlement areas in its own colonies. For Britain, a good relationship with the Reich was a priority, and the act of giving help to settle the refugees, which could be interpreted as interference in 'an internal German problem', was consequently avoided. The motivation for finding settlement places was, therefore, lacking and proposals were essentially raised to alleviate the political pressure and allay public concern.

A change in the British attitude occurred, however, at the end of 1938 when its foreign policy in Palestine was at stake. As a result of the mounting crisis there and the ensuing clamp-down on Jewish immigration to Palestine the government, despite its economic situation, changed its policy by declaring itself willing to support settlement projects in its own colonies, provided it would increase the prosperity of the empire. However, the difficulties the would-be immigrants encountered are exemplified by the following.

Jews to Africa?

Although Kenya had been mentioned as a possibility for settlement in East Africa, it was soon clear that the governor himself was not in favour of it. He indicated that the British population already settled in Kenya found a Jewish enclave to be 'an undesirable feature in a colony ... which should be developed on lines predominantly British'. The governor added however, that there might be a possibility if the right type of Jews were selected, i.e. Nordic types from Germany and Austria, for agricultural settlement and the building up of the social life of the community'.[19] Sadly, in December 1938 the Colonial Office was informed that the next group of 25 prospective settlers had been imprisoned in German concentration camps. In April 1939, in order to limit immigration, payment on admission was raised from £50 to £500. Despite all the efforts, a total of only 200 Jews was ultimately admitted.

From Northern Rhodesia, twice the size of Great Britain, the Legislative Council similarly reported that the 11,000 strong European population was opposed to Jewish settlement. Even a small initial settlement of just 150 refugees was rejected. As Britain ruled these colonies directly, we can only conclude that if the government had been more sincere in its efforts to promote settlements, they could have succeeded.

Interestingly, the British government also suggested that the German refugees be settled in the former German colonies in Africa (surrendered after World War I). Not only did the proposal provoke an outcry from Berlin, which still maintained the hope of having them returned some day; but also Zionist Jews responded negatively to the idea of living in a territory which might become German again.

In the seven years from 1933 to the end of 1939, it is significant that only 3,000 German Jewish refugees were settled in the British colonies. Equivalent to about one person per day it well illustrates the pervading attitude.

The Dominions

Regarding the dominions of Canada, Australia, New Zealand, and South Africa, the governments of these countries had, during the depression years from 1929–33, erected strong restrictive barriers to keep immigrants out. London could at best advise, but bore no responsibility for their decisions. Britain however, did try to exert some influence for the admission of German refugees.

Only Australia and Canada responded although New Zealand admitted a few families. After some negotiations, Australia informed the IGC that they were prepared to receive 5,000 German refugees annually for three years. An earlier suggestion for a colony of 60,000 Jews in the Northern Territory had, however, been turned down for fear of introducing a racial problem.[20] But in the final outcome, only 1,755 refugees, of whom 1,600 were German and 104 Czech, were able to receive landing permits in the early months of 1939, before the war put a stop to further immigration.

Canada had one of the most stringent immigration regulations and was unwilling to encourage even British immigration. The Canadian Immigration Board feared that if the rules were relaxed, the East European Jews, who comprised the majority of the Jewish group, might flood the country. Also, strong antisemitism existed in the French-speaking parts of the country. After prolonged negotiations, Canada permitted a few hundred, refugee farmers from the Sudetenland and a number of Jewish refugees with capital to enter the country.

After October 1938 South Africa only admitted a few individuals and firmly rejected any notion of large-scale refugee emigration. Previously, from the end of 1936 and during 1937, around 700 German refugees had been allowed in.

When the interim director of the IGC, S. Adler-Rudler, commented on the contribution of the British Empire, he asserted that had Britain genuinely desired to find shelter for Jewish refugees a much larger number could have been taken in. This would have made a most important contribution towards the solution of the problem. As the situation was, their contribution was none too impressive.[21]

The Mandate of Palestine

The Struggle for a 'Jewish Homeland'

After the First World War and the collapse of the Ottoman Empire, the League of Nations gave to Great Britain and France mandates to control a number of emerging Arab countries. While France was given Syria, Iraq and Lebanon, Britain was granted the Mandate of Palestine, then covering the areas known today as Israel and Jordan.

The background for the British and French interest in the Near East was mainly due to their strategic and political involvement in the Suez Canal, the vital gateway for their trade links with the Far East, as well as the growing importance of oil in the Arab countries. Added to this was the fact that during the First World War, a Jewish biochemist, Chaim Weizmann, came to the help of the British Defence Industry by inventing TNT, a plastic explosive which could be made synthetically from horse-chestnuts. In appreciation, in 1917, the British government became instrumental in supporting the establishment of a homeland for the Jews, the only reward which Weizmann requested.

The Balfour Declaration

Through the Balfour Declaration of 1917 the support for 'a Jewish national home in Palestine' was guaranteed by Britain, and later ratified by the League of Nations at the San Remo Conference on 22 April, 1920. The preamble of the Draft Mandate for Palestine acknowledged 'the historical connection of the Jewish people with Palestine'. The Jewish Agency* was set up as a public body covering administrative, economic, social and other matters, which would effect the establishment of a Jewish home.

A body known as the Permanent Mandate Commission kept watch to ensure that the countries which had the mandate bestowed upon them, kept the obligations laid down in their particular declaration, e.g. that the civil and religious rights of existing non-Jewish communities would not be hindered or endangered (article 2). The Mandate Commission was also an organ to which the peoples, as in the case of Palestine, either Arabs or Jews, could direct any grievances.

The 'Jewish Homeland' Sliced

With the Arabs forming an overwhelming majority in the Mandate of Palestine (589,000 or 79% of the population of what is now Israel and Jordan) the stability of the land was endangered. Britain soon realised that it had over-estimated

* The Jewish Agency for Israel was reconstituted in 1929 as the implementing arm of the World Zionist Organisation to represent the Jewish community in the land. Today it is the organisational expression of the relationship between the State of Israel and the Diaspora Jewry.

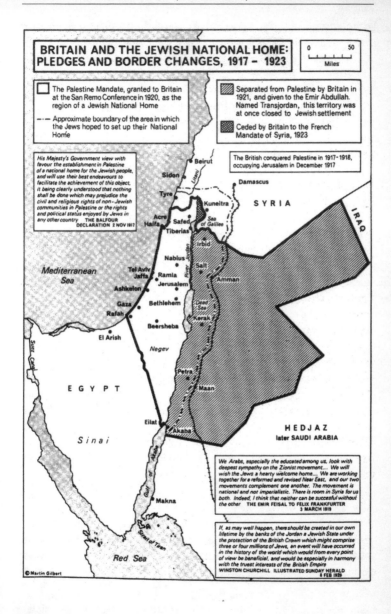

Map3
The Arab-Israeli Conflict. Sir Martin Gilbert, CBE, 1993, Routledge. Used with permission.

the influence of World Zionism. Already in 1922, in an effort to appease the Arabs, the British Colonial Office issued the Churchill White Paper whereby the Balfour Declaration was modified and the Mandate of Palestine divided. Out of the total of 45,760 square miles Britain handed over 35,222, i.e. the 77% of Palestine east of the river Jordan, to Emir Abdullah and named it Transjordan. The population was Palestinian Arab, and no Jews were permitted to settle there. Later, it became known as the Hashemite Kingdom of Jordan. The western, smaller part (the remaining 23%) was then designated as the Jewish Homeland, severely reducing the space available for Jewish settlement and reneging on the promises made in the original Balfour Declaration.

While the British rule over Palestine had been quite stable until the end of the 1920s, the drastic changes which occurred during the 1930s both in Europe and the Middle East, brought Palestine out of its relative isolation and into the centre of political events. Britain was faced with two problems not anticipated by the early policy makers of the Balfour Declaration, namely: a Jewish mass immigration and rising Arab nationalism.

Arab Attempt to Cut Jewish Immigration

During the 1920s Jewish immigration had essentially been unhindered. Then the economic recession in Europe began to cause an increased influx of Jewish immigrants from Poland and Germany. However, many of these were able to bring out some capital to build up their new homeland. As the years went by, the increase of the Jewish population led to protests from the illiterate Arab day-labourers, who were afraid of losing their work. They did not understand that, in fact, it was the Jews, who actually created their work possibilities.*

By 1929, the Jewish community had grown to 156,000 or around 20% of the Arab population, which then numbered

---

* By 1920, the Histadrut, the Federation of Hebrew workers, was established to ensure Jewish workers a basic standard of living, even under adverse circumstances. Arab workers also became members.

In 1934, Histadrut HaOvedim-Leumit (the holding company with its own bank for heavy industry and public works) was formed.

794,000. The tension culminated in an Arab rebellion aimed at stopping Jewish immigration.

A considerable number of casualties occurred in Jerusalem, and in Hebron in particular, 67 orthodox Jews were killed. In order to stop further trouble from the Arabs, the massacre in Hebron led to the swift removal by the British of the surviving Jewish residents, even though their ancestors had lived there for hundreds of years. (Not until after the 6-Day War in 1967, when the Israelis regained the land from Jordan, were the Jews able to re-settle in Hebron.)

In order to calm the Arabs, Britain issued the *Passfield White Paper* in 1930, which limited both immigration and sale of land to Jewish settlers. In order to avoid Arab unemployment a restriction was made to ensure that certain categories would not exceed the absorption capacity. Already in 1930, Britain had introduced a new regulation that at the request of the High Commissioner from Palestine, the British government in London would issue Jewish work certificates (labelled as Category C)* on a half-yearly basis. In order to prevent further rebellion, the number of certificates was to be cut.

But the British government was so severely criticised for their over-reaction in the White Paper by the Mandate Commission of the League of Nations, the English Parliament and, not least, the Jewish Agency, that the Colonial Office had to withdraw most of the effect of the White Paper. (See Appendix IV.)

The Hardship of European Jewry Increases

Between 1933–35, when antisemitic laws and growing anti-semitism began to exert heavy pressure upon Jews in Germany and several East-European countries, 135,000 were

---

* The categories for immigration to Palestine included:
  Cat. A: Persons of independent means, not less than £500 per individual. (By 1933 the fee was raised to £1,000.)
  Cat. B: Students or persons of religious occupation and orphans, whose maintenance was secured.
  Cat. C: The so-called labour schedule for persons who had definite prospect of employment.
  Cat. D: Dependants of permanent residents or of immigrants belonging to other categories.

able to escape by immigrating to Palestine. The situation was comparatively more peaceful there. Of these, 22,757 were German Jews, but the number from Poland, Rumania, Latvia and Lithuania was also considerable. In 1935, immigration reached a peak of 61,854. In the meantime, through the influence of Jewish capital and manpower, many new projects were developed in Palestine. The Arab population shared in the prosperity of the country.

Illegal Arab Immigration to Palestine

A considerable number of the Arab labourers living in Palestine during the 1920s–1930s had come across the border from Jordan, Syria and Egypt, attracted by the prospect of work possibilities which the newly arrived Jews had provided with their funds. Needing no specific British work permit for entry, they just crossed the border and worked as cheap, unskilled labour. The British authorities usually closed their eyes to this influx which they maintained amounted to just a few thousand per year. But many of these Arabs settled permanently, causing economic and political instability, adding to the growth of the indigenous Arab population.[22] However they did not permit Jews to live in Jordan.

The rising Arab nationalism led to protests in which they demanded a cessation of mass Jewish immigration and a ban on land sales. In 1933 the Jewish population was only one fifth of that of the Arabs. However, just three years later in 1936, the Jews had grown to 384,000 or one third of the Arab population, then totalling 970,000.

Arab Rebellion Erupts Again

During 1935–36, the situation in the Mediterranean intensified due to the Italian dictator Mussolini's conquest of Abyssinia (Ethiopia), where Britain was influential. Britain feared that the Arabs would see this as a weakness of the British Empire, rather than being caused by lack of support from the League of Nations. Furthermore, anti-British propaganda from Italy fuelled Arab hatred against their own British rulers and aggravated the situation. The British Foreign Office feared that Italian expansionism might extend to Egypt and the Suez Canal, and in this way endanger her interest in India and the Far East. In the wake of the Italian war came economic depression and unemployment with much tension in the eastern Mediterranean countries. In Palestine the crisis hit the Arab working class harder than the better-organised Jews and further increased antagonism against them.

In April 1936, hostile Arab riots broke out culminating in a general strike aiming to thwart Jewish immigration. Shops were closed for six months. Although the initial phase was aimed against the Jews, in which their crops were destroyed and tens of thousands of citrus trees uprooted, the rebellion soon changed character and began to be directed against British targets in Palestine. The organisers of the upheaval were the newly formed, very nationalistic, Arab Higher Committee under the Muslim leader, Haj Amin al Husseini, Mufti of Jerusalem. This gave the movement a religious emphasis.

Furthermore, since the Arabs in Palestine began to receive support from the surrounding Arab countries, this clearly indicated that the issue had now become a greater Pan-Arab issue. In the British government there was an internal conflict over goals. The Colonial Office, responsible for the Mandate, was in disagreement with the Foreign Office who, for fear of a possible war, advocated an alliance with the Arab states. The Foreign Office also took the initiative to call upon the Arab countries to seek to bring about a quick solution in Palestine.

Britain now attempted to walk the middle road by partly complying with the Arab demands to halt Jewish immigration. The number of certificates issued was severely reduced in spite of the rising need for refuge and the growing prosperity of the country. No visas were to be issued which could cause unemployment, nor was any explanation for the reduction given to the Jewish Agency. On the other hand, immigration did continue to flow and capital was still transferred through the special German *Reichflugsteur* economic transfer plan for Jewish emigrants overseas, previously mentioned. In 1936, the total immigration figure amounted to around 36,000.

When the Arab demands for the suspension of Jewish immigration had become an ultimatum, the British Cabinet decided to reassert British authority and in September 1936 martial law was declared with the arrival of 20,000 British soldiers. The Arab rebels in Palestine finally gave in at the request of the surrounding Arab States, and the strikes and disorder ended in October the same year. There were 1,300 deaths from the uprising, including 28 British and 80 Jews. Hundreds were wounded.

Palestine – Jews Not Wanted!

The Peel Commission – 1937

The future of Jewish immigration was to be decided by two British Royal Commissions dispatched to Palestine. While the tension in the Mediterranean continued to mount, inflamed by the Italian invasion of Libya in July 1937, the first Commission under the leadership of Lord Peel was sent out in order to seek a solution to the growing nationalist issue. The investigation concluded that the existing form of government only 'tended to aggravate the Jewish Arab conflict'.*

The Commission recommended that the idea of a Jewish homeland should be abandoned and the remaining 23% of the original state of Palestine, the part west of the Jordan, should be partitioned into sovereign Jewish and Arab States with a British zone around Jerusalem and Bethlehem. The Arabs would be given by far the largest portion. Even though the majority of the Zionists rejected the idea of a truncated Jewish state calling it 'a sabotage of the Balfour Declaration',[23] some Jewish leaders such as Chaim Weizmann accepted it after some consideration. The suggested Jewish State would, however, have only a small Jewish majority of 258,000 over 225,000 Arabs. The Commission further suggested that immigration to Palestine should be controlled so the proportion between Arabs and Jews could be kept at a ratio 3:1 to ensure that the Jews would remain a permanent

* The solution of partition was proposed by Reginald Coupland, professor of Colonial history, who based it on the principle deduced from his research, that two people who had developed national consciousness could not live together as equal partners in a single state. (Sykes, Christoffer, *Cross Roads to Israel*, London, 1965, 202.)

minority. For immigration, the principle of the economic absorptive capacity was maintained. As the proposed border was indefensible, this would necessitate a revision of the frontier.

Interestingly, in the light of the situation today, the Arab States completely rejected the partition plan as well as the idea of an Arab Palestinian State. The reason for their attitude was that they viewed the whole of Palestine as part of the Middle East Arab territory and did not wish to lose any of it.

The British Foreign Office feared that the partition issue might cause the Arab States to move towards the German–Italian alignment, the Axis. They argued that had it not been for the annual influx of an alien Jewish immigration, the Arabs and Jews already in Palestine would have got along satisfactorily at a local level. They felt that the country was already overpopulated and would never be able to absorb European Jewry. The Office, therefore, suggested that it would be much better if the British government would openly admit that an implementation of the Balfour Declaration was no longer possible, and instead offer the Jews a free gift of British territory somewhere else.

The Woodhead Commission – 1938

The following year, 1938, as Britain was in a dilemma and reluctant to resume the former immigration policy, the Woodhead Commission left for Palestine in order to adjust the borders of the suggested new states. In the event, the commission was unable to come up with a recommendation of boundaries for the proposed areas that could produce self-supporting Arab and Jewish States. The new Colonial Secretary Malcolm MacDonald, yielding to the Foreign Office's view, had already hinted to the committee that such a lack of decision would not be unwelcome to the British government.[24] The British government then decided to take the matter into its own hands and continue to hold the responsibility for the whole of Palestine.

Although the government was severely criticised by the House of Commons for their previous vacillation, they were also in a considerable dilemma, being faced with the choice between either intensifying the existing bitterness among the Jews or increasing the Arab opposition. To the Jews, the outcome of the Woodhead Report was a smarting disappointment as the government was withdrawing more and more from its previous support for the Jewish national home. The abandonment of partition could only be interpreted as a victory for Arab terrorism in Palestine.

Britain Makes Her Own Decision

In order to seek a further solution for the ongoing Jewish–Arab conflict, Britain decided that a conference was to be held in London to discuss future policy. This would include the touchy question of Jewish immigration into Palestine.

From 1937, the reduction of immigrant permits for labourers to Palestine began to be severely felt. Only 12,500 immigrants were permitted in all that year. Although it was clear that on economic grounds Palestine could receive a far larger quota, for political reasons London kept the figure low and reduced the quota annually. In 1938 and 1939, the quotas for legal immigration to Palestine were so severely reduced that only 13,000–16,000 visas were granted.

As an example, the lowest quota granted was in 1937. The Jewish Agency had asked for a total of 22,000 labour permits (Category C) for immigration. The annual quota was, as usual, issued on a half-yearly basis from the administration in London. In total, for the two half-year-periods, it amounted to 5,140 visas or less than 25% of the original request. To this figure would then be added visas granted for other categories, such as independent people with capital, religious students or dependants of permanent residents.[25]

In the light of the unmerciful pressures on the Jews in Europe in late 1938, the reduction of visas to their promised homeland, their only place of refuge, appears even more cruel.

The Catastrophic White Paper – 1939

After the German invasion of the Rump State of Czechoslovakia in 1939, it had become clear to the British that a war with the Reich was inevitable and that their policy of appeasement had failed. Events in Europe seemed to move towards a climax. The mounting tension in the Middle East was heightened by the danger that millions of Moslems might cause riots against the British rule in India and throughout the British Empire because of their pro-Arab sympathies, and in protest against Jewish immigration to Palestine. In the end, the British priority was to seek the strategic advantage of support from the Arab alliance – and the Jews drew 'the short straw'.

The proposed conference to discuss future British policy in the Mandate convened in London on 7 February, 1939, and lasted throughout the month. As the question about immigration into Palestine was being discussed, various Zionist groups from Palestine, Britain and the US were included. By also inviting representatives from various Arab States, the Colonial Secretary MacDonald made it clear that he viewed the conference as a Pan-Arab issue. At the conference there were no real negotiations as both the Jewish and the Arab delegates refused to meet each other, so the Colonial Office had to mediate.

When the conference was about to dissolve because of disagreement, the British government presented the MacDonald White Paper on 17 May, declaring for the first time 'that it is not part of their policy that Palestine should become a Jewish State.'[26] Their objective now was to create 'a state in which the two people in Palestine, Arabs and Jews, shared authority in governing in such a way that the essential interests of each are secured.' A single independent State of Palestine was to be established within ten years.

The British government adopted the plan for immigration which they knew was acceptable to Arabs, namely an annual quota of 10,000 Jewish immigrants on labour certificates over five years and an additional total of 25,000 'free entry', regardless of the country's economic ability to absorb them. The number of illegal Jewish immigrants discovered would be deducted from the yearly quota. After five years no further Jewish immigration would be permitted – unless the Arabs would consent to it.

By issuing the White Paper of 1939, the British policy makers had only continued the course of the previous decade when complacency and vacillation marked a retreat from the Balfour Declaration.[27] From the original goal of establishing a Jewish national home, the British government had turned right around and was now planning for an Arab Palestinian State. To the British it was just a matter of political expediency. The White Paper was a great victory for the Arabs at Jewish expense. To the Jews, it was both harsh and unrealistic to demand the sacrifice of their aspirations for a state at a time when they needed it most as a haven of refuge; and foolish to believe that the Jews would submit and abandon their struggle.

The Zionists tried to exert influence to change the White Paper, but failed. The British Parliament harshly criticised the government, while Churchill warned that 'the White Paper – a betrayal of British promises to the Jews – would cast the country, and all it stood for, one step downwards in its fortune.'[28] In June, the Permanent Mandate Commission reported to the League of Nations Assembly that 'the policy set out in the White Paper is not in accordance with what the Commission had placed on the Palestine Mandate.'[29] But before the League Assembly could meet to consider this opinion, World War II broke out in early September. Because of tension over the approaching war, the British public did not pay much attention to these issues.

In summary: During the years from 1933–39 a total of 204,000 Jewish immigrants arrived in Palestine. For political, rather than socio-economic reasons, only 58,000 (27% of the total) came from the Reich as against 79,000 (32% from Poland). Bauer asserts that if the 1938–39 flow of immigrants had persisted for a few more years, a sizeable portion of German Jewry might have been saved from the European catastrophe.[30] But the expediency of the British Arab appeasement policy prevented it.

Illegal Immigration

With the desperate situation in Europe before World War II, the hopelessness of the Jews is illustrated by the continued rise in the number of immigrants attempting to reach Palestine. From late 1938 illegal immigration was organised on an increasing scale. Out of a total quota for 1939 of 27,561 persons (including all categories), over 11,156 came in illegally – as against 3,400 in 1938. When the British authorities discovered Jewish illegal immigrants, they simply deducted the figure from their quota.[31] The available figures correspond exactly with the official statistics from the Mandate, but we must also keep in mind that the real numbers, which would be much higher, will never be known.

The whole situation appears so much more unjust when we take the unchecked immigration of unskilled Arab workers into consideration. (For a lengthy discussion, see Joan Peters, *From Time Immemorial*, 1984.)

In this connection, it should be added that illegal immigration to Palestine was officially promoted by some of the speakers at the 21st Zionist Conference at Geneva in August 1939. This was, however, in contradiction to the policy of the Jewish Agency (and contrary to the wishes of Weizmann). It led to a situation, in which the Jewish Agency and the British government were brought into direct confrontation.

During the first war years, when the German refugees were still able to flee the Reich, they sought to reach Palestine by any means possible. Cynically, the Polish, Rumanian and other governments sought, with the self-serving assistance of the Gestapo, to push the desperate would-be immigrants into clandestine travel. Faced with these attempts at illegal immigration, the British government attempted to stop the escape routes. Dilapidated ships, sailing overloaded with refugees, were intercepted by British patrol boats and the would-be immigrants placed in camps in Cyprus. Some boats unloaded their passengers outside the territorial waters of Palestine, leaving them to row ashore in small boats. Some Jewish fugitives, captured by the British upon landing on the shores of Palestine, were either imprisoned or deported. In some cases they were fired on, as they entered their homeland.

The Last Hope Quenched

At the beginning of the war the Zionists proposed to the British government that any further implementation of the White Paper be 'frozen' for as long as the military operation lasted. But despite support from Churchill, the

Cabinet decided to abide by the document. In February 1940, a severe limitation on land purchase, also envisaged in the White Paper, was introduced. Land sale to Jews was seriously cut in territories with a major Palestinian Arab population, while purchase by the Jews was permitted in an area with a small rural Arab population. But despite the war and the shortness of money, the Jewish National Fund was in fact, able to acquire a considerable portion.

During the first phases of the war, when there was a real danger that the Middle East might fall to the Axis powers, it is understandable that it was not possible for Britain to change its White Paper policy. It was indeed tragic that, even after the military attacks had stopped, and despite Britain being well aware of the atrocities taking place in German occupied territories, the British government continued its harsh *realpolitik* (practical politics) and callously refused to open the Mandate to Jewish refugees. With this decision the British effectively abandoned the Jewish refugee cause. On 5 September, 1939, just two days after the declaration of war, a Foreign Office official taking minutes wrote: 'So far as we are concerned, the position of Jews in Germany is now of no practical importance to us.' [32]

As the war progressed, the British lost a historic opportunity, not only to champion the cause of human rights, but also to help the Jewish people, and so possibly avert some of the tragic outcome of the Holocaust.

Summary: Britain's Response to the Plight of German Jewish Refugees

The Jewish problem in Europe was not primarily a matter of British concern, but during the 1930s, Great Britain, as the leading country, became deeply involved in the issue due to its responsibility for the Mandate of Palestine. However, the expediency of the British Arab policy prevented them from offering protection by allowing Palestine to be the haven of refuge so desperately needed.

It is evident that although Britain accepted a substantial number of refugees, 50,000, into the United Kingdom in the pre-war years, they did not attempt to help them in any special way or make an effort to absorb them. Since Britain was a Christian country it might have been expected that its standard of help for the refugees would be high and the English would have sympathy for their plight. However, we must, regretfully, be aware of the limitations of any government action and note that such help is generally given only when it does not run contrary to the country's political policies. Thus humanitarian help generally has to come from unofficial refugee bodies.

Although the government had issued the visas, it was the Anglo-Jewish community and their refugee organisations, which extended the invitations and shouldered the major part of the burden for their stay. Some Christian philanthropic societies such as the Quakers, and the Anglican and Catholic Churches, also helped to defray the expenses. This emergency help was commendable, but was it not merely the kind of practical care Christians ought to give?

Even if Britain's response to the German Jewish refugee problem was considered to rate quite well, it might merely be indicative of how poorly the European countries generally responded to the desperate human need. For all the nations could surely have done better.

Other Nations' Response to the German Jewish Refugee Problem

Having looked at British policy in the 1930s, it would also be interesting to see how other sovereign countries responded to the pressing refugee problem. In the Depression Years of the later 1920s and through the 1930s all Western governments struggled with the same problems which Britain faced. The difficult economic situation caused all countries to put a bar on immigration in order to protect their citizens from the increased tax burdens and the unemployment that would result from the influx of a large number of refugees. Therefore the criterion for entry into any country was whether the potential immigrant could become an economic asset. The fact that it was an immigration of German Jews also caused a social problem which gave rise to anti-alien and antisemitic feelings, and the population was not always sympathetic to the refugee's plight. This too was a restraining factor on each government's consideration of immigration.

Let us now compare Britain with the response from some of the other sovereign countries. From the onset of the first antisemitic persecution in 1933–1939 and into the early 1940s, France, Belgium and the Netherlands, all bordering on Nazi Germany, were exposed to waves of Jewish refugees. The major reason that these three countries and Britain received the highest number of German refugees was that they contained the largest Jewish communities in Western Europe outside Germany. (The Jewish centres ranged in size from 60,000–300,000 Jewish residents.) These communities then formed the basis of the refugee aid societies that, in turn, could put pressure upon their governments to admit more Jews.[33]

It seems then that it was the Jewish communities in the various countries who spearheaded the rescue of German Jews rather than, as has often been asserted that it was the Christians who helped the Jews. Certainly, in the early years of the Nazi regime, this was not the case.

It should also be noted that even if France, Holland and Belgium admitted fewer refugees than Great Britain; 88,000 between them, proportionally they responded better in the period from 1933 and October 1939. France took 10 refugees per 10,000 local residents and Belgium and the Netherlands 30 per 10,000 whereas the corresponding figure for Britain was only 7.5 per 10,000 residents.

In the United States, the situation was different again. Situated far from the war zone, and containing a Jewish population numbering 4.7 million, who would have served as a strong support group, they were in an excellent position to come to the rescue of German Jewry. However, although the US took in 85,000 refugees, the ratio of these immigrants was only 0.76 per 10,000 residents. It seems, therefore, that America could have provided a haven for a much larger number of Jews.

In total, France was probably highest on the European scale of help as it also took in 80,000 Spanish refugees. Britain was somewhere in the middle. As it was mainly the Jewish communities which responded to the plight of German Jewry, we can perhaps understand how catastrophic it was for the Jewish population of Europe when these countries too were overrun by the Germans and their Jewish communities largely destroyed.

Seen in retrospect, all the nations could surely, in one way or another, have given more help. On the other hand, none of the countries could imagine that the German Jews were heading for annihilation and the need for help was so acute.

Although the European refugee policy was in many ways similar to the British, it might be helpful to look briefly at some of the different features that characterised the various countries who, because of their geographical position, became involved in the Jewish tragedy.

France

In the 1930s France, with a population of 42 million, had become by far the most prominent refugee country in Europe. There were several reasons for this. For decades the French people had maintained a democratic and humanitarian tradition, which offered a place of asylum to political refugees compelled to leave their home country. Thus, since World War I, Paris had been the European intellectual and spiritual centre for Russian emigrants. These were later joined by Armenians, Assyrians, Italians, Turks, Saarlanders from the German border country, and other fugitives. As an example, at the peak of the Civil War in Spain, the number of Spanish refugees reached 350,000, later decreasing to 80,000. At that time, in 1936, there were already 2.5 million foreigners in the country.

In 1933, when the Nazi regime began to issue its new political doctrines and antisemitic laws, tens of thousands of German refugees fled to the border of the nearest free country, such as France, Belgium and the Netherlands. The crowds of unfortunate people included Social Democrats, Communists, Jews and others, all hoping to find work and create a new future.

With only half the population of her larger neighbour Germany, France was interested in increasing her population in order to compete economically. Being a comparatively rich country, France needed manpower and immigrants were welcomed. For several decades France had been dependent upon foreign workers. Mining alone absorbed 50–75% of the immigrants and a considerable number also found work in factories and agriculture. Furthermore, from a military point of view, France was interested in increasing its population through absorption of refugees as they were unlikely to have loyalties elsewhere.

To begin with France willingly issued not only identity cards but also travel documents to those newcomers who were willing to give up their German passports.

According to information from the Hebrew Immigration Aid Society (HIAS): 10% of the early German refugees were political. Most of the Jewish applications for asylum came from small traders and artisans. The Hebrew Aid society often set up centres giving training in various manual trades, agriculture and other occupations, which would enable the refugees to earn a living. Small loans were also distributed to immigrants to establish businesses.

One year later, however, as competition on the labour market grew, France began to change her attitude and tighten the rules for admission. The population was generally afraid of being swamped by outsiders who were not part of the French Trade Unions and who were willing to work for lower pay. Antisemitism was also rising. Complaining to the High Commission for Refugees from Germany, the French government declared that they did not want to become a dumping ground for refugees.[34]

By the summer of 1936 an intense political conflict arose within the Socialist Party when the Popular Front, headed by Leon Blum, took power. They had a more friendly policy towards refugees, and the number of expulsions, which had reached a peak in the previous years, fell appreciably. However, much of the French working class continued to remain hostile to the arrival of outcasts from abroad and this often surfaced in sweeping attacks on Jewish refugees.

The following year, when the French government again changed leadership to Edouard Daladier, it turned against the former liberal policy on refugees. After the Anschluss, when the refugees increased pressure on the international borders, a decree was issued in May 1938 under which the refugees found it increasingly difficult to obtain work and temporary residency permits. In contrast to Spanish refugees who, during the civil war, were regarded as temporary visitors, German refugees were turned back by French border officials unless they had an assured promise of emigration overseas. At the same time, Austrian refugees were entering illegally, but in spite of threats of expulsion from France, these were usually drafted into labour organisations. The kinder reception for the Austrians was probably due to the previous 70 years of Franco-German wars, and political suspicion which caused a somewhat colder attitude to the German refugees. As a new wave of exiles from Czechoslovakia joined the previous groups, the French became nervous and even low ranking frontier officials were permitted just to turn the refugees back.

By the late 1930s, several thousand Jews were still waiting in France for final repatriation to the United States, South America, South Africa and other places overseas. Tragically many of them never got there because the Nazi army began to invade the country in May 1940.

In conclusion: France was probably the European country which took in the greatest number of refugees from Greater Germany per capita, 40,000 people in all.

Belgium and the Netherlands

Since many of the features that characterised the reception of the German Jews in France were also similar for Belgium and the Netherlands, these two countries will be referred to together. Both countries, very similar in size and with a population of about 8 million, were positive towards the plight of refugees. This was expressed by attending the various Geneva Conventions and in granting asylum to the needy.

Bordering Germany, these countries were flooded with refugees right from the beginning of the Nazi persecution. From the early years of the regime, a considerable number, particularly of political fugitives, were deliberately dumped by the Gestapo mostly inside the French or Dutch border. The neighbours, from their side, tried to show that they would not tolerate such a policy by either driving these 'undesirables' back into Germany or on into Belgium. For some years this aspect soured the relationship between Belgium and its neighbours. Furthermore, the European economic recession was also an important impetus to preserve the stability of the internal labour market and restrict foreign workers' access to it.

Moreover, over the years British refugee organisations had added to the Dutch problem by using Holland as a holding area for Jewish refugees, while their applications for permanent residence were processed. By August 1937, as the backlog of German refugees destined for England increased, the Dutch at last complained. They did not appreciate being used as 'a wastepaper basket for the whole of Europe'.[35]

However, Jewish businessmen with capital were able to escape and start enterprises for export both in Belgium and Holland. As in Britain, as time went by local labourers also found work in these enterprises.

After the Evian Conference, when none of the larger countries with greater opportunities for settlement seemed to be prepared to act, Holland and Belgium chose different ways to solve the refugee issue. While the Belgian government attempted to settle a considerable number and train them in various occupations and employ them in their country, the Dutch made an effort to help them emigrate.

The sufferings of *Kristallnacht* stirred both the Belgian and Dutch people. But even though the population had much sympathy for the German refugees and urged their two governments to ease the entrance regulations, the authorities were reluctant to consent, except for the most desperate cases, such as children abandoned at the borders. With the increasing danger of war, the Dutch government, for political reasons, became reluctant to admit a large number of German citizens into their country. They were already coping with refugees from Spain. But in spite of the official hard line, the number of admissions still rose. In November 1938 Belgium adopted a resolution to give shelter to 2,000 German refugee children.

For some years international Jewish aid societies, like the American Jewish Joint Distribution Committee, had helped local Jewish communities support several thousand Jewish refugees passing through the country. By late 1938, partly due to the large number of illegal immigrants, the national Jewish Aid Committees were no longer able to care for the large number of refugees. Furthermore, the rate of transmigration overseas was far lower than expected. In order to cope with the difficulties, camps were set up much earlier than in England. These gave training for various occupations as well as agriculture.

Both in Belgium and the Netherlands the governments became involved in helping the refugees much earlier. In June 1939, when the funds of the voluntary Jewish organisations in Belgium were again very low, the Parliament granted £41,000 towards expenses for the upkeep of 10,000 refugees.

In the same year, Dutch religious groups joined in fundraising through a National Collection. In May it was decided to set up a large central training camp for 2,500 immigrants: £125,000 for this came from the government. Sir Herbert Emerson of the IGC (Inter-Governmental Committee on Refugees) commended Holland for having gone further than most countries in accepting that the refugee problem involved some charges on public funds.[36]

Because of the large influx of illegal refugees in the late 1930s, transmigration went much slower than expected. Belgium, however, made an attempt to settle a relatively large number (2,500) in Belgian Congo, but the climate was found unsuitable for whites. From the Netherlands, the majority of the emigrants went to Palestine, Australia and the United States. The more wealthy ones left for Shanghai.

While new crowds of refugees continued to cross the border, only about one third of those staying in training camps were able to emigrate before the Germans invaded the country in May 1940.

✤ ✤ ✤

Both Belgium and the Netherlands gave shelter to a comparatively large number of German refugees; 25,000 and 23,000 respectively.

Tragically, the countries which responded so well towards

German Jewry: France, Belgium and Holland, were quickly occupied by Nazi Germany at the beginning of the war. They would otherwise have been in a position to make a very considerable contribution to saving Jewish refugees.

Switzerland

Over the decades Switzerland's geographical position has exposed her to numerous refugee waves. But although she was previously an important country of asylum for political fugitives and intellectuals, during the 1920s neither Russians nor a major part of the Nansen refugees were welcomed.

Switzerland, with its 4 million population, regarded itself as a transit country. In spite of a general reluctance to accept fugitives, between April–September 1933 the Swiss Confederation admitted a large number of refugees (both Aryan and Jewish) at one frontier with Germany, allowing them to reside temporarily in Switzerland pending re-immigration elsewhere. Since the beginning of the 1930s Swiss officials feared the unemployment problem, and refugees were supposed to bring in enough capital to live from. For this reason, the number of German fugitives declined sharply after 1933.

For about 5 years this remained the essence of Swiss policy and the confederation was regarded as merely a place of transit. The various cantons, however, had the right to give temporary residence permits for up to two years. Local authorities had wide powers to refuse entry into the country, and the government in Bern could not force them to accept political refugees.

In the succeeding period the great majority of those crossing the border were Jews, as was the case elsewhere. Unfortunately, the Swiss Jewish community was not in a strong position to lobby on their behalf as they were only 0.4% of the population, about 18,000 in 1930, and almost half of these were foreigners. Yet, after 1933 local Jewish organisations began to finance re-emigration of refugees.

After the *Anschluss* in 1938, when German refugees again thronged the border, the Swiss government tightened procedures for admission. Therefore many Austrians fled illegally over the mountains into Switzerland. During that summer only the several thousand refugees who arrived via Zürich, a city with a more liberal policy, were allowed to stay because Jewish organisations there took responsibility for them. A central camp in Dupuldsau was also established.

In September, when the German authorities began to issue their own passports to Austrian emigrants, the Swiss introduced a visa system under which no German refugee would be admitted without a pass from a Swiss consulate in Germany. In October the Swiss Interior Ministry began to turn back German Jews: these were easily identified as their passports had been stamped with a red capital 'J' for Jew, three centimetres high. The historian Isaac Gutman has described this discrimination as 'criminal'.[37] According to an announcement from the Swiss police on 4 October, Germans carrying passports indicating that they were non-Aryans now had to receive special authorisation to enter Switzerland. Thus, admission was made even more difficult.

In February 1939 Switzerland introduced even more stringent police regulations, under which illegal refugees were more vigorously tracked down, so reducing the number of fugitives still further.

By the end of December 1938, there were around 10,000 stateless German people in Switzerland, of whom 5,000 were Jews. 3,000 were supported by the Jewish community or private relief organisations. About 900 refugees were kept in various camps.

During the war Switzerland, like most other neutral countries, tried not to offend Germany upon whom their economy and safety largely depended. In fact, they supplied much towards the German war effort in both arms and finance, probably in an attempt to preserve themselves. In retrospect it seems that without their help the Nazis would not have lasted nearly as long. The Allies would not bomb a neutral country, so arms manufacture for Germany continued unabated in Switzerland throughout the war.

Recently it has been revealed that the Swiss National Bank received gold from Germany during the war to a value of nearly $4 billion. Some was savings but most of it was looted.

In real terms $1.25 billion of this was Jewish property taken by the Nazis and much of it gold from Jewish teeth fillings and wedding rings belonging to Holocaust victims (744 kilograms). 80,000 relatives are, at the time of writing, filing a lawsuit demanding that the bank return all property which belonged to Holocaust victims (*Jerusalem Post*, 22 August, 1998).

The United States

The economic depression in the 1920s almost caused the USA, with its 129 million population, to close its borders to immigration. Until 1938 immigrant quotas were not filled. Although a vast country with unlimited resources, the Americans were afraid of added competition in what they deemed an exhausted labour market. They feared that foreigners might become a public liability. Only professional businessmen, industrialists or other people with some capital were admitted, together with some academics or scholars of international standing. An Emergency Committee for Dispersed Foreign Scholars was established.

When legally admitted however, there was technically no difference between refugees and immigrants. They had the same possibility of employment, education and social welfare facilities. A very high proportion of the German quota, possibly as high as 90–95% were refugees. Polish emigrants, including many Jews, also tried to gain entrance to the USA.

Although President Roosevelt was the initiator of the Evian Conference and showed much interest in the refugees' plight, several authors, including Feingold, point out that this was mainly rhetoric.[38] Just one year after the Evian Conference, when the USA raised the quota for immigration into the country, the State Department again restricted the filling of quotas and thus abandoned the potential immigrants to their fate. When mass rescue was still possible, the Roosevelt Administration did not have the incentive to follow it up, although there were individuals who did want to help.

The Child Refugee bill is an example of this. Early in 1939 a bill was presented in the Senate regarding the admission of

10,000 German refugee children under the age of 14 during 1939 and a similar number in 1940. Their entry would be considered as additional to the regular refugee quota. The youngsters, who were of different religious persuasions, would be adopted temporarily by American families, and the cost covered by various organisations or individuals. But the gracious offer was strangled with the xenophobic excuse that in case of war America 'would be swamped with spies'.[39] In June after the British White Paper was issued, the Child Refugee bill was passed, but now the 20,000 youngsters to be admitted over the next two years, would have visas issued against the German quota, not in excess of it.

While both the American government and the majority of the American people condemned Nazi actions, the majority of them supported the restrictionist view, and were opposed to letting in more of Europe's oppressed people. Antisemitism in the US continued to rise till well into the early 1940s. Surveys from 1938–41 show that between one third to one half of the public believed that 'Jews had too much power' in the country. It seems therefore that the US refugee policy from late 1938 to 1941 did reflect the wishes of the people.

The vast USA, which could have played such an important role by opening up their country to rescue German Jewry, only admitted a small portion, some 85,000, in the pre-war days. This was less than the total for France, Belgium and Holland. The ratio of the immigrants to the USA amounted only to 0.76 per10,000 of the population.

It is also important to recall, as pointed out by the Christian historian David Wyman, that during the first couple of years of the war, half of the USA immigrant quota went to applicants from Britain and Ireland. In all 84,000 out of 154,000 were granted to countries with little or no need for emigration. Conversely, from the German occupied countries of Europe, only 10% of the already small quota limits were filled. Yet, it is noticeable that between September 1939 and the end of 1941 when the exits were finally sealed, 71,500 Jews left Greater Germany. These represented about one fifth of the Jews remaining in the expanded German state.

Until July 1941 when the US entered the war, and even

later, immigration to the USA would still have been possible as ships from Europe were regularly crossing the Atlantic while Hitler expanded towards the south and east. But the gates of America had closed to the refugees even more tightly than before 1938. The best opportunity to save European Jewry had passed.[40]

The Shortcomings of American Jewry

One might wonder why American Jewry did not play a larger role in the rescue of their own fellow believers. Although there was a considerable Jewish population in the United States, around 4.8 million in 1939, the support for the German Jewish cause was not strong. There were several reasons for this. While the British Jews had for decades been used to putting pressure on their government, the American Jews had not lived long enough in the USA to be an influential group. Since American Jews were already strongly supportive of the government, the President would not have gained anything by changing his attitude to a pro-Jewish refugee policy. In fact, this would most likely have lost him general support.

When the situation in Europe was critical, the various Jewish groups became divided between Zionist and non-Zionist. While the latter simply intended to rescue Jews out of the German inferno, the Zionist Bergsonite group wanted to put pressure upon Britain to open the doors of Palestine. This, together with the trauma of domestic antisemitism, prevented the creation of a united Jewish front. The outcome was fatal. However, the assistance that was provided by the American Joint Distribution Committee to European refugees, both Jews and non-Jews, was very valuable.

For decades America had been considered a generous nation, a land of immigration. With their humanitarian government, a concerned Jewish population and a major Christian country, called by their faith to help the helpless, they could together have been a powerful influence for effective action. The only free Western countries capable of withstanding Nazi Germany were the United States and Britain, but in their fight for victory, the internal struggle against the annihilation of German Jewry was forgotten.

Scandinavian Responses

Let us then make a comparison with the Scandinavian countries. Denmark, Norway, Sweden and Finland, in spite of their small Jewish populations, only amounting to 2–3% of those of Britain and France, came to play important roles in the rescue of German Jewry during World War II. The Danish and Swedish rescue operation of 1943 is well known, and it stands as an interesting contrast to the usual European pattern.

As background information, the Scandinavian countries are among the more progressive in Europe. For several centuries a relatively small number of Jews lived there, and there was never any significant antisemitism.

In the pre-war years of the 1930s neither Denmark, Norway nor Sweden ever played much of a role in providing refuge. The post-war depression after 1929 did, of course, also affect Scandinavia. The unemployment rate was high and many of their young people emigrated to the USA and Canada in order to seek their fortunes there. Consequently, their immigration laws were restrictive as they tried to keep out foreigners. This also included German immigrants. The small Jewish population in Scandinavia was neither sufficiently large to be able to support the needs of German Jewry, nor to exert any influence. As a consequence, in the pre-war years only very small numbers of Jews were permitted to enter these countries.

As a forerunner to the Evian Conference in 1938, a refugee conference was held in Copenhagen, Denmark, where the Scandinavian countries sought mutual agreement on their refugee policies. The Swedish representatives asserted that since '... Jews were southerners, emigration to South America, for example, would be preferable, since the climate there would be much more similar.'[41] It was agreed to limit admissions as far as possible. During the 1930s, Denmark received the largest number of refugees of all the Scandinavian countries, about 4,500 (until April 1940, when the country was occupied by German troops). However, 3,000 of these only stayed there for a year to 18 months, while being trained in agriculture. They then moved on, mainly to Palestine.

Prior to the war, Sweden received only 3,000 refugees even though Sweden's economic capacity to absorb refugees was proportionally much greater than countries such as Belgium, Holland, France and Great Britain.[42] The poor reception was mainly due to the fact that the almost 7,000 Jews living in Stockholm were very assimilated and did not support an influx of Jewish refugees sufficiently. (In comparison with 1944, when Sweden would care for a total of 175,000 refugees, of whom 45,000 were Jews.)[43]

During the 1930s, Norway had a very restrictive policy towards foreigners, including Jews. It was felt that their approximately 1,750 well-assimilated Jewish citizens were sufficient. The government feared that an increase might lead to antisemitism. It was, however, clear that the Jews were discriminated against in comparison with political refugees. The main reason here was also that the small Jewish community did not have as many strong spokesmen in Norwegian society as the political ones. Even when Norwegian Quakers offered to take in some German Jews to be trained in agriculture this was refused by the Ministry of Justice as late as 1939.[44] Towards the end of the decade there were only 700 Jewish refugees in the country.

In April of 1940, the German Army occupied both Denmark and Norway. In Norway there was fierce fighting. The Norwegian King Hakon VII had to escape to England, where a government in exile was set up. Norway managed, however, to place practically their entire merchant fleet at the service of the Allies. While 700 Jews were taken to German concentration camps in Poland (mainly Auschwitz) where they died, the remaining approximately 750 Norwegian Jews were able to flee to Sweden.

The reason for Sweden's neutrality was mainly due to the strength of the Swedish army, and Germany was reluctant to undertake the risk of another heavy battle so close to the Soviet Union. An agreement with Sweden was reached whereby German troops were allowed to use 10% of their railways to transport German soldiers across the country. Besides this Germany also received valuable iron and metal ore for their war production.

The Jewish Rescue in 1943

After the Danish surrender in 1940, an agreement was made for passive collaboration as long as the Germans respected the Danish law and the authority of the government. Denmark became 'a model protectorate'. After 27 August, 1943, when martial law had been declared in Denmark, the Nazis pressed for a 'final solution' to the Jewish Question and the Danish government resigned. Any action against Denmark's 8,000 Jews, the German authorities were told, would lead to an uprising of the Resistance Movement. However, no plans to get the Jews to Sweden had been made. During the previous months several hundred Jews had themselves secured permission from the Swedish Legation in Copenhagen to move there, and the figures rose considerably to over 400 in September. The German civilian authority in Denmark had implied that a round up of all Danish Jews was scheduled for the night of 1–2 October.

Not until 30 September, did Sweden declare herself willing to receive all Jews from Denmark. The Danish people – the Resistance Movement and Lutheran National Church playing a major role – helped nearly 7,500 to make the hazardous journey in boats across the Sound between Zeeland and Sweden to safety on 3 October. The motivation for the Resistance Movement's rescue action was the fact that the German act was considered a violation against Danish citizens (whatever ethnic background they might have) rather than that they were Jews.

One cause for the success of the operation was the willingness of the German officials in Denmark to let 'the Jews slip through their fingers.[45] If it had not been for the approaching German defeat on the eastern front and the fall of Stalingrad* in January 1943, Sweden would not have dared to take the risk, and there would not have been a country of refuge to which Denmark could pass the Jews. In fact, only 50

---

* As a part of the German 'Barbarossa plan' to attack the Soviet Union, in the last half of 1942 the German Army was pressing on the Eastern front line, particularly in mid and southern Russia. At two major battles, Kursk and Rostow, the Germans had been defeated and the loss of Stalingrad on 31 January, 1943, indicated that the Germans could not win the war.

Danish Jews, deported to Germany before the rescue action took place, were killed.

Wallenberg's Unique Rescue

An exceptional rescue took place in 1944 when the Allies used the neutral governments such as Sweden to support their rescue efforts of Jews in Hungary. A Swedish diplomat, Raoul Wallenberg, led a mass venture in the struggle to counter the Nazi deportations and save Jewish lives in Budapest. He worked as a representative for the Swedish government and the US War Refugee Board, which supplied him with money. Wallenberg issued protective passports to Hungarian Jews, placing them in a number of houses, which he rented or bought. These buildings, being Swedish extra-territorial property, could thus provide shelter for them. At least 20,000 Jews were saved in this period. However, the Hungarian government soon changed to a very antisemitic Nazi puppet regime, slaughtering thousands of Jews. The Soviet army was approaching. In January 1945, Wallenberg left for the Russian occupied zone in order to request emergency relief for the Jews in the city. He was taken captive by the USSR and is presumed to have died in a Soviet prison camp although details have never been established.

Finland Also Gives Protection

As far as Finland is concerned, at the outbreak of the war, about 2,000 Finnish Jews were living there together with 300 Jewish refugees from Germany. When Finland refused to give in to Soviet territorial demands in November 1939, the USSR launched the Winter War against Finland. After the loss of Karelia, the Finns forced the Soviets back. In 1941 when Germany attacked the USSR, Finland joined them in an alliance in order to regain the lost land. Although Finland provided a base for the German operations, the Nazis did not press the idea of the 'final solution' for fear of losing military support. A few hundred of the Jews had been able to escape to England and the USA through northern Finland in 1941, and later another small group of 160 was sent to Sweden in the spring of 1944. The remaining Finnish Jews survived the war.

Let us lastly take a look at the response of two other countries, one on the side of the Axis powers and the other of the Allies. Both of them played roles of fatal significance in the tragedy of the Jewish Holocaust, namely religious Italy with the Vatican State and the atheistic Soviet Union.

Italy and the Vatican

Italy sided with Germany early in the 1930s and the Berlin-Rome power-axis was formed.

After Hitler rose to power and began issuing antisemitic laws in 1933, Italy appeared to continue its liberal policy towards the admission of German refugees. They were all well received as a large number of those who arrived in the earlier years were able to bring out some capital which they invested in Italian businesses.

During 1935–36 Italy's fight for more *lebensraum* led to expansionist wars in Africa. However, even the Italians' invasion and capture of Abyssinia (Ethiopia) could not unify the League of Nations sufficiently to put sanctions on Italy. This only made the aggressor more self-confident and the relationship between the members of the League became very tense. Britain in particular, felt that the interference in Ethiopia, rich in raw materials, endangered their interests in the upper reaches of the Nile and the Suez Canal. This placed Italy firmly on the German side of the power-balance in Europe. These two countries intervened in the Spanish Civil War in 1936 against the rising Communist influence there. In November of the same year, they signed the Anti-comintern treaty[46] aimed at stopping a further advance of the Soviet Union in Europe.

After the German *Anschluss* in March 1938, the police station in Milan reported the arrival in that town alone of some 1,600 Austrian, German and Polish Jews. By November, a total of 10,000 Jewish refugees had come to Italy.

In 1938 Italy took a decisive step and began to follow Nazi

policy. That year the Fascist government launched a general antisemitic campaign, enacting laws particularly directed against foreign Jews, making their qualifications useless and removing their means of livelihood. In March 1939 about 20,000 Jews of non-Italian origin became liable for expulsion. They were urged to leave the country and settle in the newly conquered Abyssinia (Ethiopia). These cunning plans did not materialise however as World War II broke out.

On 10 June, 1940, after declaring war on England and France, Italy joined the Axis in the battle for North Africa. However, by 1941 Britain had already defeated Italy in Ethiopia and restored Haile Selasse to his former position as Emperor. By late 1941 7,000 Italian Jews, having been stripped of their citizenship, had left Italy for other destinations.

The Vatican

Within Italy the Vatican functions as an independent, sovereign state. It maintains its own foreign service. The Pope has the highest authority as the head of the Roman Catholic Church.

Despite the Vatican enjoying the religious allegiance of Europe's many millions of Roman Catholics and possessing a unique moral authority, there is very little evidence to show that in the early years of the Nazi regime the Roman Catholic Church protested effectively against the injustices of the German regime. Adolf Hitler died a Catholic and a yearly mass is celebrated in his memory in Madrid. Many other top Nazi leaders including Himmler and 42% of the elite SS troops, were members of the Catholic church, and a statement of disapproval might have halted some of the antisemitic plans against the Jews. However, in order not to offend the new political regime in Nazi Germany, the Vatican followed its traditional line of diplomacy.

When Hitler began to issue his antisemitic laws, they were very harmful to all Jews, including Jews who had converted to other religions. In the Catholic Church they divided the Jews into three categories: the orthodox ones, still adhering to their age-old Judaism, secular Jews and baptised Jews, members of their particular Christian denomination.

It was particularly on behalf of the baptised group that the *nuncios*, the Catholic bishops in their various countries, intervened, filing protests with the government on their behalf. Later, when the pressure upon the Jews in Greater Germany increased the Vatican appears to have been generous in helping them financially and arranging for emigration. (Thus, in 1941 about 1,000 baptised Italian Jews were able to leave for Brazil.) Even if the Vatican suspected that some Jews regarded baptism as a way to escape antisemistic persecution, this was accepted as a way of protecting their lives.

Late in 1938 and into 1939, when antisemitic pressure was intensified, humanitarian concern came to play an increasingly important role. However, when Jews were not members of the established church, even though living as an oppressed people in Germany, Eastern Europe, or other mainly Catholic countries, the Catholic church was not concerned for them.

In his book *Vatican Diplomacy during the Holocaust, 1939–1943* the American priest John F. Morley points out that there is much evidence that at a very early stage the Holy See was remarkably well informed about all that took place in the various countries – from the Nazi murder of the ruling class in Poland to the 'final solution' of the Jews.[47] Although the major part of the Holocaust took place in countries where the Catholic Church was well represented – the fact did not seem to move them sufficiently to act officially. Although the Vatican was sympathetic to the plight of the Jews and occasionally acted on their behalf as in the case of the deportation of Jews from Northern Italy, the Pope never unequivocally condemned the Nazi actions.* Nor did the Vatican use its radio or extensive influence to expose the German myth of resettlement. If they had been warned, Jews

---

* In August 1944, President Roosevelt took the initiative to have his personal representative to the Vatican, Myron C. Taylor (known from the Evian Conference), together with the IGC delegate in Italy, approach the Pope. They asked him to urge the German government to stop the deportation of Jews to Auschwitz from German-occupied northern Italy and to release them to the Allied-held part of the country. Although the nuncio in Berlin made the request, he only received an evasive response. (Wyman p. 229)

would not have gone willingly to the death camps and many more Christians would have taken action to shelter them.

On the other hand, it is questionable how much the protests of the church might have benefited the Jews during the war, and probably the task would have been impossible. But it was a tragedy that the Church in the various countries, for the most part, missed their God-given opportunity to show their concern.

We are of course aware that a number of Jewish people were rescued by Catholic establishments and hidden, particularly in monasteries and convents, in German-occupied countries throughout Europe. This was a very commendable deed. However, it must be admitted that during the Holocaust the Catholic Church generally failed to live up to the high religious and humanitarian ideals it proclaims. This is also the reason why current historians pass serious judgement on the omissions and negligence of the pope of the war years, the late Pius XII.[48]

The Soviet Union

The last allied country that played an important role in World War II, was the USSR. This will be dealt with separately, partly because their ruling doctrines of Marxism and Nazism can both be regarded as post-Christian ideologies and because the Soviet Union with its Marxist ideology was very different from the Western Allies. In the fascist countries leaders claimed that their system transcended previous world systems of political thought and style of life. Consequently the Soviet and German treatment of ethnic minority groups was rather similar. Humanitarian concerns were of little interest to the Soviet government. The Stalinist policy, with its strong emphasis on antisemitism, caused Russia to become similar to Germany in several ways. The plight and sufferings of the Jewish people were completely ignored.

Because of the specific way the Holocaust developed in the USSR with its 5 million Jewish citizens, I will add a few important points. Already seven months before the outbreak of the war, Hitler had spelled out his plans for the last phase of the Final Solution. The initial stage of this was to be 'tested out' in the USSR. In his speech in the Reichtag on 30 January, 1939, Hitler said:

> 'Today, I will be a prophet: if the international Jewish financiers in and outside Europe once more should succeed in plunging the nations into a world war, the result will not be Bolshevization of the world, which would mean the triumph of Jewry, but the annihilation of the Jewish race in Europe.' [49]

This statement contained the core of Hitler's view: Bolshevism and Jewry were one and the same. He believed by liquidating Soviet Jewry, he would achieve two purposes: to undermine the foundation of the Soviet State and eliminate the sworn enemy, i.e. the Jews.[50]

However, Allied politicians either laughed at the speech or ignored it.

During the 1930s no German refugees sought asylum in the Soviet Union. On 1 September, 1939, the German Army occupied Western Poland, causing hundreds of thousands of Jews to flee into the eastern section of the country. Two weeks later, on 17 September, the Red Army marched into eastern Poland and tens of thousands of refugees managed to escape into Soviet territory.

However, at the end of October, the Soviets closed the border. When Nazi-persecuted Jews attempted to get into the Soviet section, the Russians forced them back to the German side. The 300,000–400,000 Polish Jewish refugees were then ordered to choose whether to accept Soviet citizenship or return to their previous homes in the western sector. But since the Soviet authorities gave almost no help to the homeless, the majority chose to go back, where most of them perished. The remaining Jews in the Soviet Union were deported to labour camps in the interior of the country.

On 22 June, 1941 Hitler initiated the German-Soviet War by marching into the USSR in his quest for *lebensraum*. The Soviet government then deported and imprisoned thousands of Jews together with non-Jewish 'bourgeoisie' and 'unreliable' elements from eastern Poland. This was extended to the annexed Baltic States and Rumania in order to prevent them from collaborating with the Germans. In this way many of the deportees avoided the Nazi occupation in their home areas.

In May–June of 1941 the Wehrmacht government issued orders which provided the SS with a 'legal' basis for mass extermination of their enemies, such as Bolsheviks, saboteurs and Jews in the areas under their control. By December 1941, out of a Jewish population of 253,000 in the Baltic States, 210,000 or 90%, had been murdered by the Nazis.[51]

When Stalin announced a 'scorched earth' policy in an attempt to move administrative personnel, important industries, machinery and workers from the Baltic countries to the east, the Jews were more interested in evacuating than the local population. If Jews were in possession of Soviet citizenship obtained before September 1939, they were allowed to flee eastwards. But the German army advanced very quickly leaving little time to escape. It is very difficult to estimate how many Jews got away from the Baltic States; probably no more than 10%.[52]

Soon the German army extended their occupation to other republics such as White Russia, Russia (RSFSR) and the Ukraine, where they continued their policy of eradication. An estimated 2.9 million Jews now lived within the German occupied areas and did not manage to flee.

The Tragedy of Babi Yar

Of the numerous tragic events which took place in the Soviet Union, the story of Babi Yar has become the epitome of them all.

It occurred on 29 September, 1941. All the Jewish citizens of Kiev, the capital of the Ukraine, had been summoned to gather at an outlying ravine at Babi Yar. There they would be given the opportunity to emigrate to Palestine. They were asked to gather, dressed in their best clothing and with their money and jewellery, at a certain place. Trucks came to carry them to a place outside the city, where deep ditches had previously been dug. They were ordered to undress and leave their valuables. After being permitted to say the *Kaddish*, a Jewish prayer usually said at a deathbed, they were all shot. Some Jews, who did not come, were nevertheless rounded up

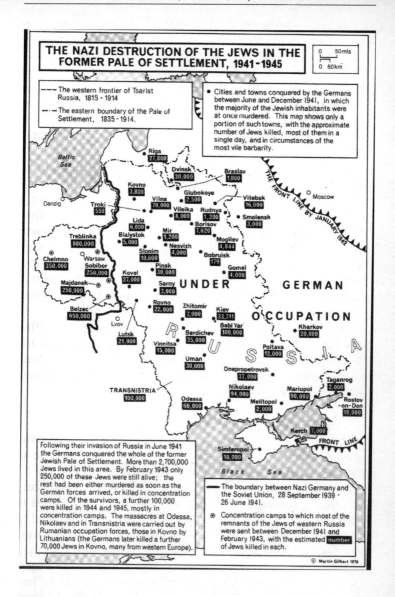

THE NAZI DESTRUCTION OF THE JEWS IN THE FORMER PALE OF SETTLEMENT, 1941-1945

0   50mls
0   50km

- - - The western frontier of Tsarist Russia, 1815 - 1914

—·— The eastern boundary of the Pale of Settlement, 1835 - 1914.

● Cities and towns conquered by the Germans between June and December 1941, in which the majority of the Jewish inhabitants were at once murdered. This map shows only a portion of such towns, with the approximate number of Jews killed, most of them in a single day, and in circumstances of the most vile barbarity.

Baltic Sea

Riga 27,800

Dvinsk 30,000

Braslav 1,800

THE FRONT LINE BY JANUARY 1942

Danzig

Kovno 3,800

Glubokoye 2,500

Vitebsk 16,000

○ Moscow

Troki 550

Vilna 70,000

Vileika 4,000

Rudnya 1,200

Smolensk 3,000

Lida 6,000

Mir 1,200

Borisov 7,620

Treblinka 800,000

Bialystok 5,000

Slonim 10,000

Nesvizh 4,000

Mogilev 4,844

Chelmno 350,000

Warsaw
Sobibor 250,000

Kovel 27,000

Pinsk 30,000

Bobruisk 179

Gomel 4,000

Majdanek 250,000

Sarny 3,000

UNDER   GERMAN

Belzec 650,000

Lvov

Rovno 22,000

Zhitomir 7,000

Kiev 33,711

OCCUPATION

Kharkov 20,000

Lutsk 21,000

Berdichev 35,000

Babi Yar 100,000

R U S S I A

Vinnitsa 15,000

Poltava 12,000

Uman 30,000

Dnepropetrovsk 37,000

TRANSNISTRIA 100,000

Nikolaev 94,000

Mariupol 90,000

Taganrog 2,000

Odessa 60,000

Melitopol 2,000

Rostov -on-Don 18,000

Kerch 7,000

FRONT LINE

Following their invasion of Russia in June 1941 the Germans conquered the whole of the former Jewish Pale of Settlement. More than 2,700,000 Jews lived in this area. By February 1943 only 250,000 of these Jews were still alive; the rest had been either murdered as soon as the German forces arrived, or killed in concentration camps. Of the survivors, a further 100,000 were killed in 1944 and 1945, mostly in concentration camps. The massacres at Odessa, Nikolaev and in Transnistria were carried out by Rumanian occupation forces, those in Kovno by Lithuanians (the Germans later killed a further 70,000 Jews in Kovno, many from western Europe).

Simferopol 10,000

Black   Sea

— The boundary between Nazi Germany and the Soviet Union, 28 September 1939 - 26 June 1941.

◉ Concentration camps to which most of the remnants of the Jews of western Russia were sent between December 1941 and February 1943, with the estimated number of Jews killed in each.

© Martin Gilbert 1976

Map 4

The Jews of Russia. Sir Martin Gilbert, CBE, 1979, Steimatzky. Used with permission. See also section on Nazi Destruction in Russia during World War II in Chapter 3.

and brought there. In just two days more than 33,700 Jews had been brutally shot.

A total of about 80,000 Jews were murdered in Kiev. Although a plaque was placed there in 1976 in memory of the Soviet citizens killed by the Germans,* no memorial was permitted for the Jewish victims there before the *glasnost* period in 1991.

The Ukraine is reputedly one of the most antisemitic republics in the Soviet Union. It is where more than 60% of the Jewish population was eradicated.[53]

Summary: the Staggering Loss

During World War II the loss of human life on the Eastern Front, for both the Soviet and German sides was enormous. This was not only among the soldiers, but it is estimated that about 10 million Soviet civilians, and among them tens of thousands of Jews, died of starvation and exhaustion and in the shelling and bombing of the major Soviet cities such as Leningrad, Stalingrad and others.

Besides this, the Jews were the targets of the specific policy of annihilation initiated by the Nazis. Recent research indicates that if we take the borders of the German-occupied territories into consideration, the losses in the Holocaust on Soviet soil would be larger than previously reckoned. Out of a total Jewish population of 2.75–2.9 million, in the German occupied territories of the USSR, about 1 million succeeded in escaping. Of the Jews who remained, only a small number survived.

Those who were fortunate enough found refuge among the local population, joined the partisans, hid in the woods or managed to survive in the dreadful camps. It is assumed that only a few thousand Jews, or less than 1% of those under the German rule of occupation, were rescued with the help of the local population. (The previous conservative number is stated as at least 1.5–1.7 million Jewish citizens killed.)[54]

---

* On the official memorial stone from 1976, only the death of 100,000 Soviet citizens is recorded, but the fact that 80,000 of them were Jews is not mentioned. The incident is commemorated by the well-known Russian poet, Yevgeni Yevtuskenko, in his famous poem *Babi Yar*.

To the victims of the genocide should be added 80,000–85,000 Jews taken captive in POW camps, who were either murdered or shot. Also between 120,000–180,000 Jewish soldiers serving in the Soviet Army fell in the war.[55]

The alarming fact is that out of the total 6 million Jews killed in the Holocaust, about 2 million or one third of them died under the German military and civilian administration in the occupied territories of the USSR. (See Appendix V.)

The Jews' centuries-old history clearly indicates: Russia is a potentially dangerous country for Jews to live in!

What Might the Western Allies Have Done?

Looking at the possibilities for the Western Allies to help the German Jews, it would be quite natural to ask the question: what more could have been done to save Jewish lives?

The Allies could have pressured their colonies to receive Jewish immigrants. The British Dominions, Canada and Australia as well as the Mandate of Palestine could have taken more. Instead Jews who emigrated to those areas on the verge of World War II, ended up in internment camps. The same was the case in the USA, where Jews fleeing Germany were regarded as possible enemies and treated as suspicious spies.

Furthermore, throughout the war the Allies, and particularly the US, might, through the neutral governments (Sweden, Switzerland, Spain and Portugal) as well as the Vatican, have shown Nazi Germany their abhorrence at the organised killing, which was known in the West as early as mid-1942. More pressure could have been applied to release their Jews. By then, 2 million Jews had already been massacred and the killing went on at great speed. With the war conditions, it might not have been possible to rescue as large a number as 1 million, but without impeding the war effort, tens of thousands or a few hundreds of thousands might have been possible.[56] Moreover, by spring of 1943, the US State Department knew from allies of the Axis that the Nazis would lose the war and some German authorities sought favourable peace terms. However, Britain would have been in a dilemma over Palestine if a large number of German Jews were to be released.

A united effort was made in July 1944, when the US War Refugee Board (WRB) launched an intensive campaign to save the Jews of Hungary. By May, deportation had already taken place of 400,000 Jews to Auschwitz. The WRB approached the neutral governments, the Pope and the International Red Cross to request the Germans 'in the name of humanity' to stop deportation of the more than 200,000 Jews still remaining in Budapest. Since a large number of them were kept in inhumane conditions, President Roosevelt promised the Nazis that their atrocities against the Jews would not go unpunished. As the Russian Army was approaching Budapest, the Hungarian Regent Miklos Horthy was considering joining the Allies. For 3 months till mid October, the deportations were stopped, while he was negotiating about emigration of the Hungarian Jews. The Germans then deposed Horthy, installed their own puppet regime and resumed deportations. The very antisemitic Nazi regime was given much power, slaughtering thousands of Jews. Disagreements between the Allies regarding the conditions for the release of the Jews also caused the matter to fall through. It was during this period that with WRB help the Swedish diplomat in Budapest, Raoul Wallenberg, saved at least 20,000 Jewish lives. In retrospect: Auschwitz was soon shut down. When the Russians entered Budapest in January 1945, only 120,000 Jews remained alive. The American War Refugee Board had played an important role. Tragically, a major opportunity was lost.

As it is known that the Western Allies had confirmed knowledge of the atrocities and of the elimination of hundreds of thousands of prisoners in German extermination camps, it would be an appropriate question to ask why allied countries did not pass on warnings to the occupied countries via the media or distribute flyers from aircraft. We can echo the words by the Jewish Czech prisoner, Rudolf Vrba, who miraculously escaped from Auschwitz and confirmed the organised murder taking place:

'Why were the Jews never told? ... Would anybody get me alive to Auschwitz if I had had the information? ... Would thousands and thousands of able-bodied

Jewish men have sent their children, wives, mothers to Auschwitz from all over Europe, if they had known?'[57]

Quite late during the war, in 1944, the British parachuted Jewish agents into Axis territory, specifically to warn the Jews, but they were too few and the action was not well enough co-ordinated.

For some reason Jews were not well liked. The following examples will throw light on the half-heartedness of Western attitudes to them. During the years from 1942 through 1944, the Allies moved 100,000 Yugoslavs, Poles and Greeks to safety in Africa, Middle East, India and elsewhere. Until the end of 1943, when the war became too intense there, large numbers of refugees were able to escape via neutral Spain and Portugal to North Africa. By 1944 9,000–12,000 Greeks, and 1,800 non-Jewish Polish refugees had been sent to Gaza in Palestine. In the early period of the war, most of the refugees were transported on ships to dozens of refugee camps that sprang into existence. While the British assisted with transport, supplies for many of the camp sites as well as staff, the USA repeatedly helped with materials and funded the bulk of the expenses through UNRRA.* While most of these refugees had, admittedly, been exposed to severe danger none of them were the object of a systematic annihilation.[58]

* The war time alliance, United Nations Relief & Rehabilitation Administration, consisted of 45 neutral nations or nations liberated from Axis occupation and functioned from 1943–47 distributing US$4 billion of aid. UNRRA is not connected with the post-war UN Organisation UNRWA.

Chapter 3

Antisemitism and the Persecution of Russian Jewry

I n our day antisemitism is again on the increase. The historian Israel Gutman asserts that the principal roots and causes of antisemitism lie in the confrontation and antagonism between Christianity and Judaism. The essence of the conflict between the two religions, which have a common root, is mainly theological, grounded in the issue of Jesus as the Messiah, and in the place of Judaism and the Jews in the Old and New Testaments.[1]

With Russia's potential for becoming a country of new, severe oppression and persecution of minority groups, it might be thought-provoking to take a closer look at Jewish history in that country.

Ancient Antisemitism in Europe

In the Early Church, and among the Church Fathers such as Justin Martyr (d. 167), Origen (d. 251), John Crysostom (344–407) and Augustine (d. 430), a 'replacement' theory was used in order to make Christianity more acceptable. It was said that in God's eyes the Church had replaced the Jews. The Church now became superior to the Synagogue. Furthermore, the Jews were accused of deicide (killing God), and relegated to an inferior status. The Church seems to have felt that it was upholding God's honour by persecuting them. This 'guilt' of deicide was not only ascribed to the Jews who lived at the time of the crucifixion of Jesus, but collectively bestowed on all the seed of Israel forever. These ideas can be clearly traced in the persecution by the Orthodox Churches throughout the centuries. Jews were thought to be the embodiment of evil and the bearers of all harm and disaster. They were considered to be associated with demonic powers, and were subject to severe persecution and killings. The stereotype image of the Jew has entered the folklore of Christian peoples, their culture and literature, creating a deep rift of suspicion between Jews and Christians.

In the Middle Ages the ill-famed crusades took place. At a call from Pope Urban II the countries of Europe were challenged to gather an army to liberate Jerusalem from the Moslems, who were considered infidels. However, the knights had several different motives, varying from religious reasons, to seeking adventure or simply easy booty. As the army went down through Europe they plundered and killed the local population. Needless to say, the unarmed Jews became an easy prey. In 1099, the crusaders arrived in Jerusalem. They massacred almost all the Jews, as well as the faithful from the Orthodox Churches and the Moslems. They rounded up the last unprotected Jews in a synagogue in the Holy City, and with the doors closed, the building was set alight. All were burned alive.

At the time of the second crusade in the twelfth century, there were two main religious accusations against the Jews, namely: ritual murder and the desecration of the host. The accusation of blood libel (ritual murder) was first made in England in 1144. In it Jews were rumoured to use the blood of Christian children for ritual purposes. (Interestingly, in the second century AD both the Roman government and the Jews persecuted the Christians, accusing them of exactly the same crime and of practising 'cannibalism.') As a rule, the story was that the Jews kidnapped a Christian child, tortured him, injured his limbs, and crucified him in memory of Jesus. The Jews were said to have drawn off his blood and distributed it among their neighbours in their preparation for making unleavened bread, '*matzot*', at Passover.

Not limited to the Middle Ages only, these fables re-surfaced from time to time and led to the so-called 'pogroms', particularly in Tsarist Russia. (The Russian word indicates an attack or an organised massacre on the Jews, including destruction or burning of Jewish property.) They occurred mainly during the Easter season. It was instigated by the clergy of the Russian Orthodox Church and carried out by ignorant Russian farmers who felt they were avenging God's honour and would thereby receive an extra blessing.

The other libel was that Jews desecrated the sacramental host. At the Fourth Lateran Council in 1215, the Roman Catholics decided that according to Christian dogma, the wafer of the sacrament was literally transubstantiated (changed) into the body of Jesus. Christians began to believe in the miraculous power of the host, in its potency for giving healing, and power for doing miracles. Since many Christians came to believe that the Jews had once slain the incarnate God who came to redeem them, the charge usually went that a Jew had bribed a Christian man or woman to give him a piece of the host. When it was brought home, the wafer was stabbed or trampled upon to fulfil their desire 'to torture Jesus again'. Whether the Jew 'confessed' or not, he was usually burnt for his blasphemous act; his family and community punished. This libel was found mainly within the borders of the German Empire, where Polish Jews suffered severely under it. Entire communities were devastated.

Antisemitism in Europe During the Middle Ages

In Europe during the Middle Ages the Jews were looked upon as outsiders, and their position was rather unstable. Their life and security was much dependent upon the favour of the king or the prince in their particular country and they could only look to him for protection. Since Jews were not permitted to own land, they were either involved in trade or often held unpopular jobs such as tax collecting or money lending. This intensified the hostility of other population groups towards them. Whenever a ruler or a hostile town population owed them too much money, they might find an excuse for killing the Jews or expelling them from their territory, and thus avoid repaying their debt. They expelled them, sometimes for considerable periods, so the Jews moved from country to country, seeking where they would be most at peace. Hence the idea of the 'wandering Jew'.

In **England**, the Catholic Church accused the Jews of being involved in usury, which resulted in their banishment in 1290. For almost 400 years they were not permitted to live on British soil, and it was not until the time of the Protestant ruler Oliver Cromwell that they were invited back in 1652. The intensity of anti-Jewish feelings is illustrated in Shakespeare's writing, by his famous caricature of Shylock the Jew, in the *Merchant of Venice*. It is unlikely he had ever met a Jew as, at that time, there were no Jews in the country to base the character on. Yet from the stereotyping it is clear that antisemitic attitudes were still rampant in England even after 300 years without any Jews.

The Jews were even blamed for various plagues and the Black Death, a rat-borne epidemic, which ravaged Europe for about a decade in the late 1340s and wiped out large segments of the European population. It was thought the Jews had poisoned the wells in an attempt to kill the Christian population. They were attacked by mobs and driven out of the towns. Under severe torture a number of Jews 'confessed' to their crime. All over Europe many Jews were massacred.

The Jews in **Germany** were more fortunate as, after only a few years, they were invited back. By 1356 the noblemen and the townships put pressure on Emperor Charles IV to issue a decree delegating power to them, including his authority over the Jews. The towns could then invite them back for tax collection! However, their right to stay in a town was often limited to 10–20 years, and they had to pay a 'golden fee' to the emperor. One condition for allowing them back was that the Jews must live close together in one section of town. Later these became known as 'ghettos'.

But further trouble was awaiting the Jews in Germany. During the sixteenth century the Protestant Reformation, spearheaded by Martin Luther, brought relief within Jewish circles for a few decades as it heralded a return to the Scriptures and an end to the Catholic Church's persecution and forced conversion of them. But the period was short. In disappointment over his inability to win them to Christianity, Luther wrote a small, virulent book, *The Jews and Their Lies*. In it he heaped all kinds of vicious accusations upon the Jews and Judaism, before finally advocating their extermination. Until the twentieth century most sections of the Lutheran Church, fortunately, only paid attention to Luther's early writings rather than those after 1543. Tragically however, it was Luther's antisemitic script that was used as Hitler's justification for his persecution and slaughter of the Jews.

In the Middle Ages, the Jews suffered much more hardship in **France** than in Germany. After a couple of shorter expulsions, in 1394 the Jews of France were expelled for two hundred years. The reason was the same as in the other parts of Europe, namely being blamed for the Plague and the Black Death epidemic and the Catholic Church's accusation of usury.

In **Spain**, both Jews and Moslems were held responsible for the Plague. As the years went by, the Catholic Church became aware that many of the Jews, who had suffered forced conversion and been added to the core of believers, in reality still adhered to the Jewish faith. In the fifteenth century, when the church wanted to cleanse itself of heresy, its attention quickly turned to these 'secret' Jews (called *Marranos* by the Spanish). In the late fifteenth century the disaster of the Inquisition struck the Jewish community. They were sought out and tortured; some even burned at the stake and their property confiscated. Finally in 1492, King Ferdinand expelled all the Jews, in spite of the fact that the Jewish population had lived there at least as long as the Christians. Because the latter were the majority, they assumed that the Jews were outsiders. About ten years later, the same tragedy occurred in **Portugal**.

Tsarist Persecution and Pogroms against Jews

In the Middle Ages

Jews have been banished from **Russia** [2] a number of times for various reasons, political or religious, or in confrontations with the Russian-Orthodox Church. In the last part of the Middle Ages (around 1450), a so-called 'judaizing heresy' had spread in the country and made an impact upon the Christian population, so they kept the Sabbath and various Jewish customs. The Jews were accused of having influenced the sect, which was found in the commercial city, Novgorod, east of Moscow and other areas. When Tsar Ivan IV, nicknamed 'the Terrible', heard of it, he ordered that all the Jews who refused to convert to Christianity should be drowned in the river. During the following centuries the Jews were, from time to time, accused of similar heresies as for example in 1742, when Tsarina Elisabeth Petrovna wanted neither Jews nor Moslems in her empire and ordered their expulsion.

Hardship in Poland

In the seventeenth century, a severe period of hardship and unrest occurred during the 30 Years' War. Polish Jews particularly, suffered much due to social injustice from their Polish overlords, and they found it increasingly difficult to earn a living. During the war a Ukrainian officer, Chmelnitzky, headed a discontented mob and went marauding into Polish territory. Although the fighting was more of a political than antisemitic nature, the Jews were spared no less than the Poles. With over 100,000 Jews killed, a migration began to the commercial centres in the West, and the Polish Jewish community had difficulty re-establishing itself.

Moreover, during the eighteenth century a weakened **Poland** was divided up three times between its stronger neighbours, Austria, Prussia and Russia. After the last partition in 1795, hundreds of thousands of additional Jews had been brought under the rule of Russia. This presaged a deterioration of the situation for the Jews, and even if Russia had, in theory, prohibited the residence of Jews for hundreds of years, by 1800 she soon found herself with the world's largest Jewish population.

Russia Re-Opened for Jews in the Eighteenth Century

After the disaster of the One Hundred Years War between England and France during the fourteenth–fifteenth centuries, the communities returned to normal living, and the Jews re-established themselves in Western Europe, settling in the countries most friendly to them. Again they resumed trade and bartered with goods between East and West. When interaction between the countries increased, the more wealthy German Jews sponsored bank loans for transactions.

In order to promote trade into Russia in 1778, the progressive Catharina II wanted to introduce some new administrative rules, by which wealthy Jewish merchants could be registered and included in the guild councils and municipalities of towns. Thus, Russia became the first country in Europe even to consider granting Jews these rights. She met, however, with strong opposition from public opinion and was compelled to reverse her decision. Nonetheless, some Jewish merchants got into Russia in this period, but it created tension with local citizens and, all the while poor Jews were banished to the villages.

Phase I: 1791–1881

When Russia received the major Jewish population group from Poland, the government adopted the view that Jews were their 'problem', to be ultimately solved by assimilation or expulsion.

In 1791, in order to confine the Jews and prevent them from leaving their areas, Russia created the notorious Pale of Settlement. It extended from parts of Lithuania, the annexed areas of Poland, and White Russia through to the uninhabited steppes of the Ukraine and the Black Sea. The area was closed off to the east, lest the Jews 'infiltrate' the main Russian areas. In order to protect the Russian peasants from being exploited, the Jews were forced to leave their homes in the surrounding villages and live only in towns and communities (*shtetls*) in the Pale. In this way, the Pale established a border inside the border. Violation was punished by exile to Siberia. In fact, the Pale became a large-scale ghetto. The area was formalised in 1812.

The Tsarist period was generally a time of hardship for Russian Jewry. By oppression, the leadership tried in various ways to make them more 'civilised' by Christianising them and forcing them to assimilate into Russian culture. This had, of course, the opposite effect. In 1827, Tsar **Nicolai I**, who became known for the cruelty with which he tried to solve the Jewish problem, introduced one of the strictest laws, the forced conscription of Jewish youth. The government used 'snatchers' to remove 12-year-old boys from their home area and compelled them to live under inhuman conditions while

THE JEWISH PALE OF SETTLEMENT IN RUSSIA, 1835 - 1917

In 1882 500,000 Jews living in rural areas of the Pale were forced to leave their homes and live in towns or townlets (shtetls) in the Pale. 250,000 Jews living along the western frontier of Russia were also moved into the Pale. 700,000 Jews living east of the Pale were driven into the Pale by 1891.

1891 2,000 Jews deported many of them in chains.

1891 20,000 Jews expelled.

By 1897 there were 5 million Jews living in the Pale, and 320,000 outside it, of whom 100,000 lived in Siberia, 80,000 in Baltic Provinces, 50,000 in the Caucasus, 10,000 in Russian Central Asia and 10,000 in Astrakhan and the Terek region.

The Pale of Settlement. Russian Jews were confined to this area by laws of 1795 and 1835. By 1897 there were more than 5 million Jews in the Pale.

Towns within the Pale which were themselves barred to Jews without special residence permits.

Towns outside the Pale with Jewish inhabitants (figures for 1897).

St. Petersburg 21,000
Novgorod 4,700
80,000
Moscow 9,000
Smolensk 10,500
Tula 2,700
Voronezh 2,700
Kursk 4,000
Kharkov 14,000
Kuban 5,000

© Martin Gilbert 1976

Map 5
The Jews of Russia, Sir Martin Gilbert, CBE, 1979, Steimatzky.
Used with permission.

being trained as soldiers or taught various trades. The compulsory service lasted for 25 years. In spite of Jewish protests from Western Europe against this cruel treatment, which alienated the youngsters from their close family and culture, the conscription was enforced for 50 more years. Later, it was substituted by a general draft into the army, but even then the Jews did not have the opportunity to achieve officer rank.

The 'Classification' Plan

By 1850, the number of Jews in Russia was estimated as 2–3 million, and the number grew rapidly. The liberal movement, which since the French Revolution had been blowing over Europe, granted equal rights to all citizens in the countries affected. This had its impact upon Russia also.

As the next stage of Russian policy, Tsar **Alexander II** (1855–1881) divided the Jews into two categories: the selected and 'useful' Jews permitted to live in the cities, and the poorer class, belonging to the 'non-useful' group, who were relegated to the Pale. The Jews, accepted by Russian society, were wealthy merchants of the first guild (paying the highest taxes), craftsmen, and agriculturists, together with some liberal professions such as lawyers, architects, physicians and pharmacists. This right to live in the Russian cities soon caused the assimilated Jewish communities to expand rapidly, particularly around St Petersburg and Moscow.

It was not long before the Russian community became opposed to the privileges granted to the Jews. In the 1870s, with hostilities increasing, the Tsar restricted the privileges again. Another reform aimed at resettling over 10,000 Jews from the crowded conditions in the Pale had already been stopped in 1866. When the Jews realised that the reforms for stimulating commerce and industry in the interior provinces of the country were due to an attempt to increase their Russification, they rebelled.

Two Ways of Jewish Life

1. The Hasidism

While the Jews of Western and Central Europe were gradually finding their place in the economic and social life of their adopted homelands, the Eastern Jews, having suffered much hardship from the Cossack Revolt and the repeated wars which devastated Poland and Lithuania, turned towards inner strengthening. Thus, *Hasidism* ('pietism') which arose in the middle of the eighteenth century was not a new movement, but rather a revival of an old one. The followers were called *Hasidim* ('pious men'). Jewish people have responded to sufferings in a similar way from ancient times. When pressured beyond measure, they have had a tendency to turn from the outer difficulties to inner piety, as for example the Maccabees in 167 BC.

The main leader of the movement was Rabbi Israel ben Eliezer, also called *The Ba'al Shem Tov* (Master of the Good Name), whose emotional teaching around 1760 moved the emphasis from the outer circumstances to a deeper, religious life. Thus, poor Jews would be led into a kind of escapism from their inferior position into an ecstatic form of worship, accompanied by miracle works, and curing with charms and amulets. His disciples, *tsadikim* (righteous men), would later take over and become a spiritual leadership. This teaching formed a barrier against modernisation.

About 50 years later a strong reaction arose when the leading rabbi of Vilna (in Lithuania), the spiritual head of the Eastern European Jews, Gaon Elijah, turned against Ba'al Shem Tov's teaching. The Gaon saw a great danger in the spread of Hasidism and stemmed the tide by emphasising that in connection with spiritual teaching, secular teaching could be helpful to understand the world and Judaism. This resulted in the Jews of Eastern Europe being divided into two groups. While the northern provinces and Lithuania, with their strong tradition on intellectualism, remained loyal to rabbinism of the traditional type, the southern areas of Poland (and the Pale) had long been supporting Hasidism, which appealed to the masses. But history's evaluation is that the Gaon's counter movement came too late to turn the tide.

Even today we find the Hasidic movement as a life-style among certain Orthodox Jews in Israel. They are easily recognised by their old-fashioned dress.

2. The Haskalah

Inspired by the liberal *Enlightenment Movement* in Europe,

Haskalah spread from Germany in the early nineteenth century, and became influential among Russian Jewry. With its emphasis on reasoning it aimed for greater freedom, tolerance and humanity. This group of Jews were educated and living in the commercial cities such as Warsaw, Riga and Odessa. In order to fit better into their new role, the city Jews spoke the national language and became assimilated. But even so they still adhered to their Jewish ways.

Thus, the Russian Jews were not only divided into wealthy and poor, but further separated between those who spoke the national language, and the poor Yiddish-speaking masses in the Pale who never became a part of the *Enlightenment Movement*. The Haskalah actually played an important role in splitting Jews from the West off from Eastern European Jewry, because of the language differences.

The appearance of Jews in economic and political life soon aroused strong protests in Russian society. The attitude even of the liberal and revolutionary elements towards the Jews was also lukewarm, and the Jews' legal status came under attack. One of the reasons for the persecution was simply envy due to their success in financial matters. Jews continued to be seen as a foreign, evil element who never truly wanted to become a part of the society in which they lived. They were suspected of secretly serving their own purpose. On the other hand, the upsurge of antisemitism resulting from the *Enlightenment* period made it even more difficult for the Jews to identify with their surroundings. The young Jews who desired secular education found, much to their disappointment, the doors to the universities closed to them.

✢ ✢ ✢

The Jew in Tsarist Literature

Although the Jewish issue was not really a preferred subject in Russian literature, some of the better-known writers and poets did refer to it. Their treatment was generally superficial, with the Jews being portrayed as repugnant or ridiculous as was the case with Chekhov, Turgenev and Pushkin. Dostoevsky's reference to Jews as being a foreign, evil element, accused of maintaining 'a state within the state' was typical of the pre-revolutionary writers.[3] On the positive side were Tolstoy and the philosopher V. Solovoyev, who joined with other leading writers in protesting against the pogroms and the reactionary policies of the Russian regime.

Many newspapers, led by the influential *Novoye Vremiya* (New Time), became involved in antisemitic agitation, particularly after the Balkan War (1877–78), when a wave of nationalism and slavophile feelings swept through Russian society.

✢ ✢ ✢

It was during this period, when the Jews were more or less attaining equal citizenship and becoming socially integrated in the European countries, that critical voices began to be raised against them in the cities. The term 'antisemitism' was coined by the German writer, William Marr in 1879. In his view, the difference between Semitic and Aryan covered the moral, cultural, linguistic and physical realms. Strangely enough, antisemitism was never levelled against Arabs, many of whom also belong to the semitic race.

In the meantime, much of the antisemitism had altered character. While the medieval religious antisemitism had disappeared and with it the stereotypical depiction of the Jews, it was replaced by a modern social and intellectual antisemitism, in which Jews were seen as both good and evil. But worse things were yet to come.

Intensification of the Persecution
Phase II: 1881–1917

During the first period of his reign, Tsar Alexander II had been guided by liberal reformers and issued laws to liberate the Jews as well as the serfs. However, around 1870 he changed his policy, becoming more restrictive and antisemitic. This led to the expression of Russian hostility in 1871 when a wave of pogroms broke out all over the country. These were fiercest in southern Russia, where Christian merchants in Odessa, being competitors of the Jews, rioted for two days.

A turning point for Russian Jews occurred in 1881 when Alexander II was assassinated by a group of revolutionaries. There was much confusion in Russia, and in order to take the pressure off the government, the Jews were again made the scapegoat for the nation's misery. In more than a hundred towns in the southern provinces pogroms broke out. Particularly hard hit were Kiev and Odessa where synagogues were destroyed, several hundred Jews were murdered, tens of thousands were robbed of their property and women were raped. It was obvious that the government instigated the riots, for the police did not intervene before the third day of a pogrom. In Western countries reports of such riots caused indignation, but the Russian government only replied that the pogroms were the people's protests against Jewish exploitation.

May Laws and Pogroms

The Tsar's son, Alexander III, was convinced that Russia needed to be purged of Western liberal influences. Since the Orthodox Church had been taking an active part in the antisemitic propaganda, the Head of the Orthodox Church, K. Probiedonostsev, formulated the official Russian policy towards Jews. In 1882, the 'May Laws' were introduced. The plan for dealing with the Jews was expressed as: to let one third die, force another third to flee and compel the last third to convert and join the Russian Church. Immediately the government set about executing these plans. Thousands of Jews were forced out of the smaller towns and back into the Pale of the Settlement, where there was no means of livelihood. This meant starvation, since the towns, to which they were forced to go, were already overcrowded with small shopkeepers and artisans. By the late 1890s, over 5 million Jews were crammed into the towns of Pale.

In 1891, a systematic expulsion of the Jews from Moscow began. Those Jews who had believed that education and assimilation would help them to secure a respected place in the Russian Empire now saw their hopes completely crushed.

The Growing Workers' Union

Towards the end of the nineteenth century, a group of younger Jews paved the way for a new avenue of influence. Being involved with political and social activities, they turned to the up-coming Russian revolutionaries and engaged in the Jewish national movement, working for socialism among their own. By 1897, a Jewish Labour Alliance of Russia, Poland, and Lithuania was formed, known under the abbreviation *Bund*. It became a branch of the underground Russian socialist movement, concealed from the Tsarist government. At first it differed from the Russian movement only by their use of Yiddish. This was employed in order to attract more Jews and as a means of propaganda.

During the next few years the Bund leadership came to the conclusion that Russian Jewry, like other ethnic groups, also deserved national recognition. With the malicious antisemitism of the time, the idea of a homeland of their own appealed strongly to the masses.

Pogroms Climaxing

Under the last Tsar, Nikolai II, the government gave free rein to the antisemitic press and agitators. This was done in order to suppress the revolutionary movement in which the radical Jewish youth played an increasing role, and resulted in several pogroms from the masses in many places in Russia during the years from 1903 till October 1906.

One of the most infamous was the pogrom in Kishinev during the Passover in April of 1903. The Jews were accused of the ritual murder of a Christian boy. The revenge broke loose upon the innocent Jews. This persecution had different features from those of the 1880s in that, from this time on, the rioters began to concentrate on murder, rape, torture and destruction. The Russian Interior Minister Plehve was believed to be directly responsible for this. According to an official report more than 50 Jews were killed in Kishinev and 500 injured, while hundreds of homes and shops were plundered and destroyed. This time the Jews defended themselves, so the rioters could not continue the acts of murder and destruction, but the authorities arrested these Jews. The conduct of the savage rioters shook enlightened public opinion in Russia as well as in the rest of the world.

The Tsar Forced to Yield – the First Duma

In 1905, in order to combat the continued revolutionary spirit, the Tsarist regime set up 'patriotic' organisations. They were composed of rowdies, known as the Black Hundreds to suppress and annihilate Jews and revolutionaries.

As a result of the first revolution on the 17 October, 1905, the Tsar was forced to issue a manifesto granting basic freedom to his citizens. An advisory assembly, the Duma, was formed in which some of his authority was delegated to the ruling class of nobility, military leaders and intellectuals. The Jews were also represented.

In protest against the new constitution, pro-Tsarist groups such as the Black Hundreds and the Cossacks, demonstrated in towns all over the country. The Tsar's picture was carried aloft in mass processions. This resulted in riots in which hundreds were killed. True to the usual pattern, the Jews were blamed for the unrest. It culminated in a pogrom in Odessa that lasted 4 days, and more than 300 Jews lost their lives. Beside the Jewish self-defence groups, members of the intelligentsia and some Russian workers supported them. Some were killed.

However, the situation in Russia did not change much. The Duma underwent several changes, each more reactionary, made in order to ensure the deputies' support. By then the opposition circles came to realise that antisemitism had been the deliberate policy of the regime, aimed at strengthening its rule and influence over a backward section of Russian society.

The Depravity of the Tsarist Government

The Infamous Forgery:
the Protocols of the Elders of Zion

In 1904 the powerful right-wing party and the Tsar's secret police produced the notorious forgery, *The Protocols of the Elders of Zion*.* (The script was actually a counterfeit and a revision of the French writer, Maurice Joly's book against Napoleon III in 1865.) [4] The serial story appeared first in the Russian newspaper, *Znamia* (The Banner), over an eleven-day period. It purported to deal with a Jewish conspiracy to

---

* Even today the book serves as fuel for antisemitism in a number of Arab countries.

destroy the Christian civilisation so that they might seize control of the whole world.

It had such an influence that on 16 July, 1918, when the revolutionary killers came for the last Tsar, Nikolai II, often called the 'little Father' of Russian Orthodoxy, two books used by him for 'devotion' were found at his bedside, the Bible and the 'Protocols'.

The Beilis Trial

The corruption of the Tsarist regime can be seen through the accusations of blood libel. Although this charge was officially outlawed in 1817, for almost 100 years it was time and again levelled against the Jews. The last time was in 1911 at the trial of Menachem Beilis. A Christian child was murdered and it was said his blood was used for ritual purposes. Although it was known that the murderers were a gang of thieves to whom the mother belonged, the government brought Beilis to trial. But strong criticism from Tsarist reactionaries brought ridicule upon Russia, so the court procedure was stopped.

Winds of Freedom Blow over Russia – Jewish Philosophers of Russia

There were, in a number of European countries, men with a Zionist vision. Simultaneously, in the last half of the nineteenth century, in countries such as England, Germany and France, several Jewish national philosophers had promoted the idea that after all, Jews belonged to one nation, based on a political and cultural heritage. They were aiming at the goal of building their own national country with a political state that would ensure them a safe future. They were convinced that in spite of education, the ever-present antisemitism in the countries necessitated such a state.

Propagation of Zionism

As with other Western countries, Russia also brought forth a number of nationalist-minded Jewish leaders. One of the best known was the physician, Leon Pinsker. Although he previously believed in the advantages of assimilation, the May Laws of 1881–82 had convinced him this was an illusion. In his pamphlet *Auto-Emancipation* he conveyed the idea that as long as Jews lived in foreign countries, they would always be exposed to antisemitism. They needed to work towards the establishment of a homeland of their own. Pinsker asserted it should be the old Jewish homeland of Palestine. The idea found a warm response in the heart of Jewish youth. Zionism soon became the most important force in Jewish life, despite the problems of having to operate underground.

At the same time Peretz Smolenskin (1842–85), a Hebrew author and journalist, had also been convinced that the Haskalah movement from Germany was a mistake. After the pogrom in 1882, he began to place great emphasis upon the idea of a Jewish awakening in the Diaspora and promoted the idea that the Jews should once more recognise themselves as a nation, and spoke about Palestine as their natural homeland.

Although it was mainly liberal Jews with socialist motivation who became involved with the Zionist projects, the orthodox Rabbi from Posen, Zevi Hirsh Kalischer, was an exception. By the 1860s, he advocated that not only Western Jews who had enough influence and wealth to support the work in Palestine, but also Eastern Jews ought to work towards the establishment of agricultural colonies which might develop into flourishing communities. He argued that the belief in the coming Messiah did not obligate the Jews to do nothing about their new homeland. Moreover, Eastern Jews were particularly in need of such a country. He thought the time was ripe for a resettlement.

Herzl and the Jewish State

An important milestone was reached on 29 August, 1897, when Jews from many countries gathered for the first Zionist conference in Basle, spearheaded by the Jewish journalist, Theodor Herzl, who was born in Budapest.

It seems the 'Dreyfus affair' in 1894 had affected him deeply, and it sent shock waves through the complacent Jewish communities of Europe. As a young journalist Hertzl was sent to France to cover the trial of a French Jewish army officer, Albert Dreyfus who was accused of treason on trumped-up charges of passing on military secrets to

Germany. As the cry 'Death to the Jews' sounded through the streets of Paris, he was sentenced to life imprisonment and deported to 'Devil's Island'. Two years later, it was proved that Dreyfus was innocent, and in 1899 he was pardoned and later acquitted.

Herzl challenged the Jewish communities that only if they recognised themselves as a nation, could they ask for a politically acknowledged homeland.

In retrospect, it is very interesting to note that the Zionist Conference gathered in Basle in 1897. Jewish leaders came from all over Europe to discuss the plight of their people. This led to the establishment of the World Zionist Organisation for the purpose of facilitating the return of the Jewish people to a legally secured and internationally recognised Jewish State in the land of Israel. With enthusiasm Theodor Herzl spoke out:

> 'We are here to lay the cornerstone of the structure that will house the Jewish nation. If I speak out today, some may laugh loudly. If maybe not in 5 years, then in 50 years the Jewish State will be a reality.' [5]

In the atmosphere and tension of increasing pogroms in Russia, Herzl was willing to accept whatever country was offered them. But in November 1947, exactly 50 years later, the United Nations voted for the establishment of a Jewish State in the land of Palestine. The following year, on 14 May, 1948, the State of Israel was proclaimed. It is interesting that according to the Bible, 50 years indicates the cycle for a year of jubilee, after which land, people and property should be restored to their original and rightful owner (Leviticus 25:8–17). That was exactly what happened.

Shortly after the Kishinev pogrom, the 6th Zionist Conference was held in Basle in 1903. The British Government had by then offered Herzl a homeland in Uganda in East Africa, the reason being that the British wanted the countries in that area and near the Suez Canal to be populated by friendly people. However, other Zionists turned the offer down.

(In retrospect, one wonders what horrors might have befallen the Jewish people if they had lived in Uganda during the fanatical reign of the Moslem ruler, Idi Amin in the 1970s (1971–79).)

Fleeing from Russia

While some Jews, as mentioned, turned towards the revolution, the poorer Russian masses, driven from their homes and facing new pogroms, were desperate. Unable even to support themselves they turned to their only possibility: emigration. During the 1870s some 30,000 Russian Jews crossed the Atlantic in order to seek a new life and refuge. Various aid organisations were established such as the Hebrew Emigrant Aid Society in New York and other charitable groups which, assisted by wealthy Jews, supplied their Russian fellow-believers with travel money and living expenses. England also became a country of asylum for Russian immigrants. In order to prevent serious antagonism they developed Jewish communities, which looked after their own. But even though the Russians had a reputation as hardworking and law-abiding, an English parliamentary commission recommended a law to restrict immigration.

During the following decade, emigration continued even more rapidly. From 1881 to 1900 about 600,000 Jews went to the USA, 10,000 left for other countries such as South America, South Africa and Australia, while some went to Palestine. By 1914, 3 million Russian Jews had settled in the United States, and only the Russian Jewish community, numbering 6 million Jews, was larger. (When a census was taken just before the close of the nineteenth century [1897], the Russian Jewish population was about 5.2 million, constituting 4.13% of the total Russian population or about half of world Jewry.)

Russian Emigrants to Zion

Lovers of Zion (*Hovevei Zion*) was a remarkable movement, which worked mainly among the Russian youth, challenging them to Jewish nationalism. But it also gained adherents in many other countries. Around 1880, BILU was one of the first organisations for Russian students to spearhead immigration to Palestine for agricultural purposes. The acronym was derived from the initial Hebrew letters of their motto: 'House of Israel, Come let us go up' (Isaiah 2:3). They were soon joined by youth from Rumania, where the persecution was severe.

It was hard work for the Jewish immigrants to cultivate the land, which was either largely malarial swamp or uninhabited, arid soil. At the same time, they were harassed by hostile Arabs and overtaxed by a corrupt Turkish officialdom. It soon became too expensive for Russian Jewry to pay the costs of buying land from the Turkish owners as well as the upkeep of the settlements, but they were helped by wealthy Jewish philanthropists in other countries.

During the first immigration wave in the 1880s a number of agricultural settlements, *moshavim*, were established and maintained through support from Baron Edmond de Rothschild of Paris. With the foundation laid, a second wave of, 40,000 Russian Jews arrived between 1904–15, still manifesting the pioneer tradition of the first immigration. The majority of the 40 settlements that existed in Palestine before the First World War were created by the 85,000 Russian Jews who had arrived during the early period.

World War I

At the outbreak of World War I in 1914, the Jews of Russia hoped that their participation in the defence of Russia would lead to an abolition of their second-class status. They defended their motherland in an admirable way, both as Russians and as Jews. Between 1914–17, about 400,000 Jewish soldiers participated in the war, 80,000 of these were at the battlefront. Their number well exceeded their ratio to the Empire's population. Although the Jewish soldiers hoped that their participation in the war would help attitudes towards the Jews, the Tsarist Government continued their old discriminatory policies. For example, Jewish soldiers wounded on the battlefield were not admitted to a hospital in the interior of Western Russia as were other soldiers, but instead were taken directly back to the Pale, which meant delays in receiving treatment and help. In spite of this, a considerable number of Jewish soldiers distinguished themselves for bravery.

In 1915, with the advancing German and Austrian armies 2.26 million Jews (40% of Russian Jewry) came under their military rule, thus freeing them from Russian oppression. Towards the end of the year most of the Pale was under German occupation. By 1917, only 3.4 million Jews still remained under Russian control. The Jews, who had hoped that the new rule would bring an end to their sufferings, were soon disappointed. The Germans pursued the usual policy of an occupying army, exploiting and robbing the local population, including the Jews. Not only did they do so for the benefit of their army, but they also sent increasingly large amounts of food and raw materials back to Germany. Major cities such as Warsaw, Vilna and Moscow suffered from starvation, and the death rate increased severely. When the Tsarist Government collapsed during World War I, the Russian Empire began to disintegrate.

The Revolution and Persecution of Jews under Communism

A second revolution took place on 12 March, 1917 (February in the Russian calendar). A provisional government under the leadership of the Duma and elected workers with soldiers' councils and Soviets, deposed the Tsar and made a brief attempt at democracy. After only a few months, a third revolution occurred on 8 November (on the Russian calendar 26 October) of the same year, where Vladimir Ilich Lenin took over the leadership and Russia began her experiment with Communism. The whole of Russia was plunged into a civil war, in which many Communist factions were fighting each other. The terrible period of bloodshed lasted until early in 1921. In the nationalist Ukraine, the Jews suffered greatly as they were caught between the strongly antisemitic right-wing White Army and the leftist Red Army. The White Army had assumed one of the slogans from Tsarist times, 'Strike at the Jews and save Russia!' The Bolshevik Régime had adopted a policy of suppressing antisemitism, and the Jews came to look to them as their protectors.

It is interesting that only a few days before the Russian Revolution started on 8 November, 1917, the Balfour Declaration was issued in England on 2 November, 1917 making provision for a Jewish homeland. It was greeted with great enthusiasm by Jews all over the world and inspired a powerful Zionist awakening, not least in Russia.

Lenin at the Top

When Lenin took over the leadership of the Communist government in 1918, he recognised the Jews as the twelfth national minority in the official statistics in Russia, and their situation began to improve. Judaism became a legal religion; and antisemitism was even outlawed as counter-revolutionary. The breathing space was, however, shortlived.

Many prominent Jews were members of the first Soviet Council of Commissars, such as the Foreign Minister and the founder of the Red Army, and Leon Trotsky (Bronstein), Commissar for Justice, I.N. Steinberg and the ministers Leo Karmenev and G. Zinoviev. Among the outstanding Jewish leaders of the Social-Democrat Party were J. Martov (Zederbaum) and the mayor of Moscow, Osip Minor. The leading ideologist of Communism, Karl Marx, was also Jewish. Although he had a rabbinic background, he was brought up as a Christian and knew little about Judaism. Strongly condemning it, he identified Jews with capitalism, believing that the Communist solution to 'the Jewish problem' was their final assimilation into Russian society.

Jewish Communists Forsake Their Own Heritage

In order to speed up the multi-ethnic assimilation of the Soviet society, a Commissariat on Jewish affairs, the Yevsektsia, was established in the years from 1918 until 1923. Since most of the members were either *Bund Poale Zion* (*Workers of Zion*) or previous Social Democrats who had recently joined the Communists, they tried to impose a proletarian dictatorship upon the Jewish masses and foster a secular Yiddish culture. It was a catastrophe for Russian Jewry as they stirred up hatred towards the Jewish religion, Hebrew language, the Bible and the Zionist movement.

Ironically, it was its own Jewish members, forsaking their heritage, who became its own worst enemy by advising Lenin to outlaw all Jewish political parties. Through this act they set an example for future Soviet leaders such as Stalin, Krushchev, Brezhnev and Andropov to follow.[6] But, fortunately, the revolutionaries represented only a small section of the vast number of Russian Jews, who generally remained attached to their tradition and religious culture.

In spite of these problems local Zionists, operating openly, had by 1918, established 1200 local Zionist groups with some 300,000 members. However, when the 2nd Conference of Jewish Communists met in Moscow the same year, they gave the death-blow to their nationalist endeavours. A resolution was adopted in which they accused Zionism of being 'an instrument of united imperialism, which combats the proletarian revolution', and called for a suppression of it. As a result, most of the 3,000 Zionist leaders were arrested and deported to political camps in Siberia.

The New Economic Period

As a consequence of uncontrolled inflation, a ruined economy, and a poor grain harvest, catastrophically reduced to only one third of the normal crop, the Bolshevik government under Lenin's regime, began their New Economic Policy, NEP, in 1921. The programme was aimed at restoring autonomy within the framework of a socialist economy and until the collectivisation in 1928 citizens were given the opportunity to develop semi-private enterprises as small businessmen and farmers. However, when these began to flourish again under the new structure, the Jews were soon accused of exploiting the situation and were the object of much envy from the rest of the population. 'We spilled our blood for the sake of the Revolution and only the Jews are benefiting from it,' stated one of the antisemitic slogans.[7]

Although Lenin severely opposed antisemitism in the matters of Zionism and Hebrew culture, for the Jewish religion he advocated – both on theoretical and practical grounds – a policy of total destruction and assimilation. Being a fervent atheist, his efforts were specifically directed at Judaism, and by destroying synagoues and religious institutions, he reckoned the bulwarks of Jewish culture would be removed. The question was, could Judaism survive without them?

In 1923, Lenin became incapacitated by a stroke and died in 1924. Yosef Stalin had already been appointed in 1922 to the new office of General Secretary of the Communist Party. Lenin had, however, many reservations about delegating too much power to him, fearing he might misuse it. Yet, Stalin became his successor to carry on the NEP policy.

Killing Russian Landowners

In order to get enough land for the new collectivisation programme, the lands belonging to the nobility, who had fled the country after the defeat of the White Army, were confiscated by the Communists. Many of the opponents of the Revolution had emigrated to Western Europe. In 1928 in need of more land for government use, the government turned to the wealthy Russian farmers, the *kulaks*. Disregarding their ownership, they merely murdered the smaller landowners, while the rich farmers were exiled to Siberia. Millions were killed in the process.

In pursuit of the Communist revolutionary goals a commission to 'fight contra-revolution and sabotage' was established in 1917, known by the Russian acronym, Tjeka. During the next two decades, time and again this police institution was sent in to attack their own people over matters such as the confiscation of land. The Tjeka was the forerunner of the much feared terror institutions of the secret police. The one best known in the West was the KGB.

The atrocities done to the Soviet Union's own citizens resulted in a number of the Communists feeling Stalin's policy ran contrary to their original goals, and had become too bureaucratic. One of the leading Jews, who dared criticise Stalin, was Trotsky. As a consequence, he was expelled from the Communist party in 1927 and exiled in 1929.*

* Still continuing his opposition against Stalinism but still fighting for world Communism, Trotsky was murdered in Mexico by a Communist agent in 1939.

The 'Golden Period' for Jewish Culture

When consolidating itself during the NEP period, the government did not push the ideological issues, thus allowing Jewish culture in Russia to flourish as their activities were still permitted on the same level as other nationalities. This began in the early 1920s and lasted until the mid-1930s. There were, reportedly, then about 100,000 pupils attending 1,400 Yiddish schools each year; and 20 Jewish theatres and theatrical groups functioning. Almost 20 daily, weekly or monthly Yiddish journals were circulated as well as the widely circulated literary review, *Sovietish Heymland*. Yiddish publishing houses had an annual output of about 2 million books and pamphlets from influential associations of Jewish writers and intellectuals. In large areas Yiddish existed as an influential language in courts and the meetings of local Soviets. But the era was shortlived.

Even if some of the ideological pressures had been relaxed during the first years of the NEP period, towards the end of the 1920s the Jews began to be disavowed in the Communist party, where they represented the third largest national group. Although a considerable number of them represented the working class, the majority of the Jews belonged to the middle class, and were therefore, regarded as enemies of the people.

As early as 1932, a central anti-religious museum in Moscow opened a special Jewish department in which they ridiculed the 'stupidity' of Judaism. As an entire generation of young people matured in the increasing atheistic atmosphere, Jewish religious loyalties quickly faded. Increasing intermarriage began to break down Jewish society and speeded up Jewish assimilation. Most Jewish teachers, journalists and writers lost their jobs and were imprisoned.

The Jews to Colonise Birobidzan in East Siberia?

In 1928 in order to undermine the powerful Zionist movement, Stalin began a Jewish colonisation programme in Birobidzan, a republic situated in the remote part of Eastern Siberia, just north of China. The republic was donated as a new Soviet 'homeland' and a substitute for Palestine, which

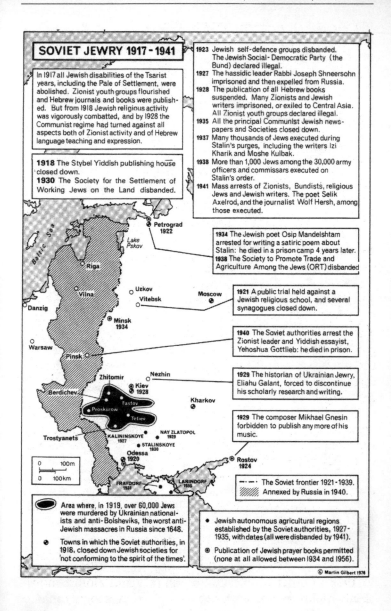

SOVIET JEWRY 1917-1941

In 1917 all Jewish disabilities of the Tsarist years, including the Pale of Settlement, were abolished. Zionist youth groups flourished and Hebrew journals and books were published. But from 1918 Jewish religious activity was vigorously combatted, and by 1928 the Communist regime had turned against all aspects both of Zionist activity and of Hebrew language teaching and expression.

1918 The Stybel Yiddish publishing house closed down.
1930 The Society for the Settlement of Working Jews on the Land disbanded.

1923 Jewish self-defence groups disbanded. The Jewish Social-Democratic Party (the Bund) declared illegal.
1927 The hassidic leader Rabbi Joseph Shneersohn imprisoned and then expelled from Russia.
1928 The publication of all Hebrew books suspended. Many Zionists and Jewish writers imprisoned, or exiled to Central Asia. All Zionist youth groups declared illegal.
1935 All the principal Communist Jewish newspapers and Societies closed down.
1937 Many thousands of Jews executed during Stalin's purges, including the writers Izi Kharik and Moshe Kulbak.
1938 More than 1,000 Jews among the 30,000 army officers and commissars executed on Stalin's order.
1941 Mass arrests of Zionists, Bundists, religious Jews and Jewish writers. The poet Selik Axelrod, and the journalist Wolf Hersh, among those executed.

1934 The Jewish poet Osip Mandelshtam arrested for writing a satiric poem about Stalin: he died in a prison camp 4 years later.
1938 The Society to Promote Trade and Agriculture Among the Jews (ORT) disbanded

1921 A public trial held against a Jewish religious school, and several synagogues closed down.

1940 The Soviet authorities arrest the Zionist leader and Yiddish essayist, Yehoshua Gottlieb: he died in prison.

1929 The historian of Ukrainian Jewry, Eliahu Galant, forced to discontinue his scholarly research and writing.

1929 The composer Mikhael Gnesin forbidden to publish any more of his music.

Baltic Sea
Lake Pskov
Petrograd 1922
Riga
Vilna
Uzkov
Vitebsk
Moscow
Danzig
Minsk 1934
Warsaw
Pinsk
Zhitomir
Nezhin
Kiev 1928
Berdichev
Kharkov
Fastov
Proskurow
Tetiev
Trostyanets
KALININSKOYE 1927
NAY ZLATOPOL 1929
STALINSKOYE 1930
Odessa 1920
Rostov 1924
FRAYDORF 1937
LARINDORF 1935

0   100m
0   100km

– – – – The Soviet frontier 1921-1939.
▨▨▨ Annexed by Russia in 1940.

⬭ Area where, in 1919, over 60,000 Jews were murdered by Ukrainian nationalists and anti-Bolsheviks, the worst anti-Jewish massacres in Russia since 1648.

⊙ Towns in which the Soviet authorities, in 1918, closed down Jewish societies for 'not conforming to the spirit of the times'.

● Jewish autonomous agricultural regions established by the Soviet authorities, 1927-1935, with dates (all were disbanded by 1941).

⊚ Publication of Jewish prayer books permitted (none at all allowed between 1934 and 1956).

© Martin Gilbert 1976

Map 6
The Jews of Russia. Sir Martin Gilbert, CBE, 1979, Steimatzky.
Used with permission.

was decried as 'a British imperialist project'. The goal was to settle 100,000 Jews there. But the climatic and soil conditions were poor.

During the first three years a few thousand Jews, mostly artisans and workers from White Russia and the Ukraine, moved to Birobidzan. By 1934 it had autonomous status. Although the Jews only amounted to 20% of the population Yiddish, together with Russian, became the official language. Although Jewish culture was permitted and schools and theatres established, the project never succeeded. Birobidzan was too far removed from contact with Jewish communities in the West. While a considerable number of Jews sought refuge there during the war, by 1960 only 15,000 of them remained among 180,000 Russian citizens. In the 1990s, an immigration movement to Israel began. Even though the official figure in 1998 was 9,000, the real number is thought to be somewhat higher.

Stalin's Purges

Around the 1930s, when Stalin took more dictatorial powers, he soon began to eradicate every trace of criticism. Not only did his paranoid suspicions affect his own party members, among whom he instigated mass purges; his enmity was aimed, in particular, at the Jews, who were considered to be a foreign element in the country. Already in 1928, many Zionist and Hebrew writers were imprisoned or exiled to Central Asia. All aspects of Zionist activities as well as the youth movements and learning Hebrew, were then prohibited.

During 1935–37, waves of terror set in, culminating in August 1936, when 14 old Bolshevik leaders, Lenin's most trusted men, were accused of plotting against the current Soviet leadership. Among these were the two Jewish ministers, Kamenev and Zinoviev, who were executed. In 1937–1938, many of the Red Army top officers and commissars were sentenced to death. Jewish leaders in Birobidzan, accused of being Troskyites and Zionists, were eliminated.

The toll was outrageous. Millions were arrested. While tens of thousands were executed, it was estimated that hundreds of thousands of people were sentenced to prison or forced labour camps, known collectively as the GULAG,* the Russian acronym for Stalin's prison network. The punitive system was run by the Soviet Ministry of Internal Affairs (MVD). All over the vast USSR, the camps containing millions of prisioners soon expanded enormously.

In the 1930s a network of work camps was established across Central Asia and Siberia. On average they held between 2,000–10,000 prisoners. Most of the camps were corrective labour colonies in which they worked on general construction projects or in mines. Such a project was the White Sea Canal built to enhance the Communists' prestige.

By 1936, the Gulag held a total of 5 million prisoners, a number which was probably exceeded each year till Stalin died.[8]

More Antisemitism under Stalin

During the 1930s, antisemitism was no longer a criminal offence, but became almost the official policy of Stalin and his regime. Synagogues were closed; holy scrolls and books of the Talmud were officially burnt in the streets. Many rabbis and Torah scholars were arrested and banished to Siberia where many leaders were killed. Because of lack of leadership and shortage of funds, Yiddish institutes were on the verge of collapse. Jews were forced to work on the Sabbath, and the people were exhausted.

Just as the Jews hoped that the purges had subsided, in 1941 another mass arrest of Zionists, members of the Bund workers, religious Jews and Jewish writers took place. A wave of terror filled the hearts of Russian Jewry.

World War II
Communist Attitudes Towards its Own People

'The Great Patriotic War', the title given by the Soviet Union to the war with Nazi Germany, began on 22 June, 1941. The military occupation by Nazi Germany has been described in the previous section. It became a severe time of testing for Russian citizens, and the death toll was very heavy both

---

* GULAG is an acronym of Chief Administration of Corrective Labour Camps.

among soldiers and civilians. The material losses were severe. During 1941 the State security function, later known as the KGB, was formed.

Stalin did all he could to play down the Nazi atrocities. The mass murder of civilians was never reported, probably because it would be difficult to explain why the Red Army had retreated into the interior, leaving the borders unprotected, and thus exposing their own people to enemy attacks. In spite of all the destruction which took place on the battlefield and occupied areas throughout the war, unyielding Stalin was set on his goal to win the war and appeared to be unmoved by the sufferings of the people. He even added to the burden by continuing his purges of foreign ethnic groups. These were the Volga Germans and the Tartars of the Crimea, who were accused of collaborating with the Germans. Kurds, together with Bulgars and Chechens from Caucasia, were deported to Siberia.

Even during wartime, Stalin did not stop banishing people to the labour camps. One of the biggest work camps, Kolyma, in the eastern part of the country, held an estimated 2 million prisoners. The prisoners simply died like flies in the camps. The Gulag system probably reached its height immediately following World War II. Even if we never know the true number of the victims of Stalin's policy, a conservative figure would be around 12 million dead in the Gulag.[9]

Communist Attitudes Towards the Jews

The official Soviet position was that there was no Jewish tragedy as such during the Second World War. They cynically asserted: 'All the people of the USSR shared in the ordeal of the Nazi occupation, and there is no reason for "separating" the Jews for a special case.' Not even at Babi Yar.

The Nazi's specific annihilation of millions of Jews was completely ignored in the reporting, lest the Soviet government be accused of fighting on behalf of the Jews. Thus, the death camps of Auschwitz and Majdanek in Poland were hardly ever mentioned in the Soviet press. No evidence has ever been found that either the Government or the Communist Party issued any appeals or sent out leaflets to underground organisations in their occupied territories in order to help Soviet citizens of Jewish background, who were subject to the Nazi extermination programme.

The figure of well over 2 million Jews, lost in the Holocaust in the Soviet territories, is based on an estimated census.[10]

(See also map of *The Nazi Destruction of the Jews in the Former Pale of Settlement, 1941–1945* in Chapter 2.)

The Last Years of Stalin

Between 1948 and the early 1950s, Stalin carried out an 'anti-cosmopolitan' campaign, which involved more purges than ever. A climax was reached in Birobidjan with an antisemitic campaign and the execution of leading Yiddish writers that took place in August 1952. Then, in early 1953 a show-trial, the 'Doctors' plot' was planned against 15 Soviet physicians (of whom 6 were Jewish). They were alleged to have acted on the orders of Western Jewish philanthropic organisations and to be plotting to murder the Communist leadership. Jewish scientists in Russia were put under pressure to denounce the 'crime'. Only Stalin's death in April three months later, followed by a communique from the Interior Minister announcing the innocence of the imprisoned doctors, put an end to the period of dread. Had Stalin lived much longer the entire Jewish population in Russia would have been in danger.[11]

The establishment of a Jewish homeland in the state of Israel in 1948 made an important impact on Soviet Jewry, and it created a hope of freedom in their hearts, which stirred their Jewish consciousness. On the other hand, it increased the hatred from the Communist leadership. When the new State was proclaimed, 2,000 Jews were brave enough to identify with it and gathered outside the Moscow Synagogue to join in the celebration.

Hoping that Israel would become a Russian satellite state in the Middle East, the Soviet Union voted for its establishment at the UN. Later, when the Communist regime realised that Israel was turning to the Western alliance, their attitude towards the new 'imperialist' state changed drastically, and it became a thorn in their eye. Another reason for opposing it was the Jewish exuberance over finally gaining a 'homeland' and their aspirations of emigrating to it.

Krushchev – a Softening of the Political Climate

After the death of Stalin, several leaders were competing for power, and after a couple of years, the first head of the Soviet Union, Nikita Krushchev, emerged in 1955. He gave the Communist Party the predominance which it held for decades until the *glasnost* period in the 1990s. He introduced a more popular style of leadership, but his colleagues were not always enthusiastic about his initiatives.

The post-Stalin era led to a new reckoning of the past and a restoration of the cultural rights of ethnic minority groups, but Jews were not included. The increased freedom also brought about the release of hundreds of thousands, probably even millions of political prisoners from camps. Many Jews had been held prisoner among the innumerable inmates. In the camps they had learned the Hebrew language as well as Jewish history and, when released, they became dissidents in the growing dissident movement.

A moment of reckoning of past history appeared to take place at the 22nd Congress of the Communist Party in 1961, when Khrushchev not only officially denounced Stalin for his crimes against the people, but also held his leadership responsible for its share in the purges of the 1930–1940s. But no charge was ever levelled against Lenin. Even if the new regime acknowledged the abuse of power against the Russian people in general in the past, they did not admit to their Communist oppression of them in the present.

As an indication of the new wind blowing, in 1962 Khrushchev permitted the publication of the book by A. Solzhenitzyn *One Day in the Life of Ivan Denisovits* (describing the life of a prisoner in a labour camp).

However, the loosening of the tight grip of the government did not last long. Already, in the early 1960s, a new shock wave was on the way when the Soviet leadership initiated another antisemitic campaign. In order to cover up for successive crop failures and the disastrous state of the country's economy, Krushchev began to accuse the Jews particularly, of 'economic crimes'. The penalty was either death or lengthy prison terms. Between 1961–63 more than

170 Soviet citizens, among whom 68 (or 40%) were Jews, were executed for these alleged crimes.

During the Krushchev years, a very limited immigration to Israel was permitted for family reunification. Usually, it was those past the retirement age of 60 who received permission to leave, together with Polish Jews who had fled to Russia during the early war years. But after the Sinai War in 1956, this came to a halt because Soviet Middle East policy had become more aggressively anti-Zionist and more pro-Arab. The war caused a climax when the Soviet envoy in Tel Aviv was recalled to Moscow as a warning. In April of 1957 he returned to Israel, shortly before the delivery of Soviet oil to Israel was stopped.

In mid-July 1957, an International Youth Festival took place in Moscow, and a 200-member Israeli delegation was permitted to participate. A huge and enthusiastic Jewish crowd, both of Muscovites and thousands of guests from the provinces, was bold enough to give an open and passionate expression of their attachment to the Jewish State and openly applauded the Israelis. They asked for Israeli postcards, stamps, and keepsakes in the streets, inviting them to their homes. Shortly after the Israeli delegation left, retribution came as thousands of Jews were declared guilty of the offence of 'fraternisation'. On various pretences some lost their jobs, while many were arrested, and others were sent to hard labour camps in Siberia.

Jewish Emigration to the West under Brezhnev

As a result of his failed agricultural policy Krushchev was deposed in 1964, and Leonid Brezhnev emerged as his successor. His willingness to listen to the aspirations of the Party and State bureaucrats was a major reason for his election. After the economic decline, they wanted a long, calm period. He was very successful in achieving concensus in the Soviet establishment, largely by avoiding the difficult problems rather than solving them. But even the exceptional abilities of Aleksey Kosygin, the Soviet Premier from 1964–80 were not enough to halt the decline in economic growth. The vast Soviet Union was moving too clumsily and slowly to keep up with the advanced technology in use abroad, particularly in manufacturing. Again, the attempts of Brezhnev to protect his position as leader conflicted with the need of the country for reforms. He feared that if he attempted a major economic reform, it would arouse such an opposition that his political career would be endangered. This resulted in bureaucratic complacency, which paved the way for increasing corruption.

As the interest in immigration to Israel grew, Hebrew study groups sprang up in many cities. The illegal *samizdat* bulletin was hand-copied and quickly spread the dissidents' viewpoints, both in their own circles as well as overseas. This movement, highly scorned by the Soviet regime, was invariably described as 'Zionist propaganda'. But, in contrast to Krushchev's fierce anti-Jewish accusations of criminal charges against the State, Brezhnev had to limit his policy to moderate campaigns against emigration, Zionism and World Jewry.

'Let My People Go' Movement

By the mid-1960s, many intellectuals in the West had become interested in the plight of the Soviet Jews and their right of reunification with their families. The movement took up the slogan 'Let My People Go' (the ancient cry of Moses to the Egyptian Pharaoh before the Israelite Exodus from Egypt, Exodus 5:1). By 1964, the main US Jewish organisations held the first American Jewish Conference on Soviet Jewry in Washington DC and established a body of the same name to keep the interest going. The first large public demonstration gained considerable support, although not such large crowds as in the 1970–80s. Soon solidarity rallies for Soviet Jewry were held in the capitals of a number of countries. Twenty years later, the *Jerusalem Post* of 30 September, 1989 notes that by 1987, these rallies drew crowds of up to 250,000 participants such as on the eve of Gorbachev's visit in December when they gathered for a mass demonstration for 'Passage to Freedom' in Washington DC. This was in some ways a symbolic atonement for the tepid political response of American Jewry during the Holocaust. These efforts were attempts to curb Soviet antisemitism.

A daring step of faith was taken by the Israeli Government in 1985, when they circulated a new money bill focusing on

Figure 1 In a bright golden yellow, the 10-shekel note depicted the first Israeli Ambassador to Moscow in 1948, Golda Meir, herself a former Russian emigrant to the USA, who later came to Israel.

Figure 2 The bill's other side showed Golda Meir in the midst of a rejoicing crowd of Russian Jews outside the Moscow Great Synagogue on the Jewish New Year. As a challenge and encouragement to the Israelis it carried the ancient cry of Moses '*Let my people go*', the slogan of the modern *aliyah* (immigration) movement!

Golda Meir later obtained high government positions in Israel, as did also a number of other Russian emigrees, and she became one of their six Prime Ministers with a Russian background. Israel has also had four Presidents who emigrated from Russia.

the release of Russian Jews at a time when the USSR had frozen Jewish emigration.

The consciousness of the free world was further stirred through a book *The Jews of Silence* by Elie Wiesel (1967), describing the utter despair and isolation of Soviet Jewry. They appeared to have lost their own voices and sought spokesmen in the West. As the author so vividly expressed it, 'I went to Russia by the silence of the Jews and brought back their cry.' [12]

After the Six-Day War in 1967, statesmen, parliamentarians and scientists in many countries increasingly began to support the cause of colleagues and others in the USSR. When Soviet Jewish dissidents staged demonstrations or hunger strikes in Soviet cities, they were followed up by solidarity rallies led by human rights activists in major capitals overseas. As leading Soviet Jews were permitted to leave, they too spoke at the Western rallies. Whenever Soviet politicians travelled abroad, they were met with human rights demonstrations, which in many cases brought pressure on them to act, pointing out to them that the issues were not solely Soviet affairs.

As a result of the political breakdown of Soviet–Israeli relations, the main Israeli Embassy in Moscow was closed. This caused great difficulty for the rising number of Jews. While they could receive exit permits to leave the USSR through the local emigration office, OVIR, the Jews still had to obtain their immigration visa for Israel. During the Brezhnev period and into the *glasnost* period, this consular task was kindly handled through the Dutch Embassy.

In 1969, the increasing Jewish desire to emigrate meant that about 3,000 Soviet Jews were permitted to leave for Israel. The following year, however, with such hurdles to overcome, the figure had dwindled to one third or 1,000 people – an average of just 80 per month. Soviet newspapers offered the explanation that it was the Jews' own decision because they simply did not want to leave. In answer, forty Soviet Jews wrote an open letter, published abroad, in which they stated that this was certainly not true. It was a difficult time for Soviet Jewry. The people having their applications for exit visas refused were named *refuseniks*. Their number grew rapidly. By 1976, the figure had reached a total of 2,000.

All this did not go unnoticed in the West, where they realised that if international pressure was exerted, increased Soviet emigration would be permitted again. From over 12,800 in 1971 to between 31,000–34,000 in 1972–73, by 1975, the figure had again fallen to 13,300, but of these only 8,500 arrived in Israel.

The reason for this development was that in the early 1970s, the Soviet Bureucracy had insisted the Jews could only go to Israel. Towards the mid-1970s, however, an increasing number of emigrants preferred to go to the USA in order to be reunited with family there. There was also the possibility of getting a better job and perhaps a more peaceful life. So when the opportunity arose, a growing number of emigrants, who had first opted for Israel, changed their destination once safely in Vienna and left for other Western countries instead, usually the USA. This so-called drop out problem, which was about 4% in 1973, later grew rapidly.

The Right to Leave the Country

Previous to the 1970s the Soviet Government would only rarely grant permission to an ordinary citizen to travel abroad, let alone emigrate. For the purpose of reunification with family abroad, only minority groups such as Volga Germans, Jews, Estonians, and Armenians might reluctantly be granted such a privilege. Soviet news media and literature of the time had strong Judeo-phobic tendencies, supporting the idea that all Russia's trouble stemmed from people of foreign roots. However, within dissident and liberal circles in the Soviet Union, it was readily agreed that minority groups should definitely be granted freedom to leave. In Alexander Solzhenitsyn [13] the political prisoners found a strong spokesman. Although having no special sympathy for the Jews and being an avowed humanist, he nevertheless, through his writings, attacked the contemporary Soviet regime for their inhumane suppression of citizens of different convictions. His criticism received a strong response among human rights supporters in the West.

The Battle of Human Rights Activists

Frequently, the activists would demonstrate in open squares

of the major cities for the right of free emigration. The gathering would quickly be broken up and sometimes the demonstrators would be beaten up by 'unknown persons' or arrested by the police and sentenced for weeks or months for 'malicious hooliganism' and 'anti-Soviet activites'.

During the 1970s or 1980s, when Western human rights supporters or tourists visited the activists or Jewish refuseniks in order to encourage them and obtain inside information, the local citizens visited would be severely beaten by the KGB (or some of their accomplices) and arrested. The Jews might be held or imprisoned for a short period on trumped-up charges. Not only would the Jews be severely punished for these contacts, but the Westerners might also risk being arrested, in which case they would be denied access to US officials or their own embassy. Thus, in the early 1980s the US State Department warned its citizens not to travel in Russia because of the danger of arrest. Leningrad and Kiev were particularly noted as dangerous cities to travel in.

Refusenik Life in the 1970s

The refusenik's fate was difficult and often tragic. Having obtained an invitation *vysof* from Israel, a would-be emigrant applied for an exit visa at OVIR, the Russian emigration office. Since such an application had to be renewed every 6 months by up-to-date invitations from abroad, the whole procedure made it very difficult to carry through in time. As mail was often inspected and confiscated by the authorities, thousands of invitations to emigrate never reached their destination. Those who turned to a foreign embassy for assistance in obtaining the necessary invitation would often be harassed.

The application procedure was very cumbersome and time-consuming. Answers were required to the following:

1. Were there objections to his departure from his close family or economic obligations such as continued payment to a divorced wife or children?
2. Was he charged with a criminal offence with a trial pending, or was he was still serving a court imposed sentence?

3. Did he have obligations of military conscription or was there any judicial sentence in custody which he had not served?
4. Or had he any knowledge of state secrets related to his work place? If so, there would be a delay of at least 5–10 years before departure.

In all instances, prospective emigrants would be dismissed from work and cut off from their profession. It would then be difficult to find even a menial job with much lower pay. Consequently, the authorities would often charge them with 'parasitism'. With the telephone cut off, they would be disconnected from their family and friends abroad. Their children were harassed, expelled from universities and made subject to conscription, which would further delay the departure. They would be exposed to severe harassment from the KGB (the Commmunist Party's political police and security agency). Their homes were often searched for incriminating material of an anti-Soviet nature. Thus, a family desiring to emigrate ran a considerable risk of having to wait in extremely difficult circumstances for an extended period, often for years. The processing of visas was often very arbitrary. Thus, to large numbers of the Jewish population the refusal of exit visas became a form of intimidation, deterring prospective emigrants from even presenting their applications.

The Notorious Leningrad Trial

The Jews' desperate struggle for freedom and escape to the West was highlighted to the world, when a group of activists from Leningrad and Riga attempted to escape to Israel on 15 June, 1970. Having seized a 12-seater civil aeroplane in Leningrad, the first planned stop was Sweden. From there the plane would be permitted to return to the USSR, while they themselves continued on. Before taking off they were caught and arrested. In the same month, several hundred Jews from Leningrad alone, had protested against the Soviet government's refusal to grant the twelve permission to leave, and other such actions continued in the West. Six months later, on 25 December, 1970, the sentences of the notorious Leningrad trial were announced.

It was an event that stirred the consciousness of the West concerning the Jewish struggle for freedom. Under Article 64 A of the Criminal Code of the USSR, the twelve were charged with 'treason', an offence punishable with death. Because of protests from the West the two pilots, Mark Dymshitz and Edouard Kuznetsov (who initially received the death sentence) had their sentences commuted to severe punishment of more than ten years in strict labour camps. In the West, the sentenced Jews became known as the first 'Prisoners of Zion', among whom were Evgeni Lein and Josef Mendelevich. Campaigns were launched to obtain their release but they remained imprisoned for ten years by which time most of their prison sentences were due to expire anyway. When freed, they were permitted to immigrate to Israel.

However, two Russian Christians who had helped the Jews to leave, Yuri Feodorov and Aleksei Murzhenko, received even stricter sentences of 14 and 15 years respectively. As a warning to the rest of the population, these two men remained imprisoned in spite of continued efforts by Jewish and Christian campaigners in the West to get them released quickly. (In appreciation for their stand with the Jews, these Russians were later termed 'Prisoners of Conscience'.) Not until late in the 1980s, were they able to immigrate with their families to the United States, where I met them. Their health had suffered severely, and the men had become very weak from their long, debilitating prison terms.

Soviet Agrees Not to Violate Human Rights – 1975

The West, and particularly American Jewry, realised that something special needed to be done to keep the Russians abiding by the human rights laws and to ensure the flow to freedom of their fellow Jews in the USSR. In the early 1970s the Soviet Union developed their policy of détente. Russia wanted to establish their position as a super power by legitimising their strong influence on their satellite countries in Eastern Europe. They also had a strong economic need for foreign supplies, technology and goods. Eventually, the Soviet Union bowed half-heartedly to Western pressures to conform to Western standards and agreed to issue a unified statement on human rights. This was set forth in the Helsinki

Agreement of 1975. In the treaty 35 countries, including the USSR, guaranteed all their citizens basic human rights in matters of emigration, reunification of divided families, and the right of dissident intellectuals to leave their country.

The West, and American Jewry in particular, lobbied to put pressure on the government to support Soviet Jewish emigration. The US Congress' proposal, which finally secured the USSR's consent, was the Jackson-Varnik Trade Amendment, offering the Soviets the attractive 'most favoured nation' status in exchange for the agreement. By linking trade advantages to the emigration issue, the USSR would receive the needed Western technology and food, particularly grain.

Soviet leaders consented to the US demand that the number of visas issued in any given year should correspond to the number of applications. Thus, there would be no refusals. To ensure the international agreement was kept Helsinki Watch groups supervised the issue.

In spite of signing the Helsinki declaration, the USSR, who for economic reasons did not want to see her manpower leaving, wanted to keep their emigration figure reasonably low. The agreement spoke in general terms about unification of minority groups for family reasons, without specific mention that Jews, for example, were only permitted to go to Israel. However this was the way the Soviet government, according to previous practice, interpreted it. To keep their figures low, an anti-emigration campaign was directed against all ethnic groups who were leaving the country in any significant numbers.[14]

Seen from a Soviet perspective, emigration involved a waste of education for which the society had paid; and the loss of working capacity in the emigrées' most productive years. Moreover, the desire to emigrate was a slap in the face of the Soviet government. In the Russian media it was described as an abandonment of the Jews' loyalties and as a contemptuous act towards their old homeland, Mother Russia, who had done so much for them – and, of all things they were leaving for the land of their enemy, the USA, instead.

Emigration Resumed After 1975

Due to the Jackson-Varnick trade amendment, emigration

from the USSR increased rapidly from 12,000 in 1976 to 28,000 in 1978.

After free emigration to the West was permitted at the signing of the Helsinki Declaration, in 1975, the drop-out rate of 4% in 1973 quickly rose. By 1979 Soviet emigration reached a peak of over 51,000 when 17,600 Jews left for Israel, while over twice as many, 34,000 (some 66%), went elsewhere in the West. In the period of good US–Soviet relationships, it was not a problem for the emigrants, because the US raised the immigration quota correspondingly.[15] Unfortunately, one year later a strain in the US–Soviet relationship caused a halt in the emigration.

Looking back over the 1970s, there is an understandable explanation for the rising number of Soviet Jews leaving for the West, and particularly the USA. The main reason was that the background of the Jews emigrating before and after 1975 was quite different. While the pre-1975 emigrants consisted mainly of Jews from the Asiatic and Western republics, settling in Israel for religious reasons, the post-1975 emigrants were well educated Jews who usually for personal, economic and professional reasons chose to live in the USA. This trend was also seen after 1985.

Emigration of Other Ethnic Groups

During the emigration wave from 1971–1980, a total of over 250,000 Jews left the USSR; 159,000 or 63.6% of them immigrated to Israel, while 91,000 went elsewhere, mainly to the United States.

It is interesting to note that in the same decade the rising interest in human rights also paved the way for the emigration of other ethnic minorities from the USSR. While 64,000 Volga Germans went to West Germany, over 34,000 Armenians left mainly to France and the US. In the following decade this trend continued. Thus, during 1981–89, 176,700 Soviet citizens departed for Germany, while 31,200 Armenians and 10,000 Greeks left for their homelands. This was actually more than the number of Jews in the corresponding years, namely 116,900.[16]

'Prisoners of Zion'

In order to muzzle the increasing desire for freedom, the Soviet government made great efforts to clamp down on the growing number of the most active Jews. Among these were 40 people who were accused of trumped-up charges and received several harsh prison sentences. These included: Felix Kochubievsky PhD, spearheading a voluntary 'Friendship association between people of the USSR and Israel'; radio engineer Vladimir Slepak, known for his letters and petitions to the UN on behalf of Soviet Jewry; and cyberneticist Victor Brailovsky who received prominent foreign scientists, and up-dated the technical knowledge of dismissed colleagues in the USSR. Not to forget the Moscow economist Ida Nudel who became known as the 'guardian angel of the prisoners' for her help to needy families of imprisoned Jews. Both before her arrest in Moscow in 1978 and during her years in exile in Siberia she continued unabated campaigning to the West about the plight of Soviet Jews.

The classic example of the struggle in this period is probably the well-known human rights activist and mathematician Anatoly (now Natan) Sharansky. Having been a refusenik since 1973, he was denied permission to emigrate when his wife Avital was forced to leave the Soviet Union in 1974. Still being denied the exit visa promised him, Sharansky was subjected to trumped-up charges and in 1977 was accused of espionage for a foreign power. The following year he was sentenced to a total of 13 years; for three of these he was to be incarcerated in the infamous Chistopol Prison followed by 10 years in a strict labour camp.

Shortly before Sharansky's arrest, the Anti-Zionist Committee presented his struggle in a TV programme called *Traders in Souls*, in which he was accused of working for the CIA. By producing such a TV programme, the media tried to give the impression that Jews were a disloyal and untrustworthy element, foreign to Soviet society. However, massive protests continued to pour in from the West. In 1986 these resulted in an early release, and Sharansky was freed in an East–West spy exchange. When emaciated and fatigued, he crossed the Glienicke Bridge connecting East with West Berlin, to freedom, a world full of human rights supporters was watching closely.[17]

The Cooling of the Emigration Climate

In the latter part of the Brezhnev regime, the Cold War between East and West was resumed. This was caused by a strain in the US–Soviet relationship in connection with the arms limitation treaty (SALT II),* but deteriorated considerably over the Soviet invasion of Afghanistan.

The Afghan war was intended as a step towards the fulfilment of the Soviet's aim to gain access to the Persian Gulf because of her oil interests. It resulted in curtailing emigration and American economic aid based on the Jackson-Varnick Agreement, ceased. A poor economy and crop failure plagued the USSR.

In spite of the difficulties, the Soviet Jews continued to request invitations from Israel. Between 1968–1980 over 630,000 Jews had asked to receive such a letter. Since it represented almost one third of the official Soviet Jewish population, it greatly alarmed the Soviet government.[18]

Oppressive Communism in the 1980s – Andropov

When Brezhnev died in November 1982, his preferred successor was the elderly Konstantin Chernenko. Brezhnev, however, was not strong enough to prevent the election of the much younger Yuri Andropov, Head of the KGB. Andropov was then only 52 years old, in marked contrast to the previous much older leadership. But Andropov was in constant need of medical treatment for a chronic kidney disease, and by August the following year he had to withdraw from public life. He died suddenly in February 1984, after a reign of only 15 months.

Under these circumstances it was remarkable what Andropov was able to accomplish by rejuvenating the Party and the State apparatus. While Brezhnev's government had

---

* SALT II relates to the Stategic Arms Limitation Treaty from 1972, dealing with negotiations between the USSR and the USA on reducing their armaments, particularly in connection with the launching of rockets.

long suffered from an elderly and incapacitated leadership, Andropov started actions against the corruption in the Soviet society. More than one fifth of the Moscow members of the Council of Ministers, and over one third of the department heads of the Secretariat of the Communist Party were removed. They were replaced with younger, and better-qualified staff members, nurtured during the Brezhnev period. But the emphasis on increased work discipline and a higher labour ethic was not popular in the ranks, since the older bureaucrats feared that they might be the next to go.

In an urge to strengthen the country during the first months of his reign, Andropov presented the watchword 'a merger of Soviet nationalities' for his nationalist policy. He was seeking to gain a proper representation for all groups, both in Party and State bodies, in the regions as well as the centre. But because of opposition, the reform was soon given up.

Antisemitism Crops up Again

The continued disastrous state of the Soviet economy, and crop failures meant that it was difficult for the USSR to see their well-educated citizens emigrate. Together with the strained East-West relations, the Israeli invasion of Lebanon in 1982 provided the background for a stepped-up anti-semitic campaign. An assimilated Jew, Lev Korneev, was put in charge of the newly established Anti-Zionist Committee for the Soviet Union (with the acronym AKSO). His vicious writings appeared in a large number of journals, newspapers and books. He alleged that the real reason these Soviet-born, well-educated Jews, who had enjoyed all the advantages of the Soviet system, wanted to leave the USSR was simply greed, and they were regarded as disloyal citizens.

He maintained that many of the invitations, extended for Jewish emigration, were simply counterfeit. At a press conference in June 1983, a considerable number of fictitious letters from 'Soviet relatives' were presented to the public. They all purported that permission to leave the USSR meant 'dooming human beings to hell'. The AKSO, therefore, worked on the idea that the Jews had to be shown that, at least for the present, emigration was out of the question. The emigration ban was therefore, in fact, only a humanitarian gesture by the government for the Jews' own benefit.

To add fuel to the fire, in his book *The Aggressive Essence of Zionism* and other writings, Korneev depicted Zionism as being the politics of the Jewish overclass, essentially anti-Communist and working towards the destruction of the USSR with the final aim of world dominion.[19] Through the Anti-Zionist Committee, Andropov created an atmosphere reminiscent of the Stalin era. This led many of the Jewish activists to feel that in the event of a serious national crisis they would again be used as scapegoats.

Oppression of its Own People

In order to make the picture more complete, it should be noted that it was not only the Jews, Germans and other minorities who desired freedom to flee the USSR, but with the increasingly oppressive situation under Andropov a number of Soviet citizens also made plans for leaving Mother Russia. As previously mentioned, there was no way these could obtain permission to emigrate. The only way to get out was by trying to escape illegally over the border without papers. A number of hijacking attempts were also reported, sometimes involving violence.

The country of choice for defection was Finland, with a long uninhabited stretch of forest north of Leningrad, along both sides of the Finnish border. Since the Finnish authorities had signed an agreement with the Soviet Union to return all escapees crossing their country, it was necessary for them to get the whole way up to the Swedish border-city, Haparanda, before reaching safety. During the early 1980s, the growing number of attempts to escape the Soviet Union increased the punishment. The first illegal crossing of the Soviet border was punishable by up to 3 years in a labour camp, while repeated attempts were punishable by as much as 5 years incarceration. By 1985, about a dozen reports of attempts to cross the border reached the West. Very few of them were successful.[20]

Refusenik Life During the 1980s

In the new decade, characterised by the Cold War, life for the

Jews went from bad to worse. Even though the outlook for emigration was bleak, the Jewish activists did not lose heart, but redoubled their efforts. They were often exposed to harassment, beaten up in the streets by the KGB and sentenced for varying periods on trumped-up charges. Demonstrations for freedom were clamped down on harder than ever and contact with Western visitors was forbidden. To the general public, the dissident movement was presented as a Jewish phenomenon, bent on undermining the foundation of the Soviet State. It was still extremely hard to obtain Israeli visas as only the Dutch Embassy in Moscow handled the requests. The matter was further complicated by the fact that in the republics only a few local OVIR emigration offices were open, and then often only part-time, in the main cities.

The State-Secret Clause

It became a characteristic of this period that Jews employed in manufacturing plants, government factories, military installations etc. were claimed by the authorities to be in possession of state secrets and considered to be a special category. Having already lost their jobs when they applied to emigrate, they would then be denied exit visas for up to 10 years or more; even though their so-called 'secret' would be declassified long before this.

Hebrew Language Learning Forbidden

Another new trend in the 1980s was that Jews, dismissed from work, often tried to earn a small income by giving private lessons in Hebrew and on subjects related to Jewish culture. This forbidden language was only taught at a few universities to which Jews, in general, would not be admitted. To pursue such studies was severely punished with fines or sometimes with prison sentences.

A well-known example from this decade was the mathematician, Yosif Begun PhD, who having applied for an exit visa in the 1970s, was dismissed from his job and served two prison sentences and exile in Siberia. In 1983, falsely accused of 'anti-soviet agitation and propaganda', Begun received his third 7-year prison sentence and a further 5 years in exile in

Siberia. This sentence of 12 years, just for teaching Hebrew, gave rise to a worldwide outcry from the human rights leaders, and Begun was later acclaimed a 'Prisoner of Zion'. In 1987, Yosif Begun was released early, and he and his family were finally able to leave for Israel.

Increasing Emigration Difficulties

During the 1980s new emigration restrictions led to a drastic reduction of exit visas. This policy was continued until the *glasnost* period. In 1981 the number of emigrants fell to 9,500 and the following year it was cut by over two thirds, so only 2,700 left the country. By 1984–85 only 900 visas were issued. Only one third of them chose to immigrate to Israel. Although the figure is probably underestimated, Dr Martin Gilbert reported that by 1985 the number of refuseniks in the USSR exceeded 10,000.[21]

Chernenko

In order to avoid instability in the regime, the 70-year-old Konstantin Chernenko, was – to the surprise of many – finally elected as Andropov's successor. This, in itself, was an extraordinary move. He was seen as the rallying-point between the old guard of the party and state officers opposed to change, and the Andropov wing of younger leadership pushing for moderate reforms. His regime was rather uneventful and the tough, oppressive line of his predecessor with regard to human rights and emigration was continued. Having spent most of his life promoting the fulfilment of other people's plans, Chernenko had little experience in economic affairs. Brezhnev's political line was continued, and Chernenko backtracked to restore some of the former privileges to old party ministers. After only a couple of years, he died from emphysema in 1985.

The Growing 'Drop-Out' Problem in the 1980s

In the 1980s, the problem of the Cold War meant that not only the Soviet Union, but also the US placed restrictions upon immigration. As some of the Soviet emigrées did not qualify for a US visas at the first selection, they were still waiting in Vienna, hoping for another chance to become united with their families in the US. During the 1980s, the drop-outs rapidly grew to two-thirds of the number of the Soviet emigrants compared with about half in the late 1970s. (But emigrant numbers were rather small by then.)*

But after some years the Austrians became apprehensive about the growing number of Soviet Jews staying temporarily in their country, and they made it known that too many Soviet Jews were not welcome.** So a majority of the emigrées went instead to Rome. In the 1980s several thousand of them were stranded there under miserable conditions. By 1989 the backlog had risen to over 7,000 Soviet Jews. Eventually some Jewish and Christian organisations took up their cause and alleviated the situation, and a few years later when the Soviet-American relationship again thawed, the US took care of the problem.

The First Reformer: Gorbachev and Glasnost

Although groomed by Andropov as his heir, Mikhail Gorbachev (then 55 years old) was actually chosen as the representative of the reform wing. More than any previous president, he shook the traditional foundation of the otherwise untouchable central government of the Soviet Union. Reared in the Communist system, it was Gorbachev's dream to reform Communism and modernise the Soviet Union, so that a healthier economy would make it more attractive to the West. So he started out on the path of *perestroika*, i.e. restructuring the socialist system. In this move he was

---

* In an interesting research Z. Gittelman has pointed out, that if Jewish emigrants want to leave for the US, but are forced to go to Israel first, an equivalent proportion will end up leaving Israel for the West anyway (Z. Gittelman, *Emigrants in the USA*, Soviet Jewish Affairs, Vol. 7, No. 1. 1977, p. 44).

** A growing antisemitic spirit was apparently prevalent in Austria. In order to gain votes at the election in 1990, one of the political parties used the slogan 'Don't let Vienna become Chicago' (S. Heitman, *Soviet Immigration in 1990, A New Fourth Wave*, Soviet Jewish Affairs, Vol. 21, No. 2, 1991, p. 19).

well supported by his politicians. Being strongly influenced by the USA, Gorbachev attempted to recreate the USSR's government on the pattern of a Western democracy. By economic subsidies and aid packages a new line of reforms and modernisation was introduced and a remarkable change from state control to privatisation took place.

Summit meetings between the United States and the Soviet Union resulted in the signing of disarmament treaties between East and West, and the arms race stopped. This led to an end of the cold war. Human rights were brought to the fore, and further great changes were in the air.

Dark Clouds Spread – Glasnost

The domestic liberalisation of *glasnost*, the openness policy, began with a revision and re-evaluation of the country's history. At last, an objective view could be taken of their former Soviet leadership, particularly of Stalin, and criticism was permitted without fear of punitive persecutions. The slogans of *perestroika* and *glasnost* became key words in the West. Incredible changes took place – in almost too short a time.

Under *glasnost*, the outlook became brighter. In order to gain support for his policy of reform, Gorbachev asked the help of the intellectuals, Russian writers and publicists. This led to an avalanche of historical, social and ideological disclosure, which in the end went so far that it undermined the very foundation of Soviet civilisation. The turning point occurred in the autumn of 1989 when, with Gorbachev's permission, Sergei Zalygin, chief editor of the journal *Novyi Mir* (New World), defied Russian bans and published Solzhenitzyn's *Gulag Archipelago*. Solzhenitzyn was the writer who dared challenge the Russian leadership.

In his book, Solzhenitzyn made ruthless disclosures and directed scathing criticism at the hypocrisy of their whole Communist system, including their treatment of the *zeks*, the political prisoners incarcerated in forced labour camps, prisons and psychiatric institutions. He also compared the Soviet treatment of their citizens with the genocidal policies of the Nazis. A supreme example of man's cruelty to man. The result was a collapse of the Communists' huge, inhuman and self-created prison system, in which they tormented innocent Soviet citizens despite their claims of wanting to liberate and serve the Russian people. In the end, the Bureau for Central Censure was closed.

Towards the end of the 1980s, Gorbachev realised that as long as the USSR controlled and dominated development in Eastern Europe, they could not win the confidence of the rest of the world. He therefore loosened the firm grip on a number of vassal states by permitting them self-rule. These included Poland, Czechoslovakia, Hungary, East Germany and the Baltic States. The culmination was probably on 9 November, 1989 with the tearing down of the Berlin Wall, the visible separation between East and West. The huge reduction of the Soviet Union, however, prompted the party apparatus to react.

Sakharov the Human Rights Advocate

Domestically, the totalitarian grip was loosened. The spokesman for human rights and Nobel Prize winner, Andrei Sakharov, was released from his exile in Gorki in December 1986. After almost 7 years forced internal exile he, together with his wife Elena Bonner, received permission to live in Moscow again.

In order to reveal the deceptions of Soviet history and to rehabilitate the political victims of Stalinism, well-known Soviet politicians formed a society in 1988 named 'Memorial'. Sakharov was its undisputed leader. (Since Sakharov's death in December 1989, his wife, Elena Bonner has directed the work of 'Memorial'.)

Amnesty Declared

In 1988, in celebration of the 70th anniversary of the October Revolution, an amnesty was granted to 200 prisoners, mainly held in psychiatric hospitals. They were freed early. Subsequently, about 50 prisoners were conditionally released from camps, with compulsory recruitment for labour, and 154 more had the remainder of their sentences halved.[22]

Antisemitism from the 'Pamyat' Group

An unforeseen result of the *glasnost* policy was that it also gave freedom to several questionable and self-appointed organs of the Soviet Press to propagate their programmes and opinions. Some of these were historical and patriotic associations, of which the Moscow-based *'Pamyat'*, ('Memory') and *'Otechestvo'* ('Fatherland') became the most well known. Pre-occupied with cultural and environmental matters, they represented extreme nationalism. Their chauvinistic and antisemitic stance is reminiscent in several ways of the monarchist (pro-tsarist) movement in the pre-revolutionary period of the early 1900s. They are convinced of a world Jewish conspiracy directed against Russia and her people.

Their ideas are similar to those being presented by anti-Zionist writers and the media in the 1970s and early 1980s.

These heavily antisemitic organisations are holding regular demonstrations in main cities like Moscow and Leningrad. Posters are put up in which Jews are accused of being the cause of all the evils in Soviet society. They are blamed for the failing economy, excessive drinking of vodka, and the recent Chernobyl disaster. The nationalists are demanding that the pogroms be resumed in order to get the Jews out of Russia. In Moscow alone, Pamyat's neo-fascist viewpoint is said to represent over 20,000 paid-up members. In the midst of the proclamation of freedom and liberty, it has been very alarming for the Jews to have these ugly reminders of intolerance reappearing – and it is an embarrassment to Soviet idealists.

Figure 3: An antisemitic poster showing a Russian bear smashing the Star of David was used in Vladivostok and various parts of Siberia in 1996–98. It was produced by the Russian National Unity Society, a group which has openly stated that it intends to persecute and kill Jewish people. The main caption reads: RUSSIA WAKE UP!

It then invites people to take part in the movement's meetings every Saturday (the Jewish Sabbath) at a city park, situated ironically 'near the Cross'.

Figure 3   RUSSIA WAKE UP!
Antisemitism strongly increasing in Russia

Emigration Policy – Intervention from the West

A new emigration law as introduced in 1987, aimed at reuniting Jews with very close relatives living abroad. Technically all 3 million were eligible, but in reality only a very limited group benefited. Criticised by the dissidents as a 'cosmetic operation', all the previous restrictive practices were brought into play. Access to 'state secrets', matters of 'public interest', and claims from family members who remained in the USSR, were all raised to block the issuing of visas. Reunion with 'close relatives' was interpreted very narrowly and a considerable number of refuseniks were turned away when they applied for visas. Some parents in long-term refusal (10 years or more) saw their children, the second generation of refuseniks, leave before them.

Even if the Jewish emigration rate did not seem to improve much in the first years of Gorbachev's regime, the issue was being openly discussed. With a renewed open relationship with the West, the Bush administration restored the 'most favoured nation' status to the Soviet Union in 1989. Before implementing this the USA had obtained the Soviet's promise to permit at least 30,000 Jews to emigrate per year. The US State Department and other countries such as West Germany introduced an annual quota. Only 50,000 Soviet emigrants were admitted to the US each year. Of these approximately 40,000 were Jews and 10,000 other Russians, including persecuted Armenians and Christians. This paved the way for the new emigrant wave.

Western Human Rights Activists to Moscow

In spite of the Soviet's poor human rights standards, the international Helsinki Commission for Humans Rights proposed that if the USSR would improve their emigration law, there might be a possibility of convening the next human rights conference in Moscow in 1991. In response, the Soviets introduced a new law on travel and emigration, under which there would be no need to obtain invitations from relatives living abroad. Adopted in 1990 before the conference in 1991, it was a big step forward as it gave the Russian emigrées an external passport instead of the former exit visa. It was valid for 5 years and provided the emigrants with the possibility of return. At the same time another important law was introduced prohibiting the incarceration of political prisoners in psychiatric institutions, sometimes for undetermined periods, to 'change' their minds.

In the meantime, several reports of Soviet violations had come to the notice of the US State Department, the US Embassy, and the Helsinki Commission for Human Rights. The West was very concerned that holding the human rights conference there would seem to indicate their acceptance of the Soviet's poor human rights policy. New violations continued to be reported, including a list of over 30 recent arrests in Soviet criminal cases suspected of having political overtones. Other complaints dealt with obstruction and limited service at the OVIR emigration offices, such as the Kiev office only being opened on Saturdays, the Jewish Sabbath. Moreover, the Kiev activists felt that the Kremlin was attempting to slow down emigration by keeping the Moscow and the Leningrad figures the same, but at the expense of the provinces.[23] On the other hand, the West feared that pressing the issues too hard might undermine Gorbachev's fragile position.[24]

However, before the proposed conference convened, the August coup took place. Had it succeeded, it would probably have caused many changes in human rights. As it failed, leaders from the 35 countries participating merely postponed the conference until September. Meanwhile hundreds of people continued to have their visa applications turned down, and more than 2,000 refusenik families – of whom 475 had been waiting for more than 10 years – watched and waited.

The Big Emigration Wave of the 1990s

At the end of 1989, Russian emigration had again risen to a total of 71,200, while only 12,900 of these went to Israel. However, this was followed by a dramatic total of well over 391,000 Russian Jews during the years 1990–91. Of these 185,000 and 140,000 immigrated to Israel in 1990 and 1991 respectively (i.e. over 80% went to Israel). The influx of Russians during these two years represented almost a 10% increase in the Jewish Israeli population in relation to the 1989 figure of 3.68 million. After a couple of years, the wave slowed down and from 1993 the yearly figure settled to about 60,000–70,000 Jewish immigrants to Israel. Sadly, Israel herself was not sufficiently prepared to absorb such a considerable number of immigrants.

Even though the Israeli government had often declared that they had emergency plans for a mass immigration, in reality when it happened not much had been organised. Housing was far from sufficient, nor was there enough space in the absorption centres. In a number of cases, hotels with poor cooking facilities were quickly crowded to capacity with newcomers. Some Israeli landlords soon took advantage of the situation, overcharging for rented accommodation that sometimes resulted in one family staying in each room of an apartment. Work opportunities for the adults and schooling facilities for their children were not sufficient. A new, difficult language had to be learned. It also meant a steep rise in accommodation prices generally, particularly in the cities, which did not make the immigrants popular with the rest of the population.

By the 1990s some government officials estimated that it cost Israel US$5,000–7,000 to absorb each immigrant – a vast amount for such a small country. Overseas Jewry, particularly in America, greatly helped to shoulder the burden. But as the years went by and the new immigrants had been absorbed, Israel soon realised the benefits of the influx of human resources and scientific knowledge for the country's economy. The gross national income per capita rose significantly from US$8,650 in 1988 to US$14,410 in 1994.[25]

The Attempted Revolt Against Glasnost

Towards the end of 1988 Gorbachev realised that it was not possible to introduce democracy into the Soviet system so quickly. By 1991, the state finances were in a shambles; money lost its value; and unemployment increased sharply. The Soviet economy was compared with that of the depression years in the late 1920s. As a result the population became dissatisfied with *glasnost* because they felt it did not include sufficient economic and agricultural reforms. When it was too late Gorbachev began to involve the citizens in his political reforms, but the internal battle with the Communists was resumed.

Shortly before Gorbachev was about to sign a union treaty which would officially have dissolved the whole of the USSR, a coup took place in August 1991. This was instigated by key right-wing members of his government, such as his Vice-President General Alexandr Rutskoi, who were against reforms. However, after a couple of days the revolt was suppressed. On the other side of the spectrum dissatisfaction was also brewing. Boris Yeltsin, the Party leader in Moscow, had for a while been very critical of Gorbachev's reforms, which he felt were neither introduced rapidly enough, nor were sufficiently thorough. This all resulted in Gorbachev's downfall. In December the same year, he was officially asked to resign as the eighth and last President of the Soviet Union. He has since become head of a Russian 'think tank', the Fund for Socio-Economic Research, trying to introduce new ideas on how to carry out reforms in the huge country.

✣ ✣ ✣

Seen in retrospect, analysts blame Gorbachev's faulty internal politics for the collapse of his regime. Although Gorbachev had opened society to intellectualism and free trade, for which he was much praised in the West, he failed domestically and could not take the next steps of creating a true multi-party society and establishing a market economy.

Down through the decades, it has usually been the grim destiny of Russian tsars and Communist leaders to leave their posts only at death, whether from natural causes or by foul means. From the Krushchev era, they began to be sent on pension; but never before *perestroika* could a previous leader return to political life.

The Second Reformer: Boris Yeltsin

Thorough and wide-ranging changes were brewing in the Soviet Union. Being the head of Russia's Supreme Soviet,

Boris Yeltsin was one of the leaders who understood the development towards a democratic country and was ready to respect the other republics' sovereignty. On 12 June, 1991, he was elected (with a 57.3% majority) president for a period of 5 years over the national republic of Russia RSFSR, which was to become the founding member state of the new Commmonwealth of Independent States (CIS).

After the coup in August the same year, Gorbachev resigned on 25 December, 1991. The following day the final dissolution of the Soviet Union was declared and the concept of the CIS proclaimed.

Despite Gorbachev's failure to form a new political union, the Commonwealth of Independent States was created in January 1992, on the initiative of three Slavic State leaders: the Ukrainian president Kravchuck, the Belorussian Supreme Court Chairman Shuskevitz together with the Russian President Boris Yeltsin. The Commonwealth was open to all the former republics of the USSR to join, and in a matter of a few days four Central Asian republics were added. This took place in spite of Gorbachev's protests.

By January 1993, the commonwealth had grown to 12 republics* with a total population of 282 million citizens. The administrative centre is in Minsk, Belorussia. On 12 December, 1993 the Russian Federation adopted a new constitution by referendum. The slow moving Russian scene was now set for new reforms. The new commonwealth's goal was to work for the development of a mutual policy on the economy, customs and migration, transportation and communication, ecology and the struggle against crime.

As leaders to help him modernise the Soviet society further, Boris Yeltsin chose mainly younger, energetic reformers as his ministers and advisers. But it was not long before the old guard of anti-reformists in the Kremlin who still held considerable power in the Duma (the Lower House), began to make their influence felt. The free market reforms had triggered

* Member states of the CIS are; the three founding states of Russia (RSFSR), Belorussia and the Ukraine, plus a further 9 adherents: Armenia, Azerbaijan, Georgia and Moldavia; the Central Asian republics of Kazakhstan, Kyrgyzistan, Tajikistan, Turkmenistan, and Uzbekistan.

scattered unrest from the consumers due to the soaring prices, and the quantity of goods available did not really increase. The mafia flourished, controlling businesses, enterprises and big interest groups in the country.

Soon Yeltsin had to make a hard choice. In order to remain in the driving seat and maintain calm in the country, he felt the need to compromise and sacrificed some of his most popular cabinet ministers and visionary reformers. Particularly painful was the dismissal in March 1993 of his Prime Minister Igor Gaidar who headed the economic programme. In December 1995, the Foreign Minister Andrei Kożyrev who was very popular in the West, was exchanged for the former KGB leader Yevgeny Primakov. The latter is known as the architect of the USSR's support programme for the Iraqi dictator Saddam Hussein. These were all indications of a harder attitude towards the West and it was such moves that caused Yeltsin to lose the confidence of the democratic countries.

In the fall of 1992, when unrest was spreading in the Russian republics, the more than 40 million Moslem citizens, some of them influenced by fundamentalist Iran, began to press for more independence. Yeltsin would have done well to learn from Gorbachev, the first reformer, whose downfall was linked to a misguided war in Afghanistan from 1979–87* and a heavy military suppression of the population in Vilnus and Riga in 1991.** In the same way, Yeltsin's 19 month-long war

* The protracted war in Afghanistan 1979–87 was heavily criticised by the Russian people for its severe loss of soldiers and army materials.

** During the 1990s, as a step to gaining independence from the USSR the three Baltic States re-introduced their old constitutions. However the Soviet Union did not recognise their right to do so, and a longer conflict with economic sanctions and threats of military intervention followed. Gorbachev suggested that the Baltic countries froze their declaration of independence from the USSR until another solution had been found. On 13 January, 1991 Soviet soldiers attacked and occupied the TV and radiostation in Vilnus, Lithuania, killing several civilians. A couple of weeks later the same action was repeated in Riga in Estonia. Gorbachev asserted he did not know about the actions beforehand, and afterwards blamed the Baltic people themselves. Many new Russian republics, which had gained independence, acknowledged the Baltic countries' independence and condemned the government actions.

in Chechnya, beginning December 1994, and the cruel ethnic suppression of its mountain people's fight for independence, lost him much confidence among the common Russian people, who strongly criticized the unnecessary slaughter of more than 30,000 Chechnyans. A considerable number of Russian soldiers were also killed. The West, afraid of destabilising Yeltsin's regime, was remarkably quiet.

Russia's Shortcomings in Human Rights

In spite of much talk about reforms, the refuseniks, even after the collapse of Communism, were still having to wage a lonely battle to emigrate. In 1993, at a summit in Vancouver Canada, international human rights activists asked President Clinton to have a discussion with Boris Yeltsin about the continual denial of the refuseniks' right to leave the CIS, stating that a list of 200 refuseniks was still pending. They requested that the Russian loan guarantee be made conditional upon improvement in human rights. The activists asserted that the new emigration law of 1991, with a passport for 'external travels' only, was a cover-up to hide the fact that the old repressive emigration policy was still being continued.

Shortly after the meetings, other lists were published with names of long-term refuseniks from all over Russia. The Moscow-based American Union of Councils for Human Rights of the Jews in the former Soviet Union had been able to get hold of a list of about 1,100 refuseniks kept by the Russian Ministry for Security (the former KGB) and withheld for security reasons. A considerable number of these names were previously unknown. The 1,000 Russian refuseniks represent an estimated 3,000–4,000 individuals affected.[26]

The Political Battle over Russia's Future

Following elections to the Duma in December of 1995, it turned out that the largest group, 24%, were old Communist hardliners.

To the surprise of many, Boris Yeltsin won the election for presidency in June of 1996. He was joined by another reform-minded group headed by General Aleksandr Lebed, known for his peace efforts in the Chechnyan war. They only gained a narrow majority over the Communist Gennady Zuyganov.

A major reason for the Communists' defeat was the economic change in the country. 40 million Russians had by then become at least nominal shareholders in 70% of the government-owned businesses and enterprises. They were not likely to let their newly achieved property go without bloodshed if the Communists attempted a return to state-controlled socialism in industry and agriculture.

Russian Roulette

After the election Yeltsin's poor health and heart operation led to an internal power struggle in the Kremlin. The unrest and instability in Russia is mainly due to Yeltsin's inability to carry out his new reform laws. This is partly because of the slow productivity apparatus, but also due to lack of funds. Even though the International Monetary Fund (IMF), has time and again bolstered the Russian Federation's ailing economy with huge loans and grants of Western money, the economic problem has become almost insoluble.

In spite of loud cries from the Communists about Yeltsin's inability to rule and the need for him to resign, even though his term as President will be over in 2000, he has been able, with surprising alertness, to remain in power by rapidly changing his ministers. His cabinet has consisted of leaders varying from the former conservative Vice-President, Victor Chernomyrdin, to the young reform-minded Sergei Kiriyenko, who took over for a few months in the summer of 1998. At the time of writing, the previous Foreign Minister and anti-Western Arabist, Yevgeni Primakov, is again in power. He is the only one acceptable to the Duma, which is strongly influenced by old hard-line Communists. For the time being it looks as if Russia is growing 'redder'.

But new faces in the Kremlin could not change the downward escalation of the Russian bonds and the rouble. By July 1998, for the second time in two months, the mining workers in Siberia blocked the Trans-Siberian Railway. In Moscow employees in the defence industry, with the scientists, marched in demonstration, because they had not received their salaries for months. Millions of workers were either jobless or unpaid. In Vladivostok a major part of the population was without water and electricity. Food prices were rapidly rising and Russian pensioners and small savers lost their money in the chaotic fall of the Russian rouble. The only ones who appeared to profit from the situation were the mafia and a group of 'newly rich' businessmen. These took advantage of the economic boom, but avoided paying taxes and quickly placed their profits securely in the West.

The political spectrum represents many shades of opinion. In a period of economic instability, there is a real threat of some extremist group grasping power. There are plenty of them in Russia. A considerable number of people want a strict regime and more law and order as it was in the former Soviet Union, and are looking for 'a strong man' to save the situation, such as Vladimir Zirinovsky who heads the ultra-nationalist group. As Russia has been losing influence as a superpower, his strong russophile ideas have quickly gained support. He wants to extend the borders to form a 'Greater Russia', including the countries in Western Europe it once ruled. It has also been said that his party, if in power, would subdue any rebellion very forcefully, and purge Russia by driving out 'foreign' elements, such as Jews. This aim of 'cleansing' Russia and the Slavic people of Jews and their influence can clearly be compared with Hitler's efforts to make Germany 'judenrein' 50 years ago.

By some ten years after Gorbachev took the first step of reforming the powerful Soviet Union, the country had undergone enormous changes, which in fact, despite a few uprisings, passed reasonably smoothly. In comparison, the same process in Europe took one hundred years. Therefore, some partial reversals might still be expected in coming years. But with the significant changes of the constitution, the introduction of democracy and the election of the president by the people in a free vote, Russia has made a huge move forward. However, the vast Russian Federation with its twelve republics and 282 million people from many different ethnic, religious and ideological backgrounds, might still prove difficult to rule.

✛ ✛ ✛

The Last Two Emigration Waves In Retrospect

Over the centuries, Russians had rarely been permitted to leave their country, compared with the relatively open borders in the West. Looking back over the last 30 years of emigration from the former Soviet Union, it is clear that the first wave of a quarter of a million emigrants in the 1970s would not have taken place without the proclamation of the State of Israel in 1948, and the thaw in the political climate after the icy years of Stalin. During these years, the Jewish masses were motivated to emigrate when domestic circumstances made it possible.

The closing doors of the early 1980s caused an abrupt halt to emigration. The Jews' desire to depart turned to desperation, so when the situation changed again under glasnost, the largest number of Russian Jews left for Israel in all the 50 years of Israel's history.

Sovietologists who have analysed the emigration waves during the 1970s and 1990s conclude that there does not appear to have been a unified Soviet emigration policy behind the two movements. At least, the emigration was never given an official sanction, but it occurred spontaneously, and when it suited the Kremlin, as in 1981–85, it just stopped. If the Soviet leaders had a coherent policy for Soviet Jewry, it was never put into writing.[27]

After the 1967 war the USSR cut diplomatic ties with Israel. It is amazing that, despite this almost insurmountable disadvantage, a Soviet Jewish emigration wave such as in the 1970s could occur under Brezhnev. It was only through the goodwill of the Dutch Embassy in Moscow that diplomatic representation and the issuing of visas was possible. The Soviet–Israeli diplomatic relationship was not restored until 1990.

Taking a closer look at the two waves, we can see that in both cases Western countries paved the way for emigration by encouraging the minority population to seek their human rights, thus making the Soviet government strongly aware of the international significance of the issue. With the background of a threatening economic crisis in the USSR, the decisive incentive for achieving Soviet emigration was provided by the USA, when they twice granted them 'most favoured nation' status. In exchange for assistance in the form of goods and technology 'open doors' were granted for ethnic minority groups, such as Jews, Volga Germans, Armenians and Greeks to leave. In the 1990s, Gorbachev opened Russia's gates to allow the largest emigration wave in modern times, in which almost 1 million Soviet Jews departed, of which over 750,000 arrived in Israel by the end of 1998.

The USSR has sometimes used the influence of World Jewry for her own ends. This happened when Brezhnev permitted the 1979 emigration of 250,000 Russian Jews, for the purpose of winning support from the American Jewish community for promoting the Varnick-Jackson trade agreement, – even though he may have overestimated their influence on US politics.[28]

Similarly Gorbachev, in his desire to combat Russia's economic crisis in the late 1980s, appealed to the USA for monetary help and offered in return, improved international human rights and free emigration.

	Jewish emigration from USSR	Immigration to Israel from USSR	Peak year	Total emigration from USSR	Immigration to Israel that year
1971–80	245,900	156,300	1979	51,000	17,600
1990–94	701,570	530,200	1990	213,400	185,200

(See Appendix IX – Emigration Statistics 1948–98.)

The first 5 years of the main Russian immigration wave in the 1990s brought an almost 15% increase to the Israeli Jewish population in relation to the 1989 figure. By the mid 1990s, the Russian emigration influx had settled to a yearly average of 60,000 immigrants to Israel. Unless specific economic or ethnic pressures are brought to bear upon the Jews, the Israeli Immigration and Absorption Committee does not expect the figure will change significantly. In the late 1990s most of the Soviet immigrants came from Russia and the Ukraine. However, due to the deteriorating economy in Belorussia, there has been an increasing immigration from there as well.

The instability of the economy in the CIS with its high inflation is a major factor which might prompt the Russian Jews to leave. Previously prized pensions and social security have devalued to such an extent that pensioners are barely able to stay alive on them.

In 1996, the Knesset Immigration Committee received information that about 1.3 million Jews, living in Russia, were eligible for immigration under the 'Law of Return'. The Jewish community in Russia is rapidly changing. As the younger families are leaving, the birth rate is falling, leaving an ageing population. Therefore, Israeli sociologists stress the need for the Russian Jews to emigrate within a reasonably short time.

It should be remembered that the Russian Jews have, indeed, been an amazing asset to the Jewish State. They tend to come from educated backgrounds to a nation which values intellectual, professional and technical attainment. 38.5% of these new immigrants have completed 13 years of education, compared with 19% of other Israelis.

An example of the contribution Russian Jewry can make is that during the 9 years of the 1990 immigration wave, they have provided Israel with more than 78,000 engineers, 16,000 doctors and dentists, 17,000 nurses and medical technicians, 36,000 teachers and 12,000 scientists.

Two Views on Russian Emigration

Russia has been called the last, large reservoir of immigration to Israel. The Jewish Agency expects that at least one third of its Jewish population, or 400,000, will have come to Israel by the end of this century. The rest are expected either to emigrate to America or stay in Russia, and in the coming 25 years, the Russian Jews remaining, will probably either assimilate or die.[29]

However, the former 'Prisoner of Zion', Natan Sharansky, holds a more optimistic view of the situation. After he became Israeli Minister of Industry and Trade in the Likud Government, elected in 1996, he led a trade delegation to Moscow, in which 80 diplomats and business men attempted to improve trade relations between the two countries. Sharansky has vowed to use his influence to improve the status of Soviet immigrants once they reach Israel and to persuade another million to emigrate in order to transform the character of Israel.[30] And so the battle for the emigration of Russian Jewry goes on . . .

Russia and Human Rights – the Reverse Side of Communism

From Tsarist times through the Communist era, and into our current period, the history of Russia appears to have been filled with suffering and deep tragedy.

An attempt to draw a picture of general life in Communist USSR would not be complete without taking a look at their inhumane punitive system. This, to a certain extent, still hangs as a threatening shadow over the life of citizens in general and is the dread of persecuted minority groups in particular. It needs, however, to be said, that while the German concentration camps ceased to exist long ago, the forced labour camp system in the vast country of the Russian Federation still continues to function in our time – although, of course, on a much reduced scale.

As previously mentioned, the Gulag system reached its height immediately after World War II. Although we will never know the true number of victims of Stalin's policies, a reasonable estimate would be around 12 million dead in the Gulag. Even though Soviet citizens were aware of the system during the whole Stalinist period (as in Nazi Germany), no official mention was made of the forced work being done by prisoners. After Stalin's death the Gulag system was not condemned, and to a certain extent the Communist leaders continued his policy.

After the death of Stalin in 1953, an amnesty was given to hundreds of thousands of political prisoners and *zeks*, from the labour camps. However, despite these releases, a considerable number of political prisoners remained in the Gulag and incarcerated in psychiatric institutions until the start of the period of glasnost at the end of the 1980s. The first attempt to demolish the Communist image was

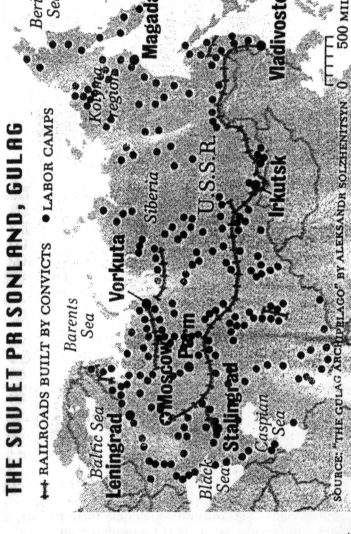

THE SOVIET PRISONLAND, GULAG

↤ RAILROADS BUILT BY CONVICTS   • LABOR CAMPS

SOURCE: "THE GULAG ARCHIPELAGO" BY ALEKSANDR SOLZHENITSYN

Map 7
Permission
applied for.

Krushchev's speech to the Congress of the Communist Party in 1961.

Just consider! As recently as 1983, under Brezhnev, the US State Department (based on CIA estimates) reported that the Soviet labour system comprised a network of some 1100 forced labour camps, not including semi-camps, prisons and paroles. The number of camps could be checked by satellites and were reckoned to contain nearly 4 million prisoners.[31]

Three years later, in 1986, in his report to the Helsinki Conference of Human Rights, Natan Sharansky stated that in his estimation there were 13 million prisoners of all types in the labour camps in the USSR. This would include exiles and so-called chemists (i.e. former prisoners who are assigned to specific work places, for example uranium mines and chemical plants, harzardous to their health). The figure also included about 15,000 prisoners of conscience and 5–6,000 people being held for religious activities.[32]

One of the worst abuses in the Soviet Union which shocked world opinion most was the forcible committal of dissidents to psychiatric institutions for indefinite periods. This practice, which had been known to the West since the mid-1960s, increased seriously during Breshnev's time as more destructive drugs and methods of psychological manipulation were used to 'remold' those who doubted the Soviet system. Besides the regular psychiatric hospitals under the aegis of the Ministry of Health, there were special psychiatric hospitals with maximum security facilities run by the Ministry of Internal Affairs (MVD).

The Human Right's report of 1986 pointed out that these 'treatments' often amount to torture. They include deliberate use of such painful drugs as neuroleptics and hallucinogens or being subjected to electric or insulin induced shocks. When administered to healthy individuals they provoke psychotic states and symptoms of Parkinson's disease with severe distortion, paranoia, catatonic stupor, severe pain and depression. Inmates are at times tied with canvas straps to the bed or to bare metal springs, or restrained with straitjackets. It is known that prisoners are sometimes incarcerated in psychiatric prisons without the family being notified.

It was against this background that Mikhail Gorbachev rose to power and attempted to change the Soviet Union by his restructuring measures. Under his *glasnost* policy the archives were opened up to the West and a wider disclosure of the Soviet's grim past began, paving the way for human rights reforms, and a radical change of the punishment system.

Before the Human Rights conference was scheduled to take place in Moscow in 1991, the West was investigating the imprisonment of at least 1,000 well-documented cases of political prisoners as well as thousands of other innocent citizens.

In order to prove that the USSR was living up to its international commitments a group from a research committee for human rights, as well as two American journalists, were invited to see one of the most infamous camps, Perm 35, situated in the Ural mountains. In honour of the visit, the camp had been painted and the punishment cells were empty. All the prisoners, although in emaciated condition, were dressed up well for the occasion. While the guests were permitted to enjoy the refreshments served by the prison committee, none of the starved inmates were allowed to come near or speak to their special visitors. The prisoners tried secretly to convey to the visitors that it was all a show and the West was aware that a number of political prisoners were still being kept in other camps of the Perm punishment complex which were not opened to Western scrutiny.[33]

Moreover, we should not forget that at a Human Rights conference held in 1992 on the issue of 'Prison Reforms in Former Totalitarian Countries', it was pointed out that Russia still has one of the highest rates of imprisonment in the world.

While there was significant improvement of human rights during the Gorbachev regime, hardly anything has changed under Yeltsin.

As Russia's policy now appears to be becoming more hardline, we need to keep in mind that the conditions for living in Russia may quickly change for the worse! These facts make an even stronger argument for the necessity of Jewish emigration from Russia as soon as possible.

Chapter 4

The Biblical Aspect of the Exodus to Israel, the Jewish Homeland

'You have to be a realist,
and believe in miracles.'

(Ben Gurion)

Having considered the issue of Soviet Jewry and their immigration to Israel from a historical and political viewpoint, it should also be remembered that the Bible, the ancient history book of the Jews, has, down through the centuries, given important pointers regarding coming events. Among many issues dealt with, the Bible gives a sketchy outline regarding the re-establishment of Israel and the re-gathering of the Jewish people in the End Times. Let us, therefore, look at the matter from a biblical perspective.

The Scattering of the Jewish People

Most of the ancient peoples such as Assyrians, Babylonians, Medes, Persians and Egyptians have vanished long ago. In some of these countries, for example Egypt and Persia, descendants of tribes from Arabia later invaded the lands and now live there while retaining the ancient name of the country. We then realise that of these ancient peoples, only the Jewish people have been preserved through the ages. The Bible says that the Jews were 'chosen' to be God's special people, not because they were bigger or better than the surrounding tribes, but because He loved them (Deuteronomy 7:6–11) and wanted to use them as a channel or an 'object lesson' to speak to other nations as well. The Jews have, therefore, been kept to this day because God has a specific future purpose for them.

Throughout the Old Testament, there is an ongoing lesson regarding God's guidelines for living. According to His Word, the reward for obedience will lead to the 'way of life', preservation and blessings, while the consequences of disobedience and sin will be punishment and curse. Those, who break God's commandments, will end up 'breaking' themselves (Deuteronomy 28).

After Moses had given God's Law to the Israelites at Mount Sinai, they were unable to keep it, as virtually no man could. (This was the reason why God had to provide an animal offering as atonement for sin in order that its blood would cleanse from guilt.) Through this, the Jews learned the hard lesson about reaping the result of their actions. If they were unrepentant and did not turn back to God, they would eventually be chastised by means of their enemies. In Deuteronomy Moses even predicts that disobedience would, in the end, result in the Jews being uprooted from the land which God was going to give them for a possession.

> *'Then the Lord will scatter you among all nations from one end of the earth to the other.'*   (Deuteronomy 28:63–64)

In God's view, the greatest sin man could commit was to break the first commandment and worship foreign gods, which the heathen around them had brought in. The best known of these were Astarte (Semite goddess of love and fertility), Asherah (Canaanite mother-goddess of fertility), Baal (Canaanite main god of fertility, storm and thunder), Molech (Ammonite god, to which live babies were offered), the host of heaven; sun, moon and stars. The Bible also warns against fortune telling and horoscopes (Deuteronomy 7:25–26). The abomination of mixing religions (syncretism) reached such a level that Asherim, wooden pillars dedicated to Asherah, were placed at altars where God was also worshipped (Deuteronomy 16:21).

Time and again, God gave many warnings. He spoke to the Northern Kingdom through the prophets, Isaiah, Amos and Hosea, while Jeremiah, Ezekiel, Micah, Joel, Zechariah and others, admonished the Southern Kingdom of Judah, with its capital Jerusalem, concerning their continued disobedience. As a consequence of their disobedience the Israelites were scattered among the nations until, far away in a foreign land, they would some day again call upon the true and living God. In the end, God's mercy and faithfulness to His promises to His ancient covenant people would prevail (Deuteronomy 4:25–31). Transcending judgement and punishment, reconciliation and restoration to the ancient homeland would take place.

After a long period of Jewish disobedience to the divine law, God's chastisement in the form of wars with Assyria began. In the end, King Shalmaneser conquered King Hoshea in 721 BC (2 Kings 17:1–5), and the ten tribes of the Northern Kingdom of Israel were taken captive to Assyria. It was a cruel Assyrian custom that after the defeat of an enemy they would, in order to prevent continued uprising, remove the majority of the conquered people from their native country and repopulate it with foreign tribes. The Samaritans were the people created from the mixed marriages between the Jews left behind at the deportation from the Northern Kingdom and the incoming foreign tribes. Being half-breeds they were always despised by the Jews of the Southern Kingdom of Judah.

For verification, 2 Kings 17:6 relates that the ten tribes were carried away to Assyria and further on to Halah (Afghanistan) and on to Habor (Pakistan), the river of Gozan (near Northern India) and *'in the cities of the Medes'* (northwest Iran). And 1 Chronicles 5:26 adds, *'They are there unto this day.'* (The Books of Chronicles were written around 440 BC in the time of Ezra and Nehemiah.) Modern anthropologists confirm that descendants of these ancient northern tribes have now begun to immigrate to Israel from these regions.

The second mighty ruler was King Nebuchadnezzar of Babylon, who conquered the remaining two tribes, Judah and Benjamin, and carried them away as exiles to an area now called Iraq. Some 150 years after Assyria's conquest of the ten northern tribes, King Josiah of Judah suffered a series of defeats by the Babylonians, between 605–585 BC (Jeremiah 25:1–9). In contrast to the Assyrians, the Babylonian attitude towards defeated countries and their people was much more humane. While the lower classes were allowed to stay in Judah, only the leadership and the upper classes were taken to Babylon. The exile only lasted for 70 years (Jeremiah 25:11–12).

On their return from Babylon, they enjoyed freedom for a comparatively short period, when they quickly began to backslide from their faith in God. Again, they were occupied by other powers; Greece and Egypt, followed by the Roman Empire. The land of Israel was then sometimes known as Israel and sometimes the Kingdom of Judah, and was, under the Romans, a province of Syria. Time and again the Jews rebelled against their foreign and oppressive rulers, to whom they had to pay taxes, but they were defeated. In 70 AD during a Jewish rebellion, Titus, the leader of the Roman army, laid siege to Jerusalem, and the city and the Second Temple were burnt. This catastrophe shook the very foundation of Judaism because the whole sacrificial system was terminated. The Temple was not rebuilt. Hundreds of thousands of Jews perished or were sold as slaves throughout the Roman Empire.

Another major Jewish uprising took place in 132–35 AD under Bar Kochba. He was falsely declared to be the Jewish Messiah who would save his people, and he had a large following which worried the Romans. In a furious attempt to crush this Jewish rebellion, another Roman army leader, Hadrian (builder of the famous Hadrian's Wall in Britain) ordered that the Jewish Jerusalem, according to Roman custom, 'be ploughed up with a yoke of oxen'. It then became a pagan city, renamed Aelia Capitolina. Jews were forbidden to live there on pain of death. As an expression of contempt for the Jews, the Romans named the land 'Palestine' after the Philistines, the ancient foe of the Jews. However, this banishment did not last long. Some Jews secretly began to live in Jerusalem, and a Jewish remnant has always been present in the land. However, it seems that after the Romans, common usage of the name Palestine was not revived until British explorers and missionaries arrived around the beginning of the nineteenth century.

It should be noted that the destruction of Jerusalem

happened about 40 years after the crucifixion and death of Jesus. Some ancient church fathers, and even orthodox churches and other denominations today, teach that the Jews were dispersed 'because they killed Jesus', but this is not wholly born out by history.

In the ancient world at the time of Jesus, there was a total of no more than 7–8 million Jews, but the majority of them, 5–5.5 million, being involved in trade, had already migrated to the thriving cities around the Mediterranean. In Alexandria alone, they numbered about 1 million, and a considerable number lived in Rome and Spain where there were plenty of opportunities for commerce. Only 2–2.5 million were left in Judah where living conditions were much poorer and taxation harder. Thus, at the birth of Jesus the majority of Jews were already living in the Diaspora.

❖ ❖ ❖

This is a bird's eye view of the history of the dispersion. From the 'scattering' we will now turn to the 're-gathering' of the Jewish people.

Restoration of the Land

After the Bar Kochba Revolt (132–135 AD) the decline continued. With the Jewish government demolished, their religious institutions destroyed, and numerous citizens carried away as slaves; the number of farmers and peasants left to till the soil also decreased. Consequently, fewer crops could be cultivated; the fields became overgrown with weeds, wasteland and desolate areas increased. For centuries, while different rulers from the neighbouring countries took turns at governing the land, the general condition deteriorated. By the seventh century, the Roman–Byzantine rule was followed by Persian and Arab conquerors. In the late twelfth century the Crusaders came, and one century later, even Mongol tribes ruled for a short period, followed by Egyptian Mameluks. By the mid-thirteenth century there followed Moslems of Turkish-Tartar origin, and for most of the last 500 years of the millennium, the Turkish Ottoman Empire controlled a mere wasteland, more or less abandoned, apart from a few stubborn Jewish communities and some nomadic Bedouins with their all-destroying goats.

In his mid-nineteenth century travel log about the Levant, *Innocents Abroad*, Mark Twain [1] described how the ancient holy places, Bethlehem, Bethany, Nazareth and Jericho in the 'Holy Land' all looked very unappealing, very desolate, barren, and with many malarial swamps. He states that there was nothing about them to remind one 'that they once knew the Saviour's presence.' Understandably, very few felt attracted to settle there.

For the Jews, however, well settled and prosperous at that time in thriving communities all over the Diaspora, a period of increasing shaking and hardship began. Many of these Jews had become very assimilated. Quite a number had adapted to the life and education of the *galut* (dispersion), they enjoyed their improved civil rights and liberty, and some even adopted the Christian faith. As a result of the apparent success and prosperity of the Jews, the non-Jewish population became increasingly envious. Even though the Jews in Russia or Poland, for example, had strong national-istic feelings and saw themselves as belonging to their particular host nation, the non-Jewish population did not share their opinion.

With that background, strong antisemitism arose at the end of the nineteenth century. Not only did it lead to severe persecution in Western Europe, but it also produced the severe pogroms in Russia and Eastern Europe discussed in the previous chapter. This gave rise to Zionism, whose purpose was to challenge and encourage the Jewish people to return to their ancient homeland. Most often the vision-ary leaders spoke from an idealistic and socialist viewpoint, only a few saw it from the religious aspect. Circumstances in their host countries caused the Jewish people to yearn for a country of their own.

In the same way as the decline during the exile to Babylon took place in stages, the restoration of Israel progressed gradually – but in the reverse order. First, the people began to return. In the previous chapter of this book is a description of the emigration movements, *aliyot*, which took place in five waves around the early part of the twentieth century. Here

returning Jews from many countries, Russia and Eastern
Europe in particular, played a major role in the restoration
and building up of the ancient homeland. Together with the
population increase and their cultivation of the ground,
the natural fertility was restored, then the economy
improved, and various administrative institutions were
established such as the parliament, *the Knesset*,* the army
(Israel Defence Force), the police, hospitals, the universities
and various schools and colleges. Although the majority of
the new-comers were not religious, many Jews living in
countries with rising persecution, felt attracted to come and
join them. They might also have realised God's hand of
blessing was upon the work. At last the country was ready for
a government and self-rule. After the proclamation of the
Jewish State in 1948, the rebuilding of the land took place
with even greater speed.

✤ ✤ ✤

The Bible speaks a number of times of the restoration
of Israel, both the natural land and the people. Many of
these references are found in the writings of the prophet
Isaiah:

> *'The desert and the parched land will be glad: the wilderness
> will rejoice and blossom.'*   (Isaiah 35:1)

> *'The burning sand will become a pool, the thirsty ground,
> bubbling springs. In the haunts where jackals once lay, grass
> and reeds and papyrus will grow.'*   (Isaiah 35:6–7)

Increased rainfall will cause water to gush forth in the
wilderness and streams in the desert. Even in the sand there
will be pools of water. Irrigation might well be in mind here.

> *'I will put in the desert the cedar and the acacia, the myrtle
> and the olive. I will set pines in the wasteland, the fir and the*

---

* It is interesting that the ancient Sanhedrin, the 120 strong religious and
legal Jewish council which was disbanded in the third century AD was,
after 1700 years, re-established in the form of the Israeli parliament, the
Knesset, again with 120 seats.

> *cypress together, so that people may see and know, ... that
> the hand of the Lord has done this, that the Holy One of
> Israel has created it.'*   (Isaiah 41:19–20)

During the latter part of the Ottoman Empire's rule in
Palestine, a large number of trees had been cut down because
the Turkish landowners taxed according to the number of
trees grown on the rented plot of land. In our time, saplings
have been replanted with the Bible as a guide to what had
previously grown in a particular area. Moreover, new trees
increased the yearly rainfall further. In some of these new
plantations cedar, acacia, pine, fir, myrtle and olives, would
be grown as prophesied. A considerable part of this work is
now being done by the Jewish National Fund.*

Another interesting verse in Isaiah relates to the rebuilding
of ancient cities.

> *'They will rebuild the ancient ruins and restore the places
> long devastated: they will renew the ruined cities that have
> been devastated for generations.'*   (Isaiah 61:4)

We have seen that ruined cities are being restored on their
former sites, and new settlements built at the ancient
places.**

As the land is restored to the Jewish people, the prediction
in Isaiah 61:5 that *'Aliens will shepherd your flocks; foreigners
will work your fields and vineyards'* is being fulfilled by, for
example, the international volunteers on the kibbutzim.

---

* Jewish National Fund, Keren Kayemet LeIsrael, was founded in 1901 to
purchase land for agricultural settlement as well as carry out development, plant forest projects and retrieve the desert in Israel. KKL began also
to employ workers at the 'national farms' on land bought by them and
sponsored by Zionist Organisations.

** Ancient cities restored include: Ashkelon in 1948; Ashdod in 1956 with
the big harbour taken into use 1965; and the new part of Tiberias 1912–14
with the rebuilding of the Jewish quarter.

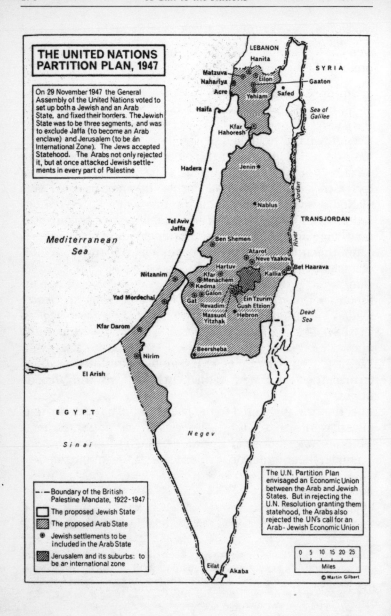

THE UNITED NATIONS PARTITION PLAN, 1947

On 29 November 1947 the General Assembly of the United Nations voted to set up both a Jewish and an Arab State, and fixed their borders. The Jewish State was to be three segments, and was to exclude Jaffa (to become an Arab enclave) and Jerusalem (to be an International Zone). The Jews accepted Statehood. The Arabs not only rejected it, but at once attacked Jewish settlements in every part of Palestine

The U.N. Partition Plan envisaged an Economic Union between the Arab and Jewish States. But in rejecting the U.N. Resolution granting them statehood, the Arabs also rejected the UN's call for an Arab–Jewish Economic Union

- - - Boundary of the British Palestine Mandate, 1922-1947
☐ The proposed Jewish State
▨ The proposed Arab State
⊙ Jewish settlements to be included in the Arab State
▦ Jerusalem and its suburbs: to be an international zone

0 5 10 15 20 25
Miles

© Martin Gilbert

Map 8

The Arab–Israeli Conflict. Sir Martin Gilbert, CBE, 1993, Routledge. Used with permission.

Key Prophecies Fulfilled

Even the remarkable 'creation' of the State of Israel had been foretold in Isaiah 66:7–8, which reads:

> *'Who has ever heard such a thing? Who has ever seen such things? Can a country be born in one day or a nation be brought forth in a moment? Yet, no sooner is Zion in labour than she gives birth to her children.'*

Exactly as the word says, the State of Israel was born in one day. The events leading up to it were as follows: On 29 November, 1947, the General Assembly of the United Nations, took a vote for the British Mandate of Palestine to be partitioned into independent Jewish and Palestinian Arab States, and for Jerusalem to become an international city (see Appendix VI). It received strong support. Thirty-three countries voted for, with 13 against (and 8 abstained). Due to disputes between the Arab States who did not want Palestine divided, the Palestinian Arabs never used the opportunity to declare their independent state, while the Jews, in contrast, proclaimed their State of Israel on 14 May, 1948. This took place almost exactly 50 years after the first Zionist Conference in Basle in 1897, where Theodor Herzl had almost prophetically, predicted that a Jewish state would be established within 50 years. (According to Leviticus 25:8–17 the 50 years indicates a year of jubilee with restoration of land and property to its original owner.)

Another amazing event was the re-establishment of Jerusalem as the Jewish people's capital. The city is one of the oldest in the world, with Jewish occupation dating some 3,000 years back to the time of King David. Even though its name, Jerusalem, means a 'city of peace', in her turbulent existence many wars have been waged over her by Gentile rulers, contesting her ownership. Over 20 times she has been besieged and conquered. Her restoration to the Jewish people and her unification is in itself an astounding miracle which took place in two stages:

1. During World War I, the British conquered the Turkish army in 1917 and the Ottoman Empire surrendered Jerusalem into their hands. For the first time in 700

years, the rule of the city passed from a Moslem nation into the hands of a Christian nation. When Israel became a sovereign state, in 1948, the rule of West Jerusalem passed into Jewish hands though the Jordanians gained East Jerusalem during the War of Independence. For the first time in almost 2,500 years, Jerusalem had come back into Jewish hands.

2. Some 19 years later, during the Six-Day War in June 1967 (50 years after the first surrender of Jerusalem by the Ottoman Empire in 1917), East Jerusalem was captured from the Jordanians by the Israeli army and Jerusalem became the united capital of the Jewish people.

> *'This is what the Sovereign Lord says: This is Jerusalem, which I have set in the center of the nations, with countries all around her.'*   (Ezekiel 5:5)

A word concerning Judah and Jerusalem:

> *'In the last days the mountain of the Lord's temple will be established as chief among the mountains; it will be raised above the hills, and all the nations will stream to it. Many people will come and say, "Come let us go up to the Mountain of the Lord to the House of the God of Jacob. The Word will go out of Zion and the Word of the Lord from Jerusalem."'*   (Isaiah 2:1–3)

Yes, even their ancient Hebrew language, which had become reduced to a liturgical and biblical language, was restored. As Jeremiah had prophesied:

> *'Thus says Jehovah the Lord of hosts, the God of Israel, Yet again shall they use this speech in the land of Judah and in the cities thereof, when I shall bring back their captivity: Jehovah bless thee, O habitation of righteousness.'*
>   (Jeremiah 31:23 ASV)

This did not happen after the return from Babylon in 536 BC when it is believed the Jews largely spoke Aramaic, which is a related language. In the days of Jesus and His disciples, there is evidence they spoke Hebrew and Aramaic as well as Greek and some Latin. Not until 2,000 years later, was the tongue of the prophets reshaped into a modern language by Eliezer Ben Yehuda, when it became the language of daily Jewish life and spoken in the streets of Jerusalem.

The Regathering of the Jews

The establishment of the State of Israel in the Middle East was a major watershed in the twentieth century, when the Jewish people were brought back and restored to their rightful place among the nations. Since then, the rebuilding of the land has taken place very rapidly.

Just as the restoration of the land and the creation of a Jewish State on its ancient site were predicted, so many other events fell in place as foretold by the prophets. While enduring exile and suffering hardship, these old seers had their eyes unswervingly fastened and their hopes staked on the end times: 'the end of days', or 'the latter days', when the Jews would return to their ancient land. About 2,500 years ago, the prophet Isaiah said:

> *'In that day the "root of Jesse" will stand as a banner for the peoples; the nations will rally to Him ... In that day the Lord will reach out His hand a second time to reclaim the remnant that is left of His people from Assyria* [northern Iraq], *from lower Egypt, from Upper Egypt* [Sudan], *from Cush* [Ethiopia], *Elam* [Iran], *Babylonia* [southern Iraq], *Hamath* [Syria], *and from the islands of the sea. He will raise a banner for the nations and gather the exiles of Israel; He will assemble the scattered people of Judah from the four quarters of the earth.'* (Isaiah 11:10–12)

(The names in brackets give the modern names of the countries.)

The quoted passage clearly indicates that *'for a second time'* the Lord will recover the remnant of His people *'from the four quarters of the earth.'* The final restoration will take place in the end times, when *'the root of Jesse'* (a synonym for King David's seed and for the coming Messiah) will be sought by both Jews and Gentiles.

The second ingathering or return will be an outstanding sign to the Jews. In Hebrew, the word is '*nes*', meaning 'miracle', but also 'a banner' for the nations to see. It will be a mighty sign, primarily to the Jews, of God's power and faithfulness to His promises towards His ancient covenant people, but also to all the Gentiles, because HE is the ruler of the whole world.

While the previous returns from their exiles in Egypt and in Babylonia were partial, at the final exodus the remnant of the Jewish people will be coming back in a mass movement from 'the four corners of the earth'.

The Pattern of a Biblical Exodus

Since the first exodus is, in many ways, said to be an example for the last return, let us take a look at what previously happened in Egypt. Naturally, information from so long ago is rather scarce, yet Egyptian historians have discovered ancient documents dating back to that event. In the deciphered papyri, the historical background of the enslavement in Egypt has been confirmed. When the taskmasters of the ancient Pharaonic labour camps increased the workloads of the Israelite slaves, smaller groups of them fled their 'prison land'.[2]

Several centuries earlier God had given the promise to Abraham, that his descendants would be enslaved in Egypt for 400 years (Genesis 15:13–14). After that He would come and lead them back to Canaan, '*a country flowing with milk and honey*' (Exodus 3:8; Deuteronomy 31:20).

The climactic event of the Exodus is central to the Bible. It is described at length in the book of Exodus, and it is estimated that the people probably reached Canaan around 1250–1200 BC. (There is much uncertainty about the date of the departure from Egypt, and dates varying from 1450 BC to 1200 BC have been seen. The latter one is thought to be nearer the date from more recent researches.)

Concerning the number of Israelites who came from Egypt to Canaan, the recognized Bible scholar, Alfred Edersheim says that at a conservative estimate, two million Israelites entered the Promised Land.[3]

It should also be kept in mind that throughout the whole journey back towards the promised land, the Israelites were attacked by their enemies. Firstly, their old rulers, the Egyptians, having given permission to allow an important part of their work-force to depart, regretted the decision and pursued them in an attempt to try to stop them or possibly kill them. As they fled on the road to the Red Sea, and by divine intervention crossed it, they came into the desert, and in this way escaped the Egyptian system of border posts, and main military and trade routes, leading across northern Sinai.

In advance, God had warned the Israelites against travelling along 'the road of the Philistines,' along the north-eastern coastal route to Egypt, where, by the twelfth century BC, the migrant Philistines from the Aegean islands, had temporarily settled (Exodus 13:17). Later, various tribal people such as the Edomites, the Amorites, the Midianites and others, attacked the Israelites as they asked to pass through their areas, or even denied them water against payment. Although they probably did not realize it, God was also testing these tribes and punished them for not helping His people.

During the whole Exodus wandering, God constantly guided the Israelites by the cloud by day and the pillar by night, leading them on. Indirectly, the opposition of the enemies also kept the Israelites to the right path so they avoided the temptation of settling too early in a wrong territory.

It is interesting to note that both the duration of the enslavement in Egypt was foretold, being 430 years (Exodus 12:40–41), as well as the exile to Babylon for 70 years (Jeremiah 25:11–12). Historical sources indicate that both the deportations of Jews to Babylon, lasting from 597–582 BC, as well as the return around 445 BC took place in stages. It was mainly the higher ranks who were taken into exile.

It was in the reign of Cyrus (559–530 BC) that the restoration of the exiles began, as he allowed them to return to Judah with the captured Temple treasures from Jerusalem. The Temple was consecrated by official permission of Darius around 520–515 BC. According to the traditional view, in

458 BC the scribe Ezra won the approval of Artaxerxes I to return with additional exiles to rebuild the walls of Jerusalem. About a decade later, he was followed by Nehemiah who became governor. According to the books of Nehemiah and Ezra, about 49,000 Jews, mainly of higher rank, came back (Nehemiah 7:66–68). Furthermore, clay tablets from the Murashu Archives at Nippur east of Babylon indicate the presence of Jews even half a century after Ezra.

It needs to be added that it is a normal pattern for emigration movements from countries to take place in larger and larger waves, until the final climax occurs. Such a wave will continue as long as there is pressure behind and there are no specific hindrances in its way. Several times in our twentieth century, movements of large population groups have occurred in Europe, because of political, racial or religious persecution. Many fled from Eastern Europe and Russia towards Western Europe and America, and later to Israel, both before World War I and during the period between the two world wars. (Examples of this have been given in previous chapters.) [4] We might, therefore, expect that the same would happen in a future emigration movement, and at the last ingathering of the Jewish people as described in Isaiah 11.

The Return of the Jews in Our Time

Though we only have scant evidence from ancient times, we do have the irrefutable fact that in the 50-some years since the establishment of the Jewish state, our generation has witnessed the return of the Jews from more than 120 countries, or biblically speaking *'the four quarters of the earth'* (Isaiah 11:12). This is a literal fulfilment of the promises spoken by Moses in the book of Deuteronomy chapter 30, that after the Jewish people had been living for centuries among the countries to which they had been dispersed, one day in the future they would again be ready to turn their hearts to the Lord and come back.

> *'... and when you and your children return to the Lord, your God, and obey Him with all your heart and with all your soul. ... He will restore your fortunes, then the Lord, your God, will*

*restore your fortunes and have compassion on you, and gather
you again from all the nations, where He scattered you. Even if
you have been banished to the most distant land under the
heavens, from there the Lord will gather you and bring you
back. He will bring you to the land, that belonged to your
fathers, and you will take possession of it. He will make you
more prosperous and numerous than your fathers.'*

(Deuteronomy 30:2–5)

Let us now look at 'the four quarters', from which the
Jewish people can be expected to return. They are further
specified in Isaiah 43:5–7:

> *'Do not be afraid, for I am with you; I will bring your
>   children from the east, and gather you from the west.
> I will say to the north, "Give them up!" and to the south,
>   "Do not hold them back!"
> Bring my sons from afar, and my daughters from the ends
>   of the earth. Every one, who is called by my name, whom
>   I have created for my glory . . . '*

If we read our newspapers with open minds, we will often
find articles dealing with part of the amazing fulfilment of
some of the quotations from the Bible. Just to give a few
examples:

From the East . . .

For background information: shortly after the State of Israel
had been proclaimed in 1948, the ancient strife between the
descendants of Abraham's two sons Isaac and Ishmael, which
had openly continued during the 1930s under the British
Mandate, resumed even more fiercely. The UN had encouraged the formation of two states, a Jewish and a Palestinian
one, but because of pressure from the Arab lands who did not
want a Jewish state at all, the Palestinians did not take the
opportunity to establish their country. Immediately after the
State of Israel was proclaimed, five neighbouring countries,
Egypt, Jordan, Lebanon, Syria, and Iraq escalated the conflict
by attacking the newborn infant state.

The Arab nations advised the Palestinians living in the new

Jewish state to flee, so they would not be destroyed as the Arab armies advanced during the War of Independence (see Appendix VII – Six Wars against Israel). They promised them that it would not take long to destroy the Jews, and they could then return to their homes in peace. 600,000 of the Palestinian Arabs fled, but since Israel was not defeated, they feared to return at the end of the war. The Palestinians got nothing, but were kept for years in refugee camps in various Arab countries under squalid conditions, and were used as pawns by their leaders to keep political pressure upon Israel, even though the Arab nations with all their oil wealth, could easily have absorbed them into the host countries. The Arab States divided the spoils between them, Egypt took Gaza, while Jordan seized Judea and Samaria. The Jordanian annexation of the West Bank in 1950 almost caused their expulsion from the Arab League. Shortly after the war, about 560,000 Jews, who had previously lived in Arab lands, began to come to Israel, and the stream continued in the following 25 years. All the Jews from Arab lands were welcomed and quickly absorbed in their ancient homeland. A marked contrast to the treatment received by the almost equal number of Palestinian Arabs who fled to Arab lands.

Some remarkable examples of immigration occurred. One of the countries situated east of Israel is Yemen. Most of the Jewish community there was brought to Israel between June 1949 and June 1950. In all, 47,000 Yemeni Jews arrived, and they were literally carried on the wings of silver birds. These people had never before seen an aeroplane, so when it landed, the Jews knelt in front of it and tried to feed the plane. How else could the ancient prophet have described the event but as in Isaiah 60:8:

> 'Who are these that fly along like clouds, and like doves to their nests.'

The Jews came to Israel in RAF planes, and the operation was given the appropriate name of 'Operation Magic Carpet'. Today, only 1,700 of the ancient Jewish community are left in Yemen, and attempts are still being made to get them out.

In almost the same period, the 2 years from 1950, another remarkable return took place, in which 104,000 Jews were smuggled out of Iraq to Iran, and thence via Cyprus, brought to Israel. This time the American-owned Near East Transport Company assisted in the airlift 'Operation Babylon'. The number of returning Jews was about twice as many as those who had previously returned from Babylon to Judah in the time of Cyrus in the sixth century BC.

From the West...

Europe and North America

Both before and after the proclamation of the State of Israel, considerable numbers of European and American Jews were instrumental in laying the foundations for the establishment of the state. Today, out of a world Jewish population of over 13.5 million, the United States has the largest number with 5.6 million. In addition, there are over one million in Western Europe. Up to now Jews living in the West have been very active and supportive in building up the state, though proportionally few have gone to live there yet.

A report on Jewish population statistics, counted at the Jewish New Year in 1998, shows that Jews are now living in more than 100 countries. Israel rates second in population size with 4.8 million.

Some of the countries with a large Jewish population are:

USA	5,600,000	Canada	360,000
Russia RSFSR, Ukraine, and White Russia	1,080,000	Great Britain	280,000
		Argentina	220,000
France	600,000	Germany	70,000

(*Jerusalem Post* 26 September, 1998; see also Appendix VIII.)

According to the Word of God, one might therefore expect, that some day in the not too distant future, they too will be shaken free of their materialistic attachment to life in the Diaspora and head for Zion. Political crises, economic depression and rising antisemitism might quickly become factors that could pressure them to emigrate to Israel.

A couple of examples of exoduses from the west come from North Africa, now more or less emptied of its Jews.

Morocco

The first Jews settled in North Africa at the time of the destruction of the First Temple in 586 BC or even before, living as a flourishing community for many centuries.

During this century, the Jews were caught between the European French rule and the Moslems, not fully accepted by either. Even though the French helped the Jews, they could not opt for French nationality. In 1948, when the State of Israel was proclaimed, the Jewish community in Morocco was the largest in North Africa, numbering 265,000, and mainly comprised of money changers, artisans and traders. The Sultan, being only a nominal ruler, appealed to the Moslems not to exert violence, but serious riots broke out in the northern part of the country. Dozens of Jews were murdered and injured; in a couple of cities the Jewish quarters were destroyed. Shortly after, mass emigration began, and between 1955–57 70,000 arrived in Israel. Even though Morocco was granted independence in 1956, emigration to Israel was forbidden, but somehow up to 1960, over 30,000 Jews managed to leave for France and America. In 1963, when the ban on emigration was lifted again, another 100,000 came to Israel.

Agitation by Moslem extremists has continued till today and caused daily life to become very difficult and insecure. Jewish schools are mainly under Moslem administration. There is no Jewish press. Today, the original flourishing Jewish community has dwindled to some 6,000, a figure that represents only 2% of the original Jewish population. They live mainly in Casablanca.

Algeria

Another ancient Jewish community from the fifth century BC is the Algerian one. During the 1930s they were subject to some severe antisemitic campaigns. In 1940, the Vichy regime withdrew French citizenship from the Jews, and their children were excluded from state schools. The Jews fought back through the Algerian Resistance movement, but when the struggle for independence began after the war, the Jews were caught between the French and the nationalists. Their efforts to remain neutral failed. In 1960, during anti-French riots, the Great Synagogue in Algiers was desecrated and destroyed; Jewish Agency officials were kidnapped and assassinated. In December 1962, the nationalist movement attacked Algeria's larger cities, where the bulk of Jews lived. Within a few months, most of the entire Jewish community's 150,000 members had fled. Over 125,000 of them poured into France, where they opted for the rehabilitation project offered by the French government to refugees from Algeria. Eventually, 14,000 of the Algerian Jews left for Israel.

In 1965, a new hard-line government caused severe anti-Jewish discrimination. Algerian Jews could no longer maintain any independent form of communal organisation. All but one of Algeria's 12 synagogues were taken over and converted into mosques. Today the number of Jews living there is minimal.

From the South...

Another unusual return of Jewish people took place from the South. On a world map with Israel placed in the centre, *'at the navel of the earth'*, Ethiopia is directly south of it. About these Jews, God promises through the Prophet Isaiah 43:6 to say to the South *'Do not hold them back!'* Also Isaiah 11:11 speaks specifically about God bringing 'the remnant' back from Cush (Ethiopia).

During 1984–85, both *Operation Moses* and *Operation Queen of Sheba* took place, in which 15,000 dark-skinned Jews were rescued from the Soviet-backed Marxist regime of Mengistu Haile Mariam and brought to Israel. Israeli press leaks disclosed that Israel had given arms to the Ethiopian regime in order to bring about the release. Those were years of terrible drought in Ethiopia, and many perished on the road to freedom. In the hope of being able to leave the country, thousands of Jews also made their way to the border and crossed into Sudan. Here they were picked up by Trans-European Airways and, via European airports, brought to Israel.

Unfortunately an early press release caused such uproar in Arab lands that the operation had to stop and many thousands were left behind. Much later, it was discovered that over 5,000 more Ethiopian Jews, having left the land on their own initiative, trekked into the Sudan in the hope of reaching Israel, but perished from starvation on the way.

This extraordinary Israeli attempt to rescue Ethiopian Jewry stirred the hopes and the hearts of the Soviet Jews, in a time of hardship and oppression, that one day they too would be able to leave for 'their ancient homeland'. When the next wave of Ethiopian Jews began heading for Israel in May 1991, under *Operation Solomon*, the flood of Russian emigration was already well under way. Ethiopia was on the verge of another Communist coup, and President Mengistu had to flee his country. The Israeli government decided they could brook no further delay. Rebel forces were closing in on Addis Ababa, and because Mengistu had used the Jews as a bargaining chip, they were a potential target for revenge attacks. Taking the tiny window of opportunity, over one single weekend 14,400 Ethiopian Jews were flown on El-Al planes to Israel. The remarkable rescue was assisted by several hundred plain-clothes Israeli soldiers, Ethiopian emigrants now repatriated in Israel, medical personnel, and volunteers distributing food and clothing. The refugees could bring nothing with them because of space on the planes. The seats had been taken out to make more room. Twenty-four planes were in the air at once ferrying their precious cargo. Within 48 hours the airport was attacked and closed by the advancing rebels. God had caused the South to 'give up' just in time.

During those years, a total of over 47,000 Ethiopian Jews were saved – an amazing rescue of the ancient tribe of Dan.

Moreover, after Operation Solomon 5,000 *Falasha Muras* (Jews converted to the Christian faith) have for family reasons been permitted to join their Jewish relatives in Israel. Since Jewish Agency responsibility is usually limited to assisting Jews to immigrate to Israel under the 'Law of Return', the organisation is principally opposed to using funds for Christian Ethiopians coming under the 'Law of Entry', as they do not regard them as a part of their religious society. Towards the end of the 1998 approximately 3,100 more Falasha Jews, who had been staying in a compound in Addis Ababa, were permitted to immigrate to Israel with the approval of the Rabbinate.

To the North...

Another example of an exact fulfilment of Isaiah 11:11 is the recent exodus movement from the area to the north of Israel, namely Syria (referred to as Hamath). For a couple of decades, leaders in Israel have been aware of the importance of rescuing as many as possible of the 5,500 Jews living in Syria before a war broke out again with that hostile country. The Israeli government feared that the Jews living in Damascus and Aleppo, could easily become hostages. (Please note Isaiah 17:1 which speaks of a future destruction of Damascus, which one day will *'cease to be a city, and will become a heap of ruins.'* This would indicate that this might occur due to a major attack in a war at some time.)

Since the beginning of the 1990s, a steady stream of Syrian Jews has been able to leave quietly, either for North Africa or the United States, where they have family. They were, however, forbidden by the Syrians to go to Israel. In the years during the preliminary negotiations between the USA and Syria concerning the Middle East Peace negotiations, the American Foreign Office was able to get the Syrian government's permission for the departure of the remaining Jews. Of these, about 1,500 have since succeeded in returning via the US to Israel and been reunited with their families there. Since 1993, only about 100 elderly Jews are, by their own choice, still left in Damascus.

Today the number of Jews living in Israel is rapidly growing and has become the second largest in the world, with 5 million, only exceeded by the North-American Jewish community of close to 6 million. It is as if we can hear the echo of the voice of the ancient prophet Ezekiel as he proclaims:

> *'This is what the Sovereign Lord says, "And I will take the Israelites out of the nations, where they have gone. I will gather them from all around and bring them back into their own land; I will make them one nation in the land, on the mountains of Israel..."'*　　　　　(Ezekiel 37:21–22a)

The Major Exodus to Come

However, the greater return of the Jewish people *'from the land of the north'* is still to become reality but has been foretold by the ancient prophets, Isaiah, Jeremiah, Ezekiel and Zechariah. Looking at a map today, Russia is the main country situated north of Israel. Jerusalem and Moscow are almost on the same longitude. Furthermore, Russia is thought to have the world's second largest community of Jews in the Diaspora, probably around 2–3 million, and is only exceeded by the USA. So the Russian Federation now apparently has fewer Jews than Israel.

According to Jeremiah, both in chapters 16:14–15, and 23:7–8 there shall come an exodus from *'the land of the north'* and *'out of all the countries, where he had banished them'*, which will be larger than the first one out of Egypt. The first passage reads:

> *'"However, the days are coming", declares the Lord, "when men will no longer say, 'As surely as the Lord lives, who brought the Israelites up out of Egypt', but they will say, 'As surely as the Lord lives, who brought the Israelites up out from the land of the north, and out of all the countries, where He had banished them'. For I will restore them to the land which I gave to their forefathers."'*

Then Jeremiah 16:16 adds:

> *'"But now I will send for many fishermen," declares the Lord, "and they will catch them. After that I will send for many hunters, and they will hunt them down on every mountain and hill, and from the crevices of the rocks."'*

For many centuries, the special event of the exodus from Egypt has been remembered faithfully by Jews world-wide during their Passover (Pesach) celebrations, just as Moses instructed the family heads to pass on the narrative to their children.

As the Scriptures have pointed towards a return to their ancient land, so it has been the Jewish prayer and hope that some day, after long years of sorrow and suffering in the Diaspora (v. 16), it would be in God's plan and purpose to lead them back. After having come out from all the countries, the prophet Jeremiah says, the Jews will no longer remember their first deliverance from Egypt – but only the second and last exodus.

According to the Word of God, the last exodus will be accompanied by many miracles, overshadowing many things which God has already done for them (as indicated by the Hebrew word *'nes'*, 'miracle' in Isaiah 11:12). Compare also Psalm 105:27–37, where a number of examples of God's miracles for His people are recalled. Firstly, the plagues He sent on the Egyptians in order to lead His people out, and secondly His provision for them through the wilderness wanderings:

> *'They* [Moses and Aaron] *performed His miraculous signs among them, His wonders in the land of Ham . . . He brought out Israel.'*

Moreover, in Isaiah 11:16, the prophet foretells that, just as safely as Moses led the Israelites across the Red Sea, God will one day open the way for the Jews to return home from the Diaspora.

The Timing of the Exodus

If we wonder when such a major exodus will happen, the prophet Jeremiah gives a good indication in chapter 23:5–6, just prior to the portion, quoted from verses 7–8. The passage is rather remarkable in that it deals with final events which will take place in connection with the Millennium or Davidic reign of peace on earth. It reads as if the prophet sees the final events of the return as occurring close to, or even in connection with, the establishment of the reign of peace on earth by the righteous Branch of King David's line – an ancient expression for the reign of the Jewish Messiah. It reads:

> ' *"The days are coming," declares the Lord, "when I shall raise up to David a righteous Branch, a King, who will act wisely and do what is just and right in the land.*

> *In His days Judah will be saved, and Israel will dwell in*
>   *safety.*
> *This is the name, by which He will be called: The Lord our*
>   *righteousness.*
>
> *So then, the days are coming," declares the Lord, "when the*
> *people will no longer say 'As surely as the Lord lives, who*
> *brought the Israelites up out of Egypt...'"'*
>
> (Jeremiah 23:5–7)

The order of these mighty events is still to be seen.

Previous Emigration Waves from 'the North Country'

If we then take a quick glance at the emigration movement
during the 50 years of Israel's statehood, we can see – as
previously mentioned – that after 1948, the emigration
waves have continued at an increased rate. Thus, during the
1970s a wave of 250,000 Russian Jews left the USSR of which
a total of 158,000 came to Israel. About one decade later, in
the 1990s the door of their 'prison land' was again thrust
open. This time over 700,000 Russian Jews were brought to
Israel, the greatest number (over 185,000) came in 1990. By
1995, the wave settled to a yearly average of 60,000.
However, with increased instability in Russia's economy
and rising antisemitism, another emigration wave can be
expected to occur any time.

How Many Jews Will Come?

There is much uncertainty as to the number of Jews living
within the Russian Federation. According to the official
Soviet census, taken in 1989, 1,450,000 Jews were living
there then. (In comparison, 10 years previously in 1979, the
corresponding census registered 1,807,000 Jews, while
the American Jewish Yearbook gave the figure as 2,678,000
for the same year.)

By the beginning of 1995, the American Jewish Yearbook
(1996 edition) indicated the number to be 729,000. However,
almost at the same time, in 1994, the Jewish Agency showed
a Jewish population of 1,434,800. Even though the official

statistics differ, the flow of Russian Jews to Israel does not seem to decrease – it just continues on!

More recent information from the Demographic Centre of the Russian Parliament in Moscow has, however, helped to throw light on the matter, admitting that the previously quoted figures appear to have been too low. Thus, in 1993, the Centre stated that an estimated 5 million Jews were living in the Russian Federation. This might be an indication that a much larger number of 'hidden' Jews are in Russia than previously realised. It appears that many have either been assimilated or had not wished to identify themselves as Jews in a country with a long history of antisemitism. If persecution should break out again, the Jews can easily be identified through their internal passports, which would mark them for discrimination. On the other hand, the opportunity to emigrate has encouraged them to admit their Jewishness during the last decade, and brought them out into the open.

A second reason why it is difficult to compare the population figures from the former Soviet Union is that after the formation of the CIS, there has, lately been a tendency only to mention the number of Jews in the largest republics, rather than the total figure. This gives a less clear picture of the situation and diminishes the true numbers.

Thirdly, another factor that needs to be taken into consideration is that, according to the Israeli Law of Return non-Jewish spouses are permitted to immigrate to Israel with the many returning Jews. Since the early 1990s about 15% of the Russian emigrants arriving in Israel have been non-Jewish. While the ultra-orthodox parties such as SHAS have been very upset over the issue, the more liberal parties defend their arrival. This has, however, increased the number of entries significantly. It is somewhat similar to what might have happened during the first Exodus from Egypt, when it says, *'many other people went up with them'* (Exodus 12:38). These left Egypt together with the Israelites and might possibly refer to such Egyptians as those mentioned in Exodus 9:20.

At a Jewish conference in Jerusalem held in January 1995 on the occasion of the twentieth Anniversary of the Jackson-Varnick Agreement, it was stated that over one million of the Jews in Russia were already in possession of visas to migrate to Israel. Even if several hundred thousands may have left since then, the major portion is still to come, and new prospective emigrants have quickly filled the places of those who have left. Most Russians are still lingering on, waiting for the right moment, but the pressure from behind is mounting.

God Calls for the Involvement of the Nations

As has already been touched upon, the Bible indicates clearly that the nations will play an important role in the final restoration of Israel.

Let us first look at the basis for the relationship between the gentile peoples of this earth, the 'nations', and the Jews. Briefly: God did not select the Jews just to be His special people, but rather to become an object lesson and a tool in His hand to speak to the nations in order that His name would be glorified over the whole earth (Ezekiel 36:36–38).

The first time the Old Testament mentions the various nations is in Genesis 10. The descendants of Noah, Shem, Ham and Japheth, eventually spread over the earth. While Jews and many Arabs come from the line of Shem (Semites), Japheth mainly refers to the European race, and Ham to Africans and Asiatic peoples. Descending from Japheth and Ham we can count 70 nations in all. According to the divine plan, God has assigned to each people, a certain place to live '*according to the sons of Israel* . . . (In Deuteronomy 32:9 some translations render the Hebrew incorrectly as 'sons of God'.) Furthermore, Acts 17:26–28 explains that God's purpose for determining allotted periods and boundaries for every nation on the earth was done in order that '*they would seek him*'.

'My People' versus 'the Nations'

In the Old Testament, the Hebrew word used for the people of Israel is '*aam*' (singular) or '*aamim*' (plural), meaning respectively 'people' or 'peoples'. The word '*goy*' (singular) or '*goiim*' (plural) for 'heathens', 'tribes' or 'nations', indicated peoples from a different cultural background, mainly worshipping other gods. This often referred to a people hostile to the Jews or Yahweh. For example Isaiah 60:12:

> 'For the nation [goi] *and kingdom, that will not serve thee*
> [restored Zion] *shall perish; yea those nations* [goiim] *shall*
> *be utterly destroyed.'* (KJV)

Yet, in some cases Israel and some friendly nations, who
may even be supportive in a war, are referred to as 'my
peoples' – *'aamim'* (plural). For example, Isaiah 51:5:

> 'My *righteousness is near. My salvation went out, and My*
> *arm shall judge the peoples* [aamim]. *The coast lands shall*
> *wait on Me, and shall hope on My arm.'*
> (J.P.Green's *Interlinear Hebrew–Aramaic O.T.*)

In modern parlance, the word *'goiim'*, 'heathens', used for
the 'nations' might seem negative. In daily Hebrew speech,
however, it is more often used of 'non-Jewish countries'.
Other words for 'people' in the Old Testament would be
'foreigners', 'aliens' or 'strangers' (sometimes 'enemies').
However, a person of non-Jewish origin, dwelling peacefully
among the Jews, would be referred to as a 'settler' or
'sojourner'.

The Abrahamic Blessing

It is important to recall that God's fundamental promise of
blessing to Abraham in Genesis 12:1–4 related to the nations,
and even before he was circumcised, symbolises the special
covenant relationship with God. It reads:

> 'I will *make you into a great nation, and I will bless you;*
> *I will make your name great, and you will be a blessing. I*
> *will bless those who bless you, and whoever curses you I will*
> *curse; and all peoples on the earth will be blessed through*
> *you.'* (Genesis 12:1–3)

Note also that the line of Abraham will be a blessing to
men. It will come through his seed. This promise came to its
complete fulfilment in Christ. The 'blessings' to all men seem
to be conditional, and there is a serious warning or divine
curse and punishment if the nations do not have a positive
relationship to the Jews.

If one reads the Bible through, paying careful attention to the many times the Old Testament mentions the word 'nation' in connection with the restoration of Israel, one gets a surprising new understanding of God's plans for Israel and the other nations; plans to bring blessings to both Gentiles and Jews. The prophet Isaiah particularly speaks of this. It has previously been mentioned that the nations, identified as foreigners and aliens, would, during the last return, help with the restoration of Israel. This would take place in connection with the rebuilding of the land and its ancient cities (Isaiah 60:10a), as well as foreigners working in the fields and caring for the domestic animals (Isaiah 61:5), which is happening on modern kibbutzim.

The Bible also says that the nations will assist in bringing back the Jews from the dispersion to Israel. These somewhat similar passages point this out:

> *'The Lord will have compassion on Jacob; once again He*
> *   will choose Israel and will settle them in their own land.*
> *Aliens will join them and unite with the house of Jacob.*
> *Nations will take them and bring them to their own place.*
> *And the house of Israel will possess the nations . . . '*
>
> (Isaiah 14:1–2)

> *'This is what the Sovereign Lord says,*
> *"See, I will beckon to the Gentiles, I lift up my banner to*
> *   the peoples; they will bring your sons in their arms and*
> *   carry your daughters on their shoulders.*
> *Kings will be your foster fathers, and their queens your*
> *   nursing mothers."'*   (Isaiah 49:22–23a)

> *'"Nations will come to your light, and kings to the*
> *   brightness of your dawn.*
> *Lift up your eyes and look about you: all assemble and*
> *   come to you; your sons come from afar, and your*
> *   daughters are carried on the arm."'*   (Isaiah 60:3–4)

At the return, some of the Jews will be carried on aeroplanes to Israel (Isaiah 60:8), while others will be brought from afar to Israel, in the ships of Tarshish, the ships of the trading nations (Isaiah 60:9).

In Jeremiah 31, we have a description of the Jewish people returning to their ancient homeland. While some will come by modern transportation, others will come walking across the borders from other countries – just as has happened previously in other mass migrations. The portion reads:

> *'This is what the Lord says:*
> *"Sing with joy for Jacob; and shout for the foremost of the nations.*
> *Make your praises heard, and say, 'O Lord, save your people, the remnant of Israel.'*
> *See, I will bring them from the land of the north and I will gather them from the ends of the earth.*
> *Among them will be the blind and the lame, expectant mothers and women in labour; a great throng will return.*
> *They will come with weeping; they will pray as I bring them back.*
> *I will lead them beside streams of water on a level path, where they will not stumble, because I am Israel's father, and Ephraim is my first-born son.*
> *Hear the word of the Lord, O nations: proclaim it in distant coastlands:*
> *'He who scattered Israel will gather them and will watch over his flock like a shepherd.*
> *For the Lord will ransom Jacob and redeem them from the hand of those stronger than they.*
> *They will come and shout for joy on the height of Zion, they will rejoice in the bounty of the Lord ... ' " '*
> (Jeremiah 31:7–12)

One of the basic foundations for the restoration of Israel is prayer as is indicated in Isaiah:

> *'I [God] have posted watchmen on your walls, O Jerusalem; they will never be silent day or night.*
> *You who call on the Lord, give yourself no rest and give Him no rest till He establishes Jerusalem and makes her the praise of the earth.'* (Isaiah 62:6–7)

Interestingly, in Jeremiah 31:6, we find that *'There will be a day, when watchmen cry out on the hills of Ephraim ... '*, the word 'watchmen' used here in Hebrew is *'notsrim'*. In Modern Hebrew, this is also the term for 'Christian believers'. Thus, Christians from many nations have felt the importance and responsibility of praying both in Israel and other countries for the re-gathering of the Jews, as well as the welfare of Israel.

Christian Response to the Exodus

In the early 1980s, a number of Christians with a biblical understanding of Israel began, mainly on their own initiative, to travel to various countries in which Jews might be in danger, particularly for political reasons. They shared Old Testament prophecies dealing with the return, reminded them that God was calling them back and warned them to leave the country and emigrate to Israel, while there was still time. The example was used of Germany in the 1930s, where the Jews continued to hope that some day things would improve – but circumstances only got worse. Suddenly, one day they found themselves trapped under Hitler's regime and could not get away: World War II was upon them – and the tragedy of the Holocaust.

In the 1980s, when human rights continued to deteriorate in the USSR, it seemed that the Jews were caught there, being denied the possibility of emigrating to Israel and suffering hardship and imprisonment on trumped-up charges. However, not only fellow Jews in the free world, but also Christians from many countries took the initiative to encourage them and help as they could. Their motivation has not merely been human concern and sympathy, but because the Bible indicates that the Russian Jews would play a key role in the Jewish return in the end times. Together, both Jews and non-Jews pursued the human rights issue in the former Soviet Union. In many Western countries, demonstrations were held on their behalf, and the plight of the Jews was presented to government leaders. As a result of these actions many wrongly accused prisoners were released early from Soviet prisons and forced labour camps.

Following this, Christian support groups and organisations formed in the Western world in order to assist the Jews to emigrate from Russia to Israel, by plane, ships, buses etc. Most of these groups work in connection with the Jewish Agency, the Jewish Government organisation that has spearheaded immigration to Israel from before the founding of the State. Another goal for the Christian organisations has been to explain events in the Middle East from a less biased standpoint than is usually used by the western media, who often show a greater sympathy with pro-Arab views. At the same time these organisations have supported hospitals in Israel, helped work for handicapped children, the sick and elderly, Holocaust survivors, soldiers, immigration of Jews to Israel, absorption of the large immigrant waves, Russian as well as Ethiopian. To a certain extent they see themselves as preparing for a time when the influx of Jews will be much larger, and they want to help Israel with the ingathering.

Moreover, for us as concerned onlookers, it has been very encouraging to hear a number of new immigrants tell how happy they are to live in Israel with a new future ahead of them, and particularly the added opportunities they have for their children's education. Not infrequently, one can also hear an immigrant say, 'In Russia, I was a Communist, but in Israel I have come to believe in God.'

Opposition to a Jewish Return (Islam)

We should not, of course, expect that such a return of the Jewish people and restoration of their ancient land of Israel, would take place without opposition from enemies in the Middle East who do not understand the Bible nor God's purpose for the Jews or Israel.

The opposition comes mainly from the neighbouring Arab countries, which consider Israel to be part of their territory, but also from the Palestinian population living in Israel today.[5] Had the Jews chosen to maintain the British name Palestine, Palestinian Arabs would never have had their propaganda tool for establishing their state.

Westerners, not knowing past history, frequently fall prey to the twisting of facts concerning a 'Palestinian people'. For propaganda purposes, Palestinian Arabs began to promote the idea that they are supposedly descendants of a previous people, the Philistines, or even the Canaanites. Historical sources show, however, that the Philistines came as waves of migrants from the Greek Islands. In the thirteenth century BC they invaded Egypt, but were driven back. By the twelfth century BC they settled for a period on the Southwest coast of Canaan (Exodus 13:17). Although King David drove the Philistines out of the hill country, they caused trouble to the monarchy for a number of years. Some sources credit their final defeat to the Babylonian army, who fought a battle in the Philistine plain and destroyed Ashkelon in 604 BC.[6] They certainly disappeared from history about that time. However, confusion was caused some seven hundred years later, around 132 AD, when the Romans, out of spite to the Jews, renamed Israel 'Palestine' after the Jews' ancient Philistine enemies.

The fact is that most of the present Palestinian Arabs came as migrants and seasonal workers from Syria (Haran), Lebanon, Jordan, Egypt, and other Arab countries during this century, and particularly in the 1930s of the British Mandate. They crossed the border in the hope of finding paid employment in the newly established Jewish industries and agricultural projects.[7]

Today, Jordan is still ruling over more than 75% of the original eastern part of the 'Jewish homeland' proposed in the Balfour Declaration. But only a relatively small number of its 4.3 million citizens are Palestinian Arabs. In contrast: in the western part of the Jewish homeland, covering less than 25% of the original mandated territory, not only are there 5 million Jews, but in addition, 1,272,900 Palestinians in the West Bank and East Jerusalem. Added to this, 893,000 Palestinians live in Gaza and Jericho. For this reason the Israeli government separated Gaza and Jericho with their large Arab populations and gave them a certain amount of independent self-rule in order to avoid Arab claims to the land. This means that in a small country a third of the size of Jordan, Israel is in reality making living space available for a total of over 2.2 million Palestinian Arabs as well as their own Jewish population. Proportionally, therefore, there is still space for considerably more Palestinian Arabs in Jordan.

With that background, the present Palestinian claim for the right to another state of their own in the previous British Mandate of Palestine seems unreasonable. Firstly, the State of Israel is the territory allotted to the Jews, and secondly, a number of politicians agree that the Palestinian Arabs already do have a state in Jordan. Finally, we have the Word of God. The Scriptures repeatedly tell us that Israel is the portion of land that the Almighty has allotted to the Jewish people for all generations as an eternal heritage:

> *'He remembers His covenant forever, the word He*
>   *commanded for a thousand generations,*
> *the covenant with Abraham, the oath He swore to Isaac.*
> *He confirmed to Isaac as a decree, to Israel as an*
>   *everlasting covenant:*
> *"To you I will give the land of Canaan as the portion you*
>   *will inherit." '*   (Psalm 105:8–11)

> *'This is what the Lord says,*
> *he who appoints the sun to shine by day, who decrees the*
>   *moon and the stars to shine by night . . .*
> *"Only if these decrees vanish from my sight," declares the*
>   *Lord, "will the descendants of Israel ever cease to be a*
>   *nation before me." '*   (Jeremiah 31:35–36)

As we are now seeing the Jews return to their ancient homeland, the Palestinians have, for largely political, military and economic reasons, become more and more opposed to the Jewish population growth in Israel. The *Intifada* (uprising) movement, which started in 1988, is such an example.

But there is nothing new in this. During the British Mandate, there were a number of such *'intifadas'* from the Palestinian Arabs. Similar situations arose in 1920–21, 1929, and particularly the uprising from 1936–38, with rioting and unrest, destruction of trees and crops, and hundreds of Arabs, Jews and British soldiers wounded or killed. (The last one resulted in the dispatch of two British Royal commissions and the disastrous MacDonald White Paper of 1939 was issued.) While previous rebellions were directed against the

British who were regarded as oppressors, permitting Jewish immigration, this time the rulers are the Israelis. Therefore, the present opposition can be viewed as part of the long battle for independence, and is part of the current Arab pattern of behaviour in the Middle East. As Ronald Nettler, a specialist in Middle-Eastern affairs, has said: 'Israel is in a constant war with her surrounding Arab neighbours – interspersed with short periods of peace.' Strangely, when offered an independent state by the UN in 1947 the Arabs refused it, preferring to attempt to oust the new Israeli State in the hopes of thereby securing the whole land.

Although the problem may appear political, military and economic on the surface, at the root the issue is religious. One of the most severe threats comes from Islamic fundamentalism. Territory, which has once been subject to Moslem conquest – even if it dates back to the seventh century – is still today considered *'holy'* to Islam, even if that particular area gained its freedom long ago. In the Moslem mind, this relates not only to the Near East, but also to the Balkans and North Africa, as well as Spain, which they conquered during the previous millennium. Because these territories are considered as belonging to *Dar-al-Islam* (the house of Islam), they must consequently be re-conquered – if need be through *jihad* (holy war). (For those of us, who have grown up in a Western, humanistic way of thinking such reasoning is quite alien.)

Even today, the presence of a Jewish State in an Arab sphere of interest is considered an affront to Allah. In line with this, a number of fundamentalist Arab States, such as Iran and until recent years Syria, have refused to recognise or even mention the name of Israel. In their minds it simply does not exist. According to the Koran, 'the House of Islam' should be in constant war with the non-Islamic world outside, *'Dar al-Harb'*.

This is the reason why Lebanon, the last Christian country in the Middle East, had to be subdued under a Moslem regime, in this case Syria, during the early 1980s. Moreover, the Moslems have declared the twenty-first century as the *'Century of Islam'* when the whole world must be submitted to their rule – if necessary, by 'holy war'.

In the same way, Israel is even more a thorn in the flesh of the Arab world. The surrounding Arab States have tried to destroy Israel throughout her existence since 1948. They initiated six wars, of which four could have been final. The Yom Kippur War on the Great Day of Atonement on 6 October, 1973, was the most dangerous. It has also been referred to as 'the countdown to Armageddon'. (See Appendix VII – The Six Wars Against Israel from 1948.)

Only under strong pressure from the USA has President Assad of Syria more recently consented to a dialogue with Israeli leaders. This has not got very far yet, and it is feared it was undertaken, not for the purpose of true peace in the Middle East, but rather with the hidden intention of reducing the size of Israel's territory and defences by forcing her to exchange 'land for peace' without the necessary guarantee of security.

In spite of some smooth talk, the Islamic fundamentalists are only waiting for opportunities to destroy the Jewish State. From the depths of their hearts, Moslems believe that it is Allah's will that Jews and Christians should only be permitted to live as second class citizens, subject to Moslem rule, guided by the Koran. They believe Islam is the highest and final revelation from God, superseding both Judaism and Christianity. There is no place in Islam for a resurgent Jewish State. It strikes at the very root of their faith and at the honour of Allah and cannot be allowed to exist, lest it prove their beliefs to be untrue.

One clear example can be seen in connection with the Palestinian political response to the issue of Jewish emigration from Russia to Israel. I will briefly touch upon it here.

In 1989, Israel's enemies in the Arab lands spoke out strongly against the Jewish return. In April of 1990, when that month's Jewish emigration from the Soviet Union reached a peak of almost 10,500, bringing the total figure up to about 33,000 for the first four months of the year, Arab countries issued a strong condemnation. They declared the Israeli immigration to be illegal and a conspiracy against the Palestinian existence in the territories. (This happened even though only a very small number, 2–3% of the Russian emigrants, requested to join their families in the West Bank. The rest preferred to settle in less troubled areas.)

With his flourishing rhetoric, Yassir Arafat accused the Soviets of making, 'a more dangerous conspiracy than Israel's establishment in 1948.'[8] He asserted that 300,000 Soviet Jews had flooded the West Bank and settled there. Statistics showed that this was one of Mr Arafat's many exaggerations, and in reality, out of the 33,000 arrivals in the first 4 months of 1990 only 200, or exactly 0.6%, had settled in Judea, Samaria and East Jerusalem. The fact is that Soviet Jews, fleeing antisemitism in the USSR, are very reluctant to settle in areas of potential trouble. With some 1,565,000 Palestinians living in the West Bank, Gaza and Jericho, in addition to 150,000 in East Jerusalem, even several hundred Russians could scarcely have posed a threat by their presence.

In April 1990, *The International Herald Tribune*, interpreted the Arab campaign as being directed more against preventing immigrants coming into Israel as a whole, rather than just to the West Bank.[9] The reason was that such an influx would 'add to the strength of the Israeli society,' – and a strong Israel is against their religion and much harder to destroy.

Arab leaders, therefore, asked President Gorbachev to halt emigration of Soviet Jewry to Israel, warning him against establishing direct flights from Moscow to Tel Aviv. Tens of thousands of prospective new immigrants to Israel, still in Moscow, were warned by the Palestinian activist, Faisal Husseini, against entering the very dangerous conflict in the 'occupied' territories.

Several terror organisations such as the *PLO*, *Islamic Jihad* and the *Popular Front for the Liberation of Palestine* (PFLP) have sent strong warnings to countries in Eastern Europe whose capitals have been used as transit airports. They also issued bomb threats to national airlines carrying Soviet Jewish emigrants. The Hungarian airline, Malev, has, particularly, been the object of much pressure.

Towards the end of 1990, the Arab Bureau for the Boycott of Israel stated that it would blacklist any airline or shipping company transporting Jewish immigrants to Israel or the 'occupied' territories. Threats to its safety were also made to a

Christian organisation carrying Jewish immigrants to Israel. Furthermore, the Arab League said they would boycott three Yugoslav companies for their role in building settlements in Israel. We can only expect such threats to increase seriously in the future.[10]

It is interesting to note, that before the peace agreement between the Palestinians and Israel was signed in Washington in September 1993, the Prime Minister of Israel, Yitzhak Rabin, said that if there had been two million more Russian immigrants in Israel, the government would not have been able to surrender any land to the Palestinians.[11]

However, in this connection some Christian leaders in Jerusalem viewed the Russian emigration wave as God's answer to the *intifada*, to show the Jews that Israel herself needs the land. In a way the *intifada* backfired because the immigration did not stop.

Thus, during the Gulf war in 1991, when the US and her Allies bombed Baghdad, Iraq, in retaliation, fired Scud missiles against Israel, particularly Tel Aviv. (See appendix VII – The Six Wars Against Israel from 1948.) In expression of their approval many Palestinians danced on their rooftops in Israel and Jordan. But in spite of the dramatic situation, Prime Minister Shamir of the Likud Party continued to encourage Russian immigrants to come. Regardless of many threats, the Jews continued to pour into the country because the pressure behind them was stronger than any fears of trouble in their new homeland.

What Might Lie Ahead for Russian Jews

In spite of Western aid, the general situation in Russia seems to deteriorate. In recent years there has been a feeling of depression among the Russians. Million of workers are either jobless or have not been paid by the state or the army for months. They survive because a lot of life in Russia is based on barter. With the rising inflation, pensioners are finding themselves unable to survive on the shrinking monthly income; an increasing number of people are literally starving. At the same time, the Mafia continues to increase in riches and power, harassing both the state and the business world, as well as individuals. Lawlessness abounds. There is a marked increase in social inequality.

With Yeltsin's prolonged illness and the leadership's inability to cope with the growing problems, there is a yearning in the society for political change and the greater stability in life which they had under a stronger government and Communism. With Moscow seemingly losing control in the republics, there is a tendency towards decentralisation. Ethnic tensions might develop into military conflicts at any time.

With the present situation in Russia, stronger features of antisemitism are developing. To an increasing extent, the Jews are becoming scapegoats for the Russian regime's failure. All the evils of the society, such as the failing economy, the rising lawlessness and Russia's loss of prestige in the West, are blamed on the Jews. With the Russian people's lack of knowledge of history and what has occurred there previously, it gives a grim outlook for the future. Added to this, the teaching of the Russian-Orthodox Church is very anti-semitic, which is just adding fuel to the fire. The danger to the Jews is imminent.

As previously during the 1930s in former Nazi Germany, the Jews seem to be oblivious to the situation and not heeding the warnings that they may again be overstaying their time. They continue to hope that the country's economy will improve and the old pattern of persecution and pogroms cease.

Why Don't the Jews Flee the Country?

One of the reasons for the Russian Jews' reluctance to emigrate quickly is that they are generally very assimilated into the Russian culture, with relatively little knowledge of the world outside. We should not forget that 70 years of Communist indoctrination which discourages individual thought, has made a deep impact. In their assimilation into Russian culture they have been taught a deep veneration for 'Mother Russia' and her traditions, with a deep attachment to the family graves. Often they have intermarried with Russians. The teaching of Jewish culture was not permitted, so the knowledge of their religion and background is often rather lacking. Furthermore, for a number of years only a few synagogues were kept open. Previously they were under the watchful eye of the KGB, and usually it was unsafe for Jews to attend. With the growing emigration movement in the 1970–80s, Jews were excluded from higher positions in society, and their children were denied education at institutions of higher learning. Clearly there is no future for them there, and again recently, a popular slogan called for *'Russia for the Russians'*.

However, for well over two decades, Jewish associations have taken considerable initiative to alleviate the problem by sending a number of educators from abroad to hold seminars on Jewish culture and religion. This has created a much deeper understanding. But sociologists assert that only emigration can save Russian Jewry from complete assimilation.

The usual pattern for emigration of the Russian Jews is that the younger generation leaves first for Israel. The newcomers will learn the language, find a job and apartment and settle there. Each one of these steps will take a long time of adjustment and can also be painful. Eventually they will help the rest of their family to follow. There are very strong family ties in Russian society. However, the sale of the parents' apartment and the difficulties of transferring the money to Israel, all take time. Particularly, when the Russians know that the prospective emigrants are making plans to leave, they often make things very difficult, offering little for the apartment and belongings, and charging high prices for visas and travel.

With this background, it is important to keep in mind the historical fact that during World War II, two million Jews – or one third of the total six million victims of the Holocaust – were killed in the Soviet Union. This is the main reason why the Jewish Agency as well as Christian organisations which have caught the vision for helping them, are warning the Jews against remaining in Russia. Currently, because of the rising antisemitism and instability in the CIS, emigration is again increasing.

Is a Significant Emigration of Russians on the Way?

Back in 1990 during the Gorbachev regime, leading Soviet economists warned of an economic disaster which might give rise to an emigration, at least temporarily, of 4–5 million Russian citizens to the West, as they now had the right to travel freely. Thus, Alexander Kolesnikov, a member of the Sociological Research Centre attached to the Communist Party's Central Committee, predicted that up to 16% of the country's 286 million population might be considered potential migrants and, at least temporarily seek better and more stable job opportunities in the West. Of these 86% were men and the majority under 30 years, with a better than average education, and little confidence in the country's economic prospects.[12]

By the end of the twentieth century, noting the chaotic situation developing in the CIS, several Western newspapers published articles about the strong possibility of migration of thousands of Muscovites to North America and Europe (*Berlingske Tidende*, 9 October, 1998.)

Early Warning Signals of a New Emigration Wave

Already in late 1995, when travelling in Eastern Europe, I learned that a new wave of Russian Jewry was expected to go to Israel. This was indirectly confirmed by the fact that the Jewish Agency was in the process of re-staffing their transit centres for air traffic in Eastern Europe. These were heavily used during the large emigration wave of the early 1990s, when Soviet Jews were trying to leave from several capitals in Eastern Europe. Later these centres were temporarily closed down and from 1993 were kept on stand-by for an emergency situation at a cost of US$250,000 per year. With the Israeli-Palestinian peace plan proposals to hand over a large portion of Judea and Samaria (the so-called West Bank) to the Palestinians, Israel may not be able to absorb large numbers of Jewish immigrants quickly. They may, therefore, be stuck in the European countries for a while.

Anticipation in Scandinavian Countries

A few years ago, when a probable breakdown of the Russian government was threatening, the possibility of an imminent migration was frequently discussed in the world press. In the beginning of 1996, one could read in Scandinavian news-papers about much anxiety in connection with an emigration from the Russian Federation. Situated close to Russia, Scandinavian countries, have in recent years, received refugees from the Baltic States, as well as a number of emigrants from Afghanistan, Iran, and Angola, seeking asylum across the sea. (At present, there are still 5,000 of these Third World refugees in the Baltic States, and they are trying to get across to Scandinavia.) It is no wonder that the subject of refugees is frequently discussed in this part of Europe.

In Finland, about 1,000 Jewish emigrants particularly from the St Petersburg area, are regularly arriving each year as transmigrants, on their way to Israel. Currently only a small number come by this route to Israel. But in the event of a crisis situation in Russia, Finland is reportedly expecting large crowds of Russian citizens, particularly persecuted minority groups such as Jews, to cross the Finnish border, seeking for a way of escape from their desperate situation.

In 1994, newspapers in Sweden stated that several counties south of Stockholm are prepared to give temporary asylum to Russian emigrants. Among these the Södertälje community is mentioned as setting up reception centres for about 4,000 Russian refugees to house them for about 6 months. An expense which the state will cover. The emergency plan relies to a certain extent, on voluntary helpers. But according to the Swedish chief of defence, T. Reuterwall, they realise that perhaps up to half a million refugees might arrive by boat.[13]

In Norway, in the fall of 1997, the Christian People's Party won the election and the new government is very positive to persecuted ethnic minority groups. A safety net is being stretched out in Northern Norway. The Norwegian Director-ate for Foreign Affairs (UDI) in Narvik, is arranging with its municipalities to establish transit offices for Russian refugees in case of emergency. The district plans a total reception capacity of 50,000 refugees. Temporary accommodation in schools, sports halls and official buildings, is under consid-eration. Kirkenes, situated close to the Russian border, is planning to have an absorption capacity of 1,500 refugees per week. (The area is very sparsely populated.)[14]

In 1998, two Christian groups, the Norwegian 'Exodus North' and the Swedish 'Marcus Organisation' already working with the Jewish Agency in the CIS on behalf of Russian Jewry, were trying to make inroads in the Murmansk area of northern Russia. 30,000 Jews are reportedly living in the Kola Peninsula. The hope is that as they are challenged about Israel, they will be stirred to emigrate there some day too. A few have already left.

In contrast to the other Scandinavian countries, in Denmark, the Interior Ministry has so far only discussed the issue of the migrants from Third World countries, still in the Baltic States. Efforts will be made to support them in Denmark until they can return home. Proportionally, there are already a considerable number of refugees from Yugoslavia, Asia and Africa in the country. There has been no discussion officially about assistance to a possible Russian influx. On the other hand, Denmark is not so immediately exposed to an influx from Russia as are the other Scandinavian countries, and since there has been much positive action on behalf of refugees here, one might expect this to continue in the future. However, the last word has not been said in this matter. In recent years, the Mafia groups from Russia and East-European countries have begun to practise organised crime in Scandinavian capitals such as Copenhagen. If this increases, it might influence the population negatively towards transmigrants coming from Russia.

One factor, however, needs to be taken into consideration. The member countries of the European Union and Norway are proposing a new refugee law, expected to take effect during 2000, which will strengthen and protect the group's outer borders against refugees coming in from Third World countries – Africa, Asia and South America. Unless exceptions are made, this will also ward off migrants coming from the Russian Federation (and the fairly large number of illegal refugees from Third World countries arriving that way).

As previously noted from earlier migration patterns, it can be anticipated that the coming exodus movement will also occur in waves. In connection with major upheavals in Russia, the Jews, fearing closing doors, will try to get out of the country quickly. At the end of 1994 about one million

Russian Jews were already in possession of exit visas. Even if a couple of hundred thousand of these have since left the country, others have quickly taken their place. With the developments in the European Union (EU) and the increased border restrictions, it is likely to be harder to emigrate there.

In order to comply with pressure arising from the Oslo Accords, the former Israeli Labour government handed over areas in Judea, Samaria and Gaza to the Palestinians during 1994–95. This has further reduced Israel's size, and it might make it more difficult for the Israeli government to find space for the immigrants to live (other than in the Negev desert, which they are now busily trying to cultivate.)

It may be during such a period, when a new immigration wave is either pressing to enter Israel, or stuck in Europe for a while, that the words from Isaiah 49:19–21 will come true:

> ' "Though you were ruined and made desolate and your
>   land laid waste,
> now you will be too small for your people . . .
> The children born during your bereavement (in the
>   dispersion) will yet say in your hearing: 'This place is too
>   small for us; give us more space to live in.' " '
>
> [Hebrew – to 'settle in']

But we should keep in mind that the international situation may soon be different. Even though a few countries, particularly Germany and the USA, are currently offering a limited number of Russian Jews permanent citizenship, the outlook might change overnight. One day, perhaps only Israel will be willing to admit them into her country.

Anticipating the Coming Emigration Wave

Sometimes when we are on a long journey it is good once in a while to size up the situation and see how close we are to our goal. There are many evidences indicating that we are on the verge of a new, large emigration wave.

At present, the Jewish Agency, as earlier mentioned, spearheads the emigration efforts from the CIS, while an increasing number of Christians organisations are being permitted to support their efforts under their supervision.

Currently, the majority of Jews fly directly from Russia to Israel, but there is already an increasing tendency to go out via another country. However, if there is a Russian government crisis with heavy antisemitism and internal economic breakdown, the situation could rapidly change, and the Christians' help in the neighbouring countries would prove extremely valuable.

Let us now try to relate our present knowledge about the Russian emigration pattern to a 'map'. This will give a general picture of what might take place. Of course, there is lots of room for unexpected events. If the usual flight routes out of Russia cannot be used, there would be an increasing tendency to scatter in various directions. The Jews would then most likely follow the same routes they have already begun to use, following friends who had already established contacts along the way. (I am now speaking of Jews; not about a possible mass flight of Russian citizens as such.)

The Jews in the northern part of Russia around the St Petersburg area, will try to go westwards, across to Finland, as long as the borders remain open. There may come a time when the Finns, perhaps fearing Russian pressure, would close it. The Jews might also leave for Sweden or Norway, as the next Scandinavian countries in the reception line, and eventually on to Denmark. Some Scandinavian governments are, as mentioned, anticipating this. During World War II, Jewish people escaped the danger in Finland by being transported across the Baltic Sea in small boats to Sweden. During the 1990s a small number of Jewish emigrant families followed the same route. They acquired motor boats and sailed from the Baltic countries to the Swedish East Coast. The trip, taking about 6 hours, lands them on the islands of Gotland and Oeland. (Previously during World War II, boats from Finland frequently brought Jewish refugees across to the Swedish shore.) From there the Israeli Embassy in Stockholm can help Jewish emigrants with further transportation.

From mid-Russia, around the Moscow area, the Jews are expected to cross to Poland and Slovakia, as the western highway from the Russian capital leads to Warsaw. This will take the Jews right into Middle Europe, where Christians in the various countries, such as Holland, Germany and

Switzerland, are hoping to be able to help the Jews get home to Israel. From Southern Russia they might pour westwards towards Hungary or the Balkans, and from the Kiev area they may also choose to go via Odessa on mercy ships, chartered by Christian organisations which are already sailing Jews home to Israel. Alternatively, they may make their way across Turkey to Israel.

As far as the Jews in the Asian republics are concerned, the Jewish Agency have arranged flight connections to Israel from various key cities in some of the Moslem republics. Regarding Eastern Siberia, for example, in the old Yiddish republic of Birobidjan (north of China), a considerable number of Jews, even though they have intermarried, are rapidly becoming aware of their Jewish heritage and have begun to prepare for departure. Although currently leaving by aeroplane, the day may not be far off, when they might sail by ship, perhaps from Vladivostok. Also, a route is now being prepared across the Bering Straight to Alaska and the north-western islands of Canada, where American Christians are preparing to help.

All over the CIS, a number of Christian organisations and Church groups are already assisting the Jewish Agency in finding the 'hidden' Jews, telling them about the possibility of leaving the country and helping them out. Voluntary workers are transporting the emigrants to their airport or ship for transit. At present, Jewish Agency workers as well as Christian 'fishers' are challenging and warning the Jews to get out before 'the time of the hunters', a time of severe persecution, sets in (Jeremiah 16:14–16).

Also outside Russia, concerned Christians are becoming increasingly involved and making themselves ready to help a large crowd of Jewish refugees if the coming exodus reaches their country. They are preparing in a way they never did 50 years ago. It is as if a 'safety net', is in the process of being spread outside Russia and 'a highway' prepared for the Jewish returnees to walk on. As the prophet Isaiah exhorted the watchmen of Jerusalem:

> '...*Prepare the way for the people.*
> *Build up the high way! Remove the stones.*
> *Raise a banner for the nations.*' (Isaiah 62:10)

God's plan is that the nations will see this exodus as a mighty sign from God as He rescues His people. But the story outlined in Isaiah 35:8–10 in which, among other things, *'the ransomed of the Lord, will return,* [and] *will enter Zion with singing...'* still lies largely in the future, and we are now only in the preparation stage...

By challenging the nations to help the Jews to return to Israel, God wants to give the various countries a great blessing according to the Abrahamic promise,

> *'I will bless those, who bless you, and whoever curses you I will curse...'*   (Genesis 12:2)

As the ancient tribes in the Sinai lost out on the possibility of blessing by opposing the Israelites during the first exodus, in the same way most of our countries fell short, only half a century ago. The people of the nations may soon be faced with their last opportunity to stand up for His chosen people.

This raises the natural question: when will these new emigration waves of the exodus take place? The Bible gives some indication that they will occur in the end times. When we look more closely at the biblical references to the last wars of the age, we will realise that though these events might in some ways seem far away, the scene is actually in the process of being set and might be much closer than we think. Just consider that during the 9 years, 1990–1998, over 1 million Russian Jews poured out of the former Soviet Union. However, we should also keep in mind that it is not only a question of getting the Jews out of the 'land of the north', but also that they shall be *'gathered from many nations to the mountains of Israel, which had long been empty'* (Ezekiel 38:8).

✤ ✤ ✤

In summary we can see that the biblical exodus from Egypt occurred in stages. So did the return from Babylon. All modern emigration waves also tend to take place in stages, usually dependent on the pressure building up behind the emigrants, causing them to leave.

In recent years this has been exemplified by Ethiopian Jewry, 1984–85 and 1991. There have also been two Soviet waves in 1979 and 1990. Now it seems, a new one is approaching. Although the next one might not be the final exodus, it is likely it will exceed the one million who came out in the 1990 wave. Increased immigration is vitally important to strengthen the Jewish State as she faces hostility from all directions.

The Last Wars – the End in Sight!

The order of the various events is difficult to predict, but a careful Bible reader can already see a number of the pieces in the huge jig-saw puzzle, 'the end times', falling into place.

Modern Israel has been built with a secular, democratic government and a presidential leader. With its biblical and historical background the country stands, for many people, as a symbol and proof of the reality of God's direct intervention in history. Both the Old and New Testaments, inspired and penned in Israel, set divine standards for Judeo-Christian conduct, as well as conveying a code of ethics and civil law to the world in general. As such the tiny Israeli State's effort to keep these standards has put it increasingly at odds with the secularised world, which is moving in a post-Christian and anti-Jewish direction. Already today, many nations would prefer to do away with Israel in order to stifle the quiet voice of God to their conscience. The last wars, outlined in the Bible, can therefore be viewed as encounters between anti-godly powers on earth and Israel, which is still a mouthpiece of the Almighty to speak to men.

We can, therefore, expect to see several wars between the countries in the Middle East that will threaten Israel's survival. Interestingly, one of the last battles spoken of in Ezekiel chapters 38–39 as the Gog-Magog War, is found between two known signposts. On the one hand we have chapters 36 and 37, that deal with the restoration of Israel and the allegory of 'the valley of dry bones'. On the other, the collection of prophecies in chapters 40–48, relating to the Temple in the Millennium and God dividing up the land according to the tribes of Israel. This in itself broadly indicates the timing for this war.

According to Ezekiel, one day, after some wars have been fought, Israel will live in a condition of apparent peace (maybe an artificial one with the Palestinians and surrounding Arab countries). It will then be a land, *'that has recovered from war, whose people were gathered from many nations to the mountains of Israel, which had long been desolate'* (Ezekiel 38:8). It is described as *'a land of unwalled villages . . . a peaceful and unsuspecting people, all of them living without walls and without gates and bars,'* when suddenly the enemy will fall upon them (Ezekiel 38:11).

The Gog-Magog War

The major and mighty enemy attacking Israel is referred to as Gog and Magog. The name probably relates to two tribes, rather than countries. In the genealogy in Genesis 10, Magog is referred to as descending from Japheth. Ezekiel 39:6 also relates to it as a people. In Hebrew, the prefix *'ma-'* as in 'Magog' can also be interpreted as 'from' or 'the place of'. It would then simply mean 'Gog from the land of Gog'.

Gog and Magog probably went from the Black Sea area northwards before the eighth century BC and settled near Moscow. (Today, their shield of armour can still be seen in the city.) The ancient historian, Josephus (living in the first century AD) identified Magog with the Scythians, a horse-riding, nomadic warrior tribe, who came to Southern Russia both from the west via the countries known today as Rumania and Bulgaria and from the east of Russia, via the Crimea. They probably drove the Cimmerians westwards. (See Gomer later.) Other sources date the Scythians as arriving in Persia around the seventh century BC and well settled in southern Russia by the fifth century BC.[15]

Other Invaders in the Trail of Gog-Magog

Rosh. In older translations of the Bible, Gog was described as *'the prince of Rosh'* (Ezekiel 38:2–3 and 39:1). Some scholars previously related it to Russia, but this name is not attested in the area. Many have also identified it with the Assyrian *'Rasu'* on the north-western border and with Elam (in Media).[16] However, *'rosh'* in Hebrew simply means 'head' or 'leader', and more modern biblical translations render it as '*Gog, chief prince of Meshech and Tubal*'.

Meshech, Tubal, Gomer and Togarmah were all old enemies of the Assyrians. At the time of Ezekiel they were hostile, invading tribes, all living in the territories north of Israel in Asia Minor, from where they oppressed the surrounding area. Meshech and Tubal, the sons of Japheth, can probably be located in eastern Asia Minor. In the eighth century BC, the annals of Sargon describe Meshech as an Asiatic tribe, imposing themselves as rulers upon the indigenous people of Asia Minor, in the neighbourhood of Anatolia (formerly Armenia). Today the territory belongs to the eastern part of Turkey.[17]

Gomer is the oldest son of Japheth, and the father of Ashkenaz and Togarmah (Genesis 10:2–3) and can probably be identified with the ancient Cimmerians, an Aryan group, who conquered Urartu (Armenia) from the Ukraine, some time before the eighth century BC.[18] In the Middle Ages there was a tendency to equate Germany with Ashkenaz, and this is the reason why some people today interpret Gomer as Germany and the east European states, former vassals of the Soviet Union.

Togarmah. By the twelfth century BC, this country was situated on the main trade route through South-western Armenia. It supplied horses and mules to Tyre as well as soldiers to Lydia in western Asia Minor.[19] Apparently Beth Togarmah (The House of Togarmah) can more or less be identified with modern Turkey.

In modern times there is much tension between the Moslem countries of the Middle East. Turkey is one of the few Moslem countries which is positive to the West. Much to the consternation of the Arab states, Turkey, which is the largest moderate Sunni nation in the area, signed a military support alliance with Israel in February 1996. This provided for a joint military manoeuvre on land and sea as well as permitting Israeli planes to use Turkish air space to conduct military exercises. In the middle of 1996, an Islamic fundamentalist government took power. They tried, in vain, to undo the treaty with Israel. However, after a year, the president was requested to step down after strong protests from the military, who hold more secular Islamic viewpoints and have pro-Western sympathies. Turkey is a member of NATO, and is hoping some day to enter the EU. This will probably not take place, certainly not in the near future, because of the country's low economic standard.

Ezekiel chapter 38 further relates that these countries will be joined by:

Persia. Late in the second century Indo-European nomads from Southern Russia entered and settled in the Iranian plateau. The Arab tribes did not come into Iran before the seventh century AD with the advance of Islam. Today, the people are Moslems, and it is the leading Islamic Shi'ite fundamentalist country, aspiring to become the pre-eminent power in the Middle East and spread its fundamentalist Moslem doctrines. Iran is a sworn enemy of Israel and, together with Syria and Iraq, one of the main conspirators for the eradication of Israel. Senior Israeli officials have declared that Iran's nuclear capability is the most serious threat facing Israel. If Iran's programme is not halted, they would be forced to consider attacking Iran's nuclear reactor just as they did to Iraq in 1981. (*Jerusalem Post*, 6 January, 1995.) Since Iran is very close to the production of a nuclear bomb, an uncontrolled Islamic fundamentalist leader might easily cause a catastrophe.

Cush (Ethiopia), probably also includes Sudan, their northern neighbour. Until recently, Ethiopia has been Communist. Sudan is becoming fanatically Islamic, and there is strong persecution of Christians. After the former Soviet Union ceased to be the training base for international terrorists, Sudan continued this role, and has now a considerable number of training camps. There is a real danger that Ethiopia might fall prey to Islamic fundamentalism.

Put (Libya), like fundamentalist Iran, is today a sworn enemy of Israel. Its profits from oil exports are used for the sole purpose of the destruction of Israel, and Libya like Syria, plays host to international terror groups, aiming for the destruction of Israel.

Not only will the peoples and countries mentioned above participate in the war against Israel, but twice in chapter 38 it is foretold that they are joined by *'many nations'*, *'goiim'*. As an interesting aside, an example from Jewish mysticism which attributes a numerical value to the Hebrew letters and words in the Old Testament, pointed out that *'Gog and Magog'*, representing the whole horde of nations attacking Israel, had the numerical value of 70. This is the same number of nations, counted in Genesis 10.[20]

Furthermore, Ezekiel 38:13 indicates that Sheba and Dedan (Saudi Arabia) as well as the merchants of Tarshish will be spectators to the scene. Tarshish could possibly refer to the 15 member countries of the European Union, with their increasing economic and political influence and their trading ships. We appear to be moving rapidly towards such a scenario today.

In conclusion, in modern-day terms, the armies of Gog and Magog, could be interpreted as representing a coalition of former Communist-related and Islamic powers against God's people, Israel. It is interesting that the previous Regional Co-operation for Development, formed in 1985, was expanded in 1992 to become a 10-nation Economic Co-operation Organisation, called ECO. This economic union now stretches from Turkey through the Central Asian republics to Pakistan and Iran, promising to create the world's biggest trading bloc in terms of both population and area.

Even more noteworthy has been the establishment of the Organisation of the Islamic Conference, OIC, formed back in the 1970s. Beyond a general agreement of economic, technical and commercial co-operation, the OIC has given its goals a heavy political and Islamic emphasis. It has thus, incorporated the 'Palestinian question', and is working towards the establishment of a Palestinian State and 'the liberation of Al-Quds' (Jerusalem). The OIC, which counts 52 member states, stretches from North Africa across the Asian republics, Afghanistan and Pakistan as far as Indonesia.

The prophet Ezekiel emphasised that the enemies' purpose for attacking Israel is to destroy the country and *'to seize spoil'* (Ezekiel 38:13). It is predicted that the enormous army of Gog and Magog will come mainly on horseback, crossing the Caucasian mountains, where no army tanks can pass (Ezekiel 38:15).

It needs to be added, however, that the 'Gog-Magog war' of

Ezekiel is not 'the last battle'. It should rather be considered as a third world war and an attack by northern, anti-God forces upon the 'Holy Land'. It seems they will not get near Jerusalem, but finish up outside the eastern border of Israel in the Travellers' Valley or the Averim Valley (Ezekiel 39:11). In Hebrew this just means 'on the other side' of the Jordan River. Perhaps it will be a major war in a series of ongoing battles. The assault will fail, because the Lord Himself will defeat them by plagues and supernatural disturbances of the weather, hailstorms and lightning (Ezekiel 38:22). It will take seven years to destroy the military equipment and seven months to bury the dead and ritually cleanse the land after the war (Ezekiel 38:9–12). This can, therefore, not be the last battle.

The Final Battle of This Age

The final battle has often been referred to as Armageddon (derived from Har-Magiddo, the Mountain of Megiddo). Located roughly between Mount Carmel and Nazareth, in the Jezreel Valley, the plains below Megiddo have seen innumerable battles and, over the centuries been the gathering point for major nations such as Egypt, Assyria and the Babylonians for their wars against Israel.[21]

Today, on a clear day the view from Megiddo is breathtaking over the vast wheatfields in the plains below. Several passes enter the Jezreel Valley from the surrounding mountains. One day this area will witness the world's most crucial battle. Today, Megiddo attracts about 150,000 Christian tourists every year.

According to the Old Testament prophets, the final war could consist of one, two or more battles. Also the Rabbinic tradition predicts that Gog will come to Israel two or three times.[22] Even if some confrontations are likely to take place in the valley of Jezreel, the major battles will probably be fought in Judea and around Jerusalem (in Benjamin). In modern media parlance biblical Samaria and Judea are called *'the West Bank'* (of the Jordan). This territory is, at the time of writing, the object of discussion under a global peace effort in which the EU, Russia and the US are all trying to force the government of Israel to exchange the land for an artificial peace treaty with the Palestinians. If it can ever be agreed upon, it is unlikely to last long. The Palestinians wish to create their own sovereign state with Jerusalem as its capital and these aspirations are likely to lead to much bloodshed in the region.

In the apocalyptic scene of the 'Day of the Lord', the judgement day for the nations, Armageddon will again be the assembly point for the armies of the nations predicted in Revelation 16:16. The Old Testament appears to narrate a growing intensity in the stages of the war, moving from *'many nations'* (Ezekiel 38:6), to the battle around Jerusalem, in which representatives of the armies of *'all the nations'* will be fighting in valleys around the Jewish capital (vividly described in Joel 3:2). In the last and most important phase, the prophet Zechariah clearly says that *'all nations'* will be coming against Jerusalem (Zechariah 12:3–9). This is in contrast to the *'many nations'* of the previous Gog-Magog war.*

The prophet Joel foretells that the last phase of the war will take place in the Valley of Jehoshaphat, which means *'God is Judge'* (Joel 3:1–2), a symbolic name for a valley near Jerusalem. The Bible says the wrath and judgement of God will be poured out upon the nations because of their attitude and continued hatred of God's people and their division of the land. In Joel 3:2b, God calls the Jews *'my inheritance, my people Israel'*, and complains that *'they scattered my people among the nations'*. It is exactly such attempts to divide up God's land according to the mistaken standards of humanistic 'justice', which we see in the political world today. In this connection, the Bible only speaks about a return of Israel, i.e. the Jewish people, to the land, not a gathering of Palestinians there. God has many rich promises for the children of Ishmael, but the promises regarding the land of Israel are to the Jewish people, the children of Isaac and Jacob (Genesis 17:18–21; 26:3–5 and 28:13–14).

Perhaps we can relate Joel's pronouncement about God's judgement in chapter 3, to Zechariah's vivid and climactic

---

* The term Gog Magog is also mentioned in Revelation 20:7–9 where it is a symbolic name for anti-God forces *'surrounding the camp of God's people, the city He loves'* (Israel and Jerusalem). It appears to relate to the end of the millenium and depicts the final battle and destruction of Satan.

description of the final battle in chapter 14:2–3, which in the first instance, will result in half the city going into exile. The Scriptures give no indication of another exile for the Jewish people, and it appears that they will remain in the promised land. But the situation might develop so dangerously that the enemy comes against Jerusalem and half the citizens might have to flee to the mountains (Zechariah 14:2; Matthew 24:16).* In all the adversity the Lord Himself will be a shield for those who live in Jerusalem (Zechariah 12:8) and will destroy all the nations, that attack Jerusalem (Zechariah 12:9).

Zechariah 14:3–5 then gives a description of how God in His divine wrath will rise to avenge the nations' last evil attempt to destroy Jerusalem at this time and, if possible, to wipe out the Jewish people in a new Holocaust attempt. But the Lord will supernaturally intervene to deliver His people. As God's fury is being poured out from the Mount of Olives, Israel's enemies will be scattered in all directions.

Time and again the Old Testament points out that the Lord will vindicate His Jewish people in the face of the nations as foretold in Joel and Zechariah. Also the prophet Isaiah speaks about *'a day of vengeance and a year of retribution to uphold Zion's cause'* (Isaiah 34:8), where God will judge the countries for their attitude to Israel on a national level (Isaiah 63:4–6).

For us, living today, it might be difficult to understand the concept of divine judgement. It is perhaps spelled out in a more understandable way as exemplified in the New Testament parable in Matthew 25:31–46. According to this, the individual nations will appear before the throne *'of the King'* (usually a synonym for Jesus) and be judged according to their attitude to and treatment of Israel and His Jewish people. On the Day of the Lord, the King will divide the nations according to the peoples' attitude to *'these brothers of mine'* (Matthew 25:40). Not only is this said in relation to Israel, but the Jews living in the Diaspora, are also included.

---

* Recalling previous history, some Bible scholars believe that, just as believing Jews fled from Jerusalem to the mountains in Pella, across the Jordan, during the Roman siege, shortly before 70 AD, so the Jews will also flee to the mountains in the future tribulation.

On a more individual level, the ideal for Christian living is to do good towards the Jews, feed them if hungry or thirsty, clothe them if need be or give them hospitality and shelter if that is needed (Matthew 25:31–46). The King concludes, *'I tell you the truth, whatever you did for one of the least of these brothers of mine, you did for me'* (Matthew 25:40). This will be the dividing line for divine justice between the righteous and unrighteous nations, executed at the Day of the Lord.

God will, at last, return the Jews left in *'the land of the north, and all the other countries'* somewhere between the end time wars and before God's Spirit is poured out, to their ancient homeland. As Ezekiel 39:28–29 clearly points out: *'I* [the Lord] *will gather them to their own land, not leaving any behind'* (in the Diaspora). It might be thought that those Jews who have not returned, will either be assimilated or annihilated in the Diaspora. Therefore, Ezekiel states that all Jews will be gathered in the land of Israel, because God will not leave any behind. In his holy land, there the Almighty God of all generations, the God of Abraham, Isaac and Jacob, will finally reveal Himself to them (Ezekiel 39:29).

During the end-time wars, God's repeated intervention on behalf of His Jewish people, will eventually lead to Israel realising her position before God, as they will mourn together before Him as a nation (Zechariah 12:10–14). The Jews will then be ready for the overwhelming revelation and acknowledge God as the Holy One of Israel and His Messiah as their Saviour. As the physical birth of Israel previously took place in one day (Isaiah 66:7–9) the spiritual birth will also happen in one day, as described in Zechariah 12. The Jewish people will then have their hearts circumcised, not just their flesh, as foretold by Moses (Deuteronomy 30:1–6) – and will be ready to enter the New Covenant (Jeremiah 31:33–34) and truly *'know'* God. The Jewish people, having returned to their land and to their God, will finally then become the true nation of Israel and the blessing to all the other nations, which He intended from the beginning.

The end result has been highlighted in Ezekiel's inspired prophecy, chapter 36, which predicts the sequence of Israel's change of heart, and how God's mercy and anointing will finally be poured out, and, by His Spirit, Israel will *'be His people, and He will be their God'* (Ezekiel 36:28) – a people conveying His glory. God's great name will be vindicated to the surrounding nations as they see His holiness and power displayed on the earth.

Many awesome events and wars might still be ahead of us, before all the Jewish people are back in their ancient homeland. It needs also to be kept in mind that Israel will need a much larger territory in order to be able to absorb them all. Each of Israel's wars has so far given her more territory, so they may also gain this as a result of the coming battles.

God's Judgement Expressed

Obadiah, one of the Minor Prophets, has predicted an example of the coming encounters. This remarkable little book, consisting of only one chapter, describes God's judgement and defeat of some of the hostile forces represented by Edom or Esau (currently Moslem), *'because of their violence against your brother Jacob'* (Obadiah 1:10).

The time setting is the approaching day of the Lord (Obadiah 1:15), when the people of Israel will rise again and possess the land promised them by God. The passage deals with the punishment of Edom and Gilead, which is Jordan, as well as the land of the Philistine, Samaria and Ephraim, covering the present Palestinian areas, Gaza and the West Bank (possibly larger Moslem areas are included) because they divided the 'Promised Land'. For centuries Israel's foes, living in these areas, have crossed the border and plotted evil against the Jews. (In modern parlance we may call these men 'terrorists.') Obadiah warns:

> ' *"The Day of the Lord is near for all nations.*
> *As you have done it will be done to you; your deeds will be turned upon your own head....*
> *But on Mount Zion will be deliverance; it will be holy, and the house of Jacob will possess its inheritance.*
> *The house of Jacob will be a fire and the house of Joseph a flame; the house of Esau will be stubble and they will set it on fire and consume it.*
> *There will be no survivors from the House of Esau."*
>   *The Lord has spoken.*

People from the Negev will occupy the mountains of Esau and people from the foothills will possess the land of the Philistines.

They will occupy the field of Ephraim and Samaria, and Benjamin will possess Gilead [east side of the Jordan River, allotted to the two and a half tribes after the exodus from Egypt].

This company of exiles, who are in Canaan [Israel] *will possess the land as far as Zarephath* [Lebanon], *the exiles from Jerusalem who are in Sepharad* [Iraq] *will possess the towns of the Negev.*

Deliverers will go up on Mount Zion to govern the mountains of Esau and the kingdom will be the Lord's.'
(Obadiah 1:15–21) [23]

✤ ✤ ✤

The Hope of Israel – and for the Nations

As dark clouds have been gathering over Israel during the last few years, the surrounding Arab countries, particularly Egypt and Syria, have been pressuring Israel to surrender land to build up a Palestinian State. At the same time, the Islamic fundamentalist countries, Iraq, Iran and Libya, have threatened the very existence of the land of Israel.

But, on the other hand, we should keep in mind that Israel has already passed another remarkable milestone in the divine timetable and been able to celebrate her 50 years of statehood, from the proclamation on 14 May, 1948 until 1998. We should, however, note that the 50th year of statehood was not a year of jubilee according to the biblical calendar, but only with regard to the ownership of land. According to Jewish reckoning, 1998 is equivalent to the Jewish year 5758 (which began at Jewish New Year 1997).

As has been mentioned previously, the jubilee of Israel's statehood also contains another 50-year circle from 1897, when the first Zionist conference took the initiative to propagate the idea of a Jewish State, until the nations in the

UN voted for the establishment of a Jewish State in 1947. After the devastating destruction in the Diaspora, the Jewish people miraculously arose from the ashes of the Holocaust to a new life in the State of Israel.

Looking back at the 50 stormy years of statehood, it is amazing that Israel has been able to survive 6 wars in its short existence in a sea of hostile Arab countries. At the anniversary, the Israeli Prime Minister, Benjamin Netanyahu, said that the country's past 50 years' history **'is the greatest victory for the Jewish people. What happened in the Land of Israel has been the story of the most amazing revival of the twentieth century**.' Moreover, the fact that the year of celebration passed in relative peace and without a major Middle East War, is in itself a great miracle.[24]

God's faithfulness has led His people through many stormy waters in the past. Therefore, the year of jubilee of their statehood was an encouragement to believe that, in spite of fierce threats from the surrounding enemies, Israel has God's safe assurance that through all circumstances He will, in the end, *'foil the plans of the nations, and thwart the purposes of the peoples. But the plans of the Lord stand firm forever, the purposes of His heart through all generations'* (Psalm 33:10–11).

The Only Hope for the Nations

It is God's ultimate purpose that all men come to salvation and see His glory. As the nations see His mercy poured out over Israel and judgement over the evil powers, God's great name will be vindicated.

> *'When I bring them* [the Jews] *back from the peoples and gather them from the land of their enemies,* **then I shall be sanctified through them in the sight of many nations.** *Then they will know that I am the Lord their God.'*
>
> (Ezekiel 39:27, NASB)

Since October 1998, pressures in Russia have caused a new upsurge in emigration, leading to the doubling of the number of Jews leaving the country. A new wave is on the way and the Israeli Government is enthusiastic about it.

Isn't it a privilege to be alive so close to the end times and see some of the pieces fall into place – even if we may only fully understand the significance of the events in retrospect.

With the approaching return of the Jewish people in the prophesied exodus from the north, the end is within sight. With our spiritual eyes we can discern that a new dawn is approaching for the House of Israel as well as all the peoples of this earth: God's Kingdom of Peace. At last the bright morning star, prophesied many ages ago, will ascend on the horizon over His Israel (Numbers 24:17 and Revelation 22:16). They will then believe in their God and Yeshua, His promised Messiah.

Epilogue

Lessons from the Holocaust

For those, who have caught some of my intentions with this book and the burden for events still to come, this post-script has been written for your sake.

Some years ago, I attended a course on 'Antisemitism and the Holocaust' at the Yad Vashem Holocaust Memorial Centre in Jerusalem. One of the lasting lessons from World War II, which stuck in my mind, is related to the three categories of people involved in the tragedy of destruction during the Holocaust.

The first two were more or less permanent groups, and not much could be done about them:

1. **The main persecutors – the SS-Nazis together with the perpetrators or collaborators on a national level**; those who carried out the German orders in all the occupied countries in Europe, whether for ideology, money or other advantages. Without them the mass destruction could not have taken place.

2. **The victims**, be they Jews, gypsies or other political and religious opponents of the Nazi regime. These were more or less helpless in the hands of the Nazi regime. Not much could be done about them.

3. The only group who could make a difference in the issue of genocide was the ordinary citizens. Lives depended on whether they were only spectators to one of the world's worst tragedies or chose to enter the conflict as participants on behalf of the victims. **The bystanders, acting as rescuers, made the whole difference**.

Historical analysts assert that World War II was fought on two levels: a military and conventional war, but also an ideological war, fought in ghettos, concentration and death camps, in order to eradicate the Jews. Today, not many people are aware of this. The Allies reasoned that if they dealt with the Nazis on a military level to defeat Germany as quickly as possible, the death threat to the Jews would consequently also be overcome. The result was that Europe and the USA were mainly bystanders to the Jewish tragedy. In retrospect, a number of historians such as Feingold, Gilbert, Lacquer, Morse, Wasserstein, and Wyman have pronounced their verdict that the effort to rescue the Jews was 'too little, and too late'.

The Rescuers

We should not forget that while today we look at the rescue of Jews in German-occupied countries as an heroic deed, during the war, the act of rendering assistance to any Jews, Gypsies or other unwanted political or religious people, was seen as detestable. The German occupying forces or their government considered it to be a very unsociable act, directly harmful to their goals, and it was therefore highly dangerous.

By early 1942, it was not an easy task to shelter a Jew. The country was usually governed by a fascist regime, and rescuers were surrounded by a hostile neighbourhood, with many willing to betray them for personal gain.

Under those circumstances it was very difficult for a hunted person to find a hiding place. Jews were hidden in such places as secret cupboards or rooms in houses, in unused cellars or factories, huts in the forest, pits under the house, under chicken coops, in mineshafts or sewers. Not only were the lives of the victims in danger, but also the attempted rescuer and his family's lives were at risk. The obstacles involved in hiding people for short periods, let alone months, or even years were overwhelming. The outside world must have no idea what was going on. At a time when food was rationed, the food portions in the house had to be further reduced; suitable clothes had to be found, washed and dried unnoticed by the neighbours; babies and children kept silent; additional water for washing provided, and human waste products needed to be discarded. Also, in case of sickness, medicine had to be obtained.

The rescuers were ordinary people from all walks of life, there were idealists and clergy among them, but also thieves became involved in these humanitarian acts. They were by no means all saints. Remember they also included a German collaborator and scoundrel, Oscar Schindler. But they knew how to act in a world of cruelty and depravity and did so at a time when the Jews were very unpopular. First and foremost, they maintained their humanity and intervened at the appropriate time. The rescuers acted as one human to another, often not even aware of their altruism. They did it for a righteous cause and to preserve the sanctity of life. No wonder the Jews have honoured their rescuers, and given them the title of 'righteous Gentiles'.

Was it a hopeless task? In retrospect: not at all – but it was a risky one which demanded commitment and courage. Was it effective? Undoubtedly. For example, after the war ended, to the astonishment of many, out of the ruins of Berlin emerged over 1,100 Jews, who had been hidden away in the city, kept safe despite being so near the centre of Hitler's regime.

As we are seeing the early warning signals of coming times of crisis, now some 60 years after World War II, there may again be roles waiting for us to fill in our generation. Whether in wars or where ethnic minority groups are persecuted, will we be willing to offer shelter and food in order to preserve their lives? Will we be available to help, despite possible inconvenience and danger, or will we close our eyes and be indifferent to the return of the Jewish people to their land? **Will we dare to stand in the gap?**

As a well-known Talmudic saying reads:

> 'He, who saves one life is likened to
> the one, who has saved the whole world.'

Do remember: There may still be a need for the by-standers! They can make *all* the difference!

Organisations Involved in Supporting the Exodus Movement

'For the revelation awaits an appointed time;
it speaks of the end
and will not prove false.
Though it linger, wait for it;
it will certainly come and will not delay.'

(Habakkuk 2:3)

As many believers are aware, God has been speaking through past history for, in a way, the Old Testament is also the Jewish people's history book. But if we have an open mind and are tuned in to listen, God also speaks through various events today, both in Israel as well as in the history of the nations. While it is easier for us to see the move of His hand in retrospect, regarding future events we are limited in our understanding of timing. We need, therefore, to have an open mind and be assured that His promises will come true.

As it is surely a challenge to our faith to see the biblical prophecies fulfilled, I will be honest and say that it is even more exiting to get involved ourselves. Since the early 1980s, as Christian groups have become aware of what is happening with regard to the Exodus, they began to form organisations to help Russian Jews from 'the land of the north' back to Israel. This important work can only be done in co-operation with the Jewish Agency. Besides the vital importance of praying for the activities and spreading information, there are many other ways of helping, such as financing help with travel and support during the immigrants' first, difficult phase of absorption in Israel.

During my years in Jerusalem, I became acquainted with a number of excellent organisations, working on behalf of Russian Jewry. One moving example of Christian concern is the British-based Ebenezer Emergency Fund which, since 1991, has been helping prospective Jewish emigrants. It brings them either by train or bus from their homes in Russia to the port of departure. It hosts them during their stay in

Odessa, helps process their luggage, often up to 250 kilos, through customs (as against the 45 kilos permitted by aeroplane), and finally sailing them the last part of the way, a 3-day voyage, to Haifa. Throughout the journey, both young and old, healthy as well as handicapped are well cared for by a Christian voluntary staff. Christians from many countries pay all the expenses.

In December 1996, Ebenezer celebrated their 50th sailing on the Odessa–Haifa route, having carryied a total of 12,000 Jewish emigrants from Russia in their first 5 years. On that ship, about 300 Russian Jews were brought 'home'. The event was celebrated in Haifa port, where the city's Deputy Mayor and the Minister of Immigration and Absorption Yuli Edelstein.[1] himself an emigrant from the USSR, were present to greet the new arrivals. And the sailings continue.

Ebenezer has also brought Russian emigrants by plane from remote areas in Siberia, either to connect with the shipping route in Odessa or link up with Jewish Agency chartered planes directly to Israel. The areas included are Armenia, Uzbekistan, Kazakhstan, Birobidjan and Magadan. In total, from 1991 to early 1999, Ebenezer has helped more than 30,000 emigrants come to Israel.

It is a daring step of faith in 'the land of the north', relying totally on God's promises and provision. But being involved one really feels a part of the Lord's plans for the future.

A few of the Israel-based organisations for Soviet Jewry, which you might contact, are:

Soviet Jewry Zionist Forum
2 HaOr St
Romema
Jerusalem 94389

Tel: (972)-(0)2-385823/24
Fax: (972)-(0)2-385813

Keren Klitah – Aid for Russian Immigrants
PO Box 4629
Jerusalem 91044

Tel: (972)-(0)2-5666957/5669722

'Mother to Mother'
Director Ida Nudel
PO Box 1119
76110 Rehovot
Israel

Tel: (972)-(0)89287329
Fax: (972)-(0)89286210

Some international Christian organisations helping Russian Jews which you can contact for up to date information:

Bridges for Peace
12 Ibn Ezra Str.
PO Box 7304
Jerusalem

Tel: (972)-(0)2-669 865
Fax: (972)-(0)2-666 675

Christian Friends of Israel (Jerusalem)
23 Shivtei Yisrael
PO Box 1813
Jerusalem 91015

Tel: (972)-(0)2-6264172/187
Fax: (972)-(0)2-6264955

Christian Friends of Israel (UK)
PO Box 2687
Eastbourne
E. Sussex, BN22 7LZ
England

Tel: (44)-(0)1323-410810
Fax: (44)-(0)1323-410211

Ebenezer Emergency Fund
5a Poole Road
Bournemouth BH2 5QJ
England

Tel: (44)-(0)1202-294455
Fax: (44)-(0)1202-295550

Exobus
PO Box 1030
Hull HU2 8YL
England

Tel: (44)-(0)1482-217153
Fax: (44)-(0)1482-216565

The International Christian Embassy
PO Box 1192
20 Rachel Imanu Street
Jerusalem 91010

Tel: (972)-(0)2-566 9823
Fax: (972)-(0)2-566 9970

A Personal Postscript

My Auschwitz Experience

In May of 1986, I went to Poland for the first time. It was shortly after the Chernobyl disaster, and only a few people travelled towards the east for fear of nuclear contamination. My purpose in going to Poland was to share at some meetings about Israel and the coming exodus from Russia. Because of the critical situation in the country, I took dried milk powder and tinned food for needy ones. At the same time I felt an urge to take the opportunity to visit Auschwitz. My Polish friends, however, tried to discourage me from the trip, because they felt it was a tragic and distressing place to visit.

The day before our visit I had a very strange experience. Now I am not usually given to visions, but late that night I had a very strong spiritual experience which I shall never forget. I believe the Lord took me back in time to Auschwitz during World War II. It was the cold, cruel winter of 1943 when there were so many victims in that death camp that the crematoriums clogged up. For that reason the bodies were transported to the neighbouring camp of Birkenau where they were simply dragged out and dumped, 'buried' in the already overfull marshy lakes. I still recall the horrible impression of the black mire and slime, from which a terrible stench emanated. The sides of the lakes were very slippery and the bottom of them covered with people lying side by side like rotting tree trunks. (It was in Jerusalem 6 months later, when I saw the authentic film 'Shoah' (The Holocaust), that I understood the experience better.)

When I woke, the sun was shining brightly into the room. I did not tell my friends about the night's harsh experience. I wanted to think it through a bit more. So we went, as planned, to Auschwitz.

Later that day, when my friends accompanied me to the death camp, I saw the horrors of injustice committed by one nation against another: man's crime against man. I saw the ramps at the end of the railway where victims were selected for the extermination process. I saw the mounds of little children's shoes, heaps of shaved hair, piles of spectacles telling their mute story, and the house for 'medical experimentation with humans'. All of it made a deep impression upon me.

Towards the end of the visit, I came to the building housing the Hall of Memory for the Jewish people. The room was dimly lit, with a Star of David set in the floor. Softly a cantor's melodic voice sang an elegy in a minor key, for the dead. I felt such a pressure on my throat I could hardly swallow. A burden of deep sorrow overwhelmed me and I could only bow down, weep, and pray to the Almighty for mercy.

While there I 'saw' a kind of 'picture' before my eyes. This time of a large golden pair of scales in which one nation after another was placed, and weighed according to their actions in relation to the Jewish people. There was the strong superpower of the USA, the leading European countries of England, France and Germany, and also the smaller Scandinavian countries, including my own country of Denmark. All were weighed in the balance and found wanting. It was my deep concern that, before it is too late, God in His mercy, would grant each of the nations another opportunity to redress the balance. To stand up and help His Jewish people in a time of testing – and not just be spectators at the arena.

It was there at the memorial of anguish in Auschwitz that I received my burden to alert the nations so that we can all play a more positive part in the coming exodus.

Appendix I

Statistics

I am grateful to the Israeli Government Statistics Office for their valuable help in providing statistical material.

It should be understood that statistics, particularly from the 1930s, given in this book, reflect the incomplete and limited information available. The refugees' country of origin (the Reich) seldom recorded all cases of emigration, particularly after *Kristallnacht*, and the forced expulsion in November 1938, as it was impossible to keep track of such data. Furthermore, there was no specific record-keeping by either governments or refugee organisations of the actual number of refugees, in either Germany or Great Britain.

Jewish organisations maintained the most accurate statistics, but only of individuals applying for help. Moreover, statistics did not distinguish between the ordinary traveller and the refugee, between German 'non-Aryan' and Jew, or for that matter between German Jew and Polish Jew.

Governments and refugee organisations often deliberately understated the figures in order not to create antisemitic feelings. On the other hand, some countries' immigration figures were inflated to avoid assuming greater responsibility. Since refugees admitted to Great Britain were accepted as trans-migrants or on permits for domestic work, the number for remigration fluctuated. Only the figures for work permits are available to give an impression of the influx into Britain.

While in Palestine the government figures are more reliable. Again the recordings from the Jewish Agency are held at the lowest possible level in order to protect the yearly quota. Illegal immigration numbers are notably inexact.

Appendix II

Jewish Population in Europe and Other Countries Around 1933

	General population	Jewish population	Per cent
Europe			
Austria	6,759,062	191,408	2.83
Belgium	8,092,004	60,000	0.74
Bulgaria	6,090,215	46,431	0.76
Czechoslovakia	14,729,536	356,830	2.42
Denmark	3,350,656	5,690	0.16
Finland	3,667,067	1,772	0.05
France	41,834,923	240,000	0.57
Germany	66,030,491	499,682	0.76
Great Britain and Northern Ireland	46,178,884	300,000	0.65
Greece	6,204,684	72,791	1.17
Hungary	8,688,349	444,567	5.11
Irish Free State	2,971	3,686	0.12
Italy	41,176,671	47,435	0.12
Luxemburg	299,782	2,242	0.75
Netherlands	8,392,102	156,817	1.86
Norway	2,814,194	1,359	0.05
Poland	31,927,773	3,028,837	9.49
Portugal	6,825,883	1,200	0.02
Rumania	18,023,037	984,213	5.46
Serb-Croat-Slovene State	13,934,038	68,405	0.49
Spain	23,563,867	4,000	0.02
Sweden	6,141,571	6,469	0.11
Switzerland	4,066,400	17,973	0.44
Turkey (Europe)	1,185,719	55,592	4.69

	General population	Jewish population	Per cent
*Russia**			
Crimea	713,823	45,926	6.43
Estonia	1,126,413	4,302	0.38
Latvia	1,950,502	93,479	4.79
Lithuania	2,340,038	155,125	6.63
Northwest Russia	13,450,533	326,363	2.43
Russia (RSFSR)	74,384,273	170,693	0.23
White Russia	5,439,400	407,059	2.43
Ukraine	31,901,400	1,574,428	4.94
All countries of Europe and Russia	508,699,031	9,390,113	1.85
United States	122,775,046	4,228,029	3.44
Canada	10,376,786	155,614	1.50
Australia	6,630,600	23,553	0.36

* The Russian census is from 1926.
Source: American Jewish Year Book, Vol. 38, 1936–37.

By 1939 the statistics do not show an increase of Jewish refugees in Europe as most were not registered. However, Germany having annexed both Austria and the Sudetenland, had an increased general population of more than 10 million, of which 192,000 (0.90%) were Jews, despite their best efforts to rid themselves of their Jewish population.

Appendix III

Countries Invited to the Evian Refugee Conference, 1938

The United States – host country
Great Britain
Belgium
France
The Netherlands
Switzerland
Scandinavian countries:
   Denmark
   Norway
   Sweden
Australia
Canada
New Zealand

Argentina
Bolivia
Brazil
Chile
Colombia
Costa Rica
Cuba
Dominican Republic
Ecuador
Guatemala
Haiti
Honduras
Mexico
Nicaragua
Panama
Paraguay
Peru
Uruguay
Venezuela

Italy refused to come because of the previous war in Ethiopia.
Germany sent observers.
Poland and Rumania sent an observer each.

Source: Proceeding from the Intergovernmental Committee, Evian, Verbatim Record, Conference, Annex V, p. 56.

Appendix IV

Jewish Emigration and Immigration

Table 1 Jewish Emigration from Central Europe, 1933–39

Year	Germany	Austria	Czechoslovakia Bohemia, Moravia	Total
1933	37,000			
1934	23,000			
1935	21,000			
1936	25,000			
1937	23,000			
1938	47,400	62,958		
1939	68,000	54,451	43,000	
	244,400	117,409	43,000	404,809

Source: Bauer, Yehuda. *American Jewry and the Holocaust* (Detroit, 1982), p. 26. Used with permission from Wayne State University Press, Detroit, Michigan.

Table 2 Jewish Immigration from all countries to Palestine 1930–39

Year	Jews	Christians	Moslems	Total
1930	4,944	1,296	193	6,433
1931	4,075	1,245	213	5,533
1932	9,553	1,524	212	11,289
1933	30,327	1,307	343	31,977
1934	42,359	1,494	290	44,143
1935	61,854	903	1,390	64,147
1936	29,727	675	1,269	31,671
1937	10,536	743	1,196	12,475
1938	12,868	473	1,922	15,263
1939	16,405	376	1,652	18,433
	222,648	10,036	8,680	241,364

Source: Adapted from Anglo-American Committee of Inquiry, *A Survey of Palestine*, Vol. 1 (Palestine Government Printer, 1945–46), p. 185.

Appendix V

Estimated Number of Jews Killed
in the Final Solution

Table 1   Estimated number of Jews killed in the final
solution, 1939–45.

Country	Estimated pre-final solution population	Estimated Jewish population annihilated	
		Number	*Percent*
Poland	3,300,000	3,000,000	90
Baltic countries	253,000	228,000	90
Germany/Austria	240,000	210,000	90
Protectorate	90,000	80,000	89
Slovakia	90,000	75,000	83
Greece	70,000	54,000	77
The Netherlands	140,000	105,000	75
Hungary	650,000	450,000	70
SSR White Russia	375,000	245,000	65
SSR Ukraine*	1,500,000	900,000	60
Belgium	65,600	40,000	60
Yugoslavia	43,000	26,000	60
Rumania	600,000	300,000	50
Norway	1,800	900	50
France	350,000	90,000	26
Bulgaria	64,000	14,000	22
Italy	40,000	8,000	20
Luxembourg	5,000	1,000	20
Russia (RSFSR)*	975,000	107,000	11
Denmark	8,000	–	–
Finland	2,000	–	–
Total	8,861,800	5,933,900	67

* The Germans did not occupy all the territory of this republic.
Source: Dawidowicz, Lucy. *The War Against the Jews* 1933–1945. New
York, Holt, Rinehardt and Winston, Inc., 1975, p. 403.

Table 2 Estimated losses of the Jewish population in the Soviet Union under the German occupied territories (according to Dawidowicz)

	Number killed
Russia RSFSR, White Russia, the Ukraine and Baltic countries	1,480,000
Eastern Poland: out of 300,000 who fled east into Russia	120,000
Rumania: Bessarabia, Bukovina and Transnistria and others occupied by Germany after June 1941	360,000
Total	1,960,000

According to Yitzhak Arad between 1,950,000 and 2,165,000 Jews were killed in these areas (Yad Vashem Studies, XXI, p. 47).

Appendix VI

The Nations Vote in the UN for the Establishment of Israel in 1947

On 29 November, 1947, the vote in the General Assembly of the United Nations taken for Partion of the British Mandate of Palestine into independent Jewish and Palestinian Arab States, and for Jerusalem to become an international city, was as follows:

33 for: Australia, Belgium, Bolivia, Brazil, White Russia, Canada, Costa Rica, Czechoslovakia, Denmark, Dominican Republic, Ecuador, France, Guatemala, Haiti, Iceland, Liberia, Luxembourg, Netherlands, New Zealand, Nicaragua, Norway, Paraguay, Peru, Philippines, Poland, Sweden, Ukraine, Union of South Africa, USSR, United States of America, Uruguay, Venezuela.

13 against: Afghanistan, Cuba, Egypt, Greece, India, Iran, Iraq, Lebanon, Pakistan, Saudi Arabia, Syria, Turkey, Yemen.

8   abstentions: Argentine,   Chile,   China,   Ethiopia, Honduras, Mexico, Great Britain, Yugoslavia.

Appendix VII

The Six Wars Against Israel from 1948
(mentioned in Chapter 4)

1. The War of Independence, 1948–49

Less than 24 hours after the proclamation of the State of Israel, war was declared by seven Arab countries. Five of these, Egypt, Jordan, Syria, Lebanon and Iraq, invaded the new-born state, forcing it to defend its sovereignty. In a miraculous way the newly formed, and poorly equipped Israeli Defence Forces (IDF) were able to stop the Arab invaders. Although Egypt took Gaza in 1948, and Jordan seized the West Bank areas of Judea and Samaria as well as East Jerusalem in 1949, the annexation almost cost them expulsion from the Arab League.

2. The Sinai Campaign, 1957

In contravention of the UN Security Council Resolution of 1 September, 1951, Israeli-bound ships were prevented by Egypt from using the Suez Canal. In October 1956 Egypt, Syria and Jordan formed a military alliance, which was a threat to Israel's very existence. At President Nasser's request the UN peace-keeping forces were removed, opening the way for an Egyptian attack on Israel.

As France and Britain (the UN forces) lost control of the Suez Canal, the IDF captured Gaza and Sinai in an 8-day campaign, halting only 10 miles (16 km) east of the Suez Canal. After a UN emergency force was again positioned at the Egyptian–Israeli border, Egypt gave assurance of free use of both the Suez Canal and the Gulf of Eilat. In November 1956, Israel agreed to a withdrawal in stages.

3. The Six-Day War, 1967

Upon President Nasser's request the UN peace-keeping force was again asked to withdraw from Sinai, opening the way for

Egypt and Syria to 'drive Israel into the sea'. Concerned by threatening troop build-ups in the Sinai, Israel made a lightning pre-emptive attack in June. In six days Israel amazingly gained control over the Arab-controlled areas previously used as bases for terrorist attacks in Judea, Samaria and Gaza. They also gained the Golan Heights which was of great strategic importance. East Jerusalem was regained from Jordan and came under Jewish control for the first time in some 2,000 years.

4. The Yom Kippur War, 1973

On *Yom Kippur*, the Great Day of Atonement, 6 October, when the whole country was fasting, the joint Egyptian and Syrian forces' attack on Israel almost cost her very life. With very extensive loss of life, Israel miraculously gained the upper hand. During the next three weeks, the IDF advanced its forces, crossed the Suez Canal, and were standing on the Egyptian side. They were also within 20 miles (32 km) of the Syrian capital Damascus.

This was the most ferocious attack on Israel so far and has been called the count-down to Armaggedon.

5. Operation Peace for Galilee, 1982

After the Palestine Liberation Organization (PLO) was expelled from Jordan in 1970, it re-deployed itself in Lebanon, repeatedly attacking towns and villages in Northern Israel, resulting in many casualties. In order to safeguard its population, the IDF entered Lebanon, removing the bulk of the PLO's organizational and military infra-structure from the area. They reached the outskirts of Beirut before withdrawing. Since then, Israel has maintained a small security zone in the mainly Christian Southern Lebanon, adjacent to its northern border.

6. The Gulf War, 1991

Threatened by a nuclear attack from Iraq, Israel bombed and destroyed their atomic reactor in June 1981. Because of the Iraqi aggression and occupation of Kuwait with its rich oil resources in 1991, the USA together with Western Allies and Arab supporters, began the Gulf War.

Jordan was one of the few countries, which sided with Iraq. They permitted supplies of food and weapons etc. to be transported from the port of Aqaba across Jordan to Iraq. Jordan also allowed Iraqi missiles to be fired from moveable ramps at their mutual border.

It was feared that Iraq would bomb Israel under cover of the hostilities and in retaliation against the West. The USA requested that, in order to dimish losses, Israel should not participate in the military attacks, but remain passive and let the US take care of their defence. It was very hard for Israel to stand by while being attacked and she did suffer extensive material damage from scud missiles, but with miraculously little loss of life.

Appendix VIII

The World Jewish Population

According to the Jewish Year Book, the total world Jewish population, shown in the 1996 edition, is 14,343,910.

The largest Jewish population groups are as follows:

1. Countries

USA	5,800,000
Israel	4,420,000
Former Soviet Union	1,449,117
France	600,000
Canada	360,000
Great Britain	300,000
Argentine	250,000
South Africa	114,000
Australia	100,000
Brazil	100,000
Hungary	85,000
Moldova	65,000
Germany	60,000
Mexico	48,000

2. Major cities of Jewish population

New York	1,450,000
Los Angeles	490,000
Paris	350,000
Jerusalem	346,100
Tel Aviv-Jaffa	308,700
Fort Lauderdale (Florida)	284,000
Philadelphia	254,000
Chicago	248,000
London	215,000
Haifa	210,000
Boston	203,400
Moscow	200,000
Buenos Aires	200,000
Toronto	175,000
Washington DC	160,000
Odessa	120,000
Kiev	110,000
St Petersburg	100,000

Appendix IX

Jewish Emigration from the Former USSR 1954–1998

Total USSR		To Israel		To USA
1948–69	11,573	1954–69	10,208	–
1970	1,027		992	135(a)
1971	13,022		12,839	214
1972	31,681		31,652	453
1973	34,733		33,447	1,449
1974	20,628		16,816	3,490
1975	13,221		8,531	5,250(b)
1976	14,261		7,279	5,512
1977	16,736		8,348	6,842
1978	28,865		12,192	12,265
1979	51,320		17,614	28,794
1980	21,471		7,570	15,461
1981	9,447		1,770	6,980
1982	2,658		782	1,327
1983	1,315		399	887
1984	876		367	489
1985	1,139		362	570
1986	914		202	641
1987	7,776		2,096	3,811
1988	19,343		2,283	10,576
1989	71,343		12,932	36,738
1990	213,437		185,227	31,283
1991	178,026		147,839	34,715
1992	108,292		64,057	45,888
1993	102,134		66,048	35,581
1994	99,681		67,025	32,622
1995	106,612		64,847	24,765
1996	94,220*		59,049	20,171
1997	88,654*		54,602	14,620
1998	71,803*		46,703	7,319

(a) Indicates HIAS-assisted émigrés, who accounted for most of the total Jewish immigration.

(b) The difference in the total is mainly because some emigrants left their country of origin at the end of the calendar year, while the arrival date in the new country was the following year.

* The total from the CIS is not available since 1996.

Notes and Bibliography

Abbreviations

CAB   Cabinet papers
CO   Colonial Office
FO   Foreign Office
HC   House of Commons
HO   Home Office
PRO   Public Relations Office

Chapter 1

1. Feingold, H. 'Who shall bear guilt for the Holocaust: The Human Dilemma', *American Jewish History*, Vol. LXVIII, no. 3. Waltham, MA: American Historical Society, 1979, 269.
2. Littell, F. *The Crucifixion of the Jews*. Macon, GA: Mercer University Press, ROSE edition, 1986, 48.
3. Bauer, Y. *A History of the Holocaust*. New York: F. Watts, 1982, 349.
4. *Historical Atlas of the Holocaust*. New York: MacMillan Publishing, 1996, 14.
5. Lehmann, Henning, *Armenierne, Kultur og Historie* (The Armenians, Culture and History). Toender, Denmark: Centrum, 1984, 115–116.
   Smith, Roger W. 'Genocide and Denial: The Armenian Case and its Implications', *The Armenian Genocide in Perspective*. Ed. Hovannisian, Rich. G. New Brunswick, NJ: Transation Books, 1987.

6. Bauer, Y. *Holocaust and Genocide Studies*, Seattle:
    University of Washington Press, Vol. 2, 216.
    Littell Fr., op. cit. 40 and 65.
    Shawcross, W. *The Quality of Mercy*. New York: Simon &
    Schuster, 1984, 421.

Chapter 2

1. The League of Nations was founded in Geneva in 1919
    at the wish of President Wilson, USA. The main
    intention was to be an instrument for all countries in
    the world to intervene as mediators, whenever peace
    was threatened.
       The 32 victorious allied powers were the founding
    members, led by the USA, England and France. To these
    a number of neutral countries, including Scandinavia
    were quickly added. Later, Germany joined in 1926 and
    the Soviet Union in 1934. By the time Hitler rose to
    power in 1933, the peace-preserving influence of the
    League had dwindled considerably.
2. The transversion from German Reich Mark to British
    Pound has been based on figures from A.J. Sherman,
    *Island Refuge: Britain and the Refugees from the Third
    Reich, 1933–39*, Berkely: University of California Press,
    1973, 24–25; 167–68.
3. Bland Minute, 21 May, 1938, FO 372/3283, T 6797/
    3272/378, quoted Sherman, op. cit., 90.
4. *Encyclopedia Britannica, Vol. 3*, cols. 277–78.
5. Winterton to Halifax, 8 July, 1938, FO 371/22530,
    W 9531/104/98, quoted in Sherman, op. cit., 113.
6. The move to restore the US immigration quota was an
    important gain for the refugees and this ended the
    policy begun in 1930, limiting the admission for fear
    that immigrants might become a public charge. David
    Wyman, *Paper Walls, American and the Refugee Crisis,
    1938–41*, Amhurst: Amhurst University Press, 1968, 50.
7. *Proceedings of the International-Governmental Committee,
    Evian, Verbatim Record, July 1938*, Chambery: Reumies,
    42.

8. Adler-Rudler, S. 'The Evian Conference on the Refugee Issue,' *Yearbook XIII of the Leo Baecke Institute*, London, 1968, 250–51.

9. Sherman, op. cit., 121.

10. Marrus, Michael R. *The Unwanted, European Refugees in the Twentieth Century*, Oxford: Oxford University Press, 1985, 172.

11. Lindsey to Halifax, 17 November, 1938, FO 371/21637, C 14092/1667/62, quoted Sherman, op. cit., 177.

12. Makins minute, 8 December, 1938, FO 371/22539, W 16411/1104/98, quoted Sherman, op. cit., 187.

13. Marrus, op. cit., 181–82.

14. Wyman, David. *Paper Walls, America and the Refugee Crisis, 1938–41*, Amhurst: Amhurst University Press, 1968, 55.

15. Moore, Arthur D. *While 6 Million Died*, New York: Ace Book, 1968), 229.

16. 348 H.C., Deb. 1111–1112, 13 June, 1939, quoted in Sherman, op. cit., 252–53.

17. Moore, op. cit., 234.

18. Sherman, op. cit., 43.

19. ibid., 108.

20. ibid., 175.

21. Adler-Rudler, op. cit., 260.

22. ESCO Foundation for Palestine Inc., *Palestine, A Study of Jewish, Arab and British Policies*, Vol. 2, New Haven: Yale University Press, 1942, 680–84.

23. Cohen, Michael J. *The Retreat from the Mandate, The Making of British Policy 1938–45*, London: Elek, 1978, 37.

24. Ballagay Memorandum of 13 August, 1937, in FO 371/20811 quoted in Cohen, op. cit., 39–40.

25. ESCO., op. cit., 680.

26. Palestine, A Statement of Policy, MacDonald White Paper, Cmd. 6019 of 1939, art. 4, 4.

27. Cohen, op. cit., 86.

28. ESCO, op. cit., 927.

29. Wasserstein, Bernard. *Britain and the Jews of Europe, 1939–45*, Oxford: Clarendon, 1979, 25.

30. Bauer, op. cit., 127.

31. ESCO., op. Cit., 682.
    Peters, Joan. *From Time Immemorial*, New York: Harper
    & Row, 1984, 336–37.
32. A.W. Randall minute 5 September, 1939, PRO FO371/
    24078, quoted in Wasserstein, op. cit., 52.

Other nations' response:
33. Sherman, op. cit.: the author describes the activities of
    the Anglo-Jewish community, taking the lead in raising
    funds for the establishment of refugee organisations to
    the rescue of German Jewry. The Jewish community
    was prepared to guarantee adequate means for the
    refugees during their stay. 25 and 32.
34. Marrus, op. cit., 147.
35. Moore, Bob. *Refugees from Nazi Germany in the
    Netherlands, 1933–40*, Dordrecht, Lancaster: M. Niihoff
    Publishers, 1986, 42–43.
36. Hope Simpson, John. *A review of the situation since
    September 1938*, Oxford: Clarendon Press, 1938, 80–81.
37. *Encyclopedia of the Holocaust*, Vol. III, 1990, 1441–42.
38. Feingold, op. cit., 298.
39. Moore, op. cit., 215.
40. Wyman, David. *The Abandonment of the Jews, America
    and the Holocaust, 1941–45*, New York: Pantheon Books,
    1985, 6.
41. Johansen, Per Ole. *Oss sjælv nærmest* (Closest to
    ourselves, Norway and the Jews), Oslo: Gyldendal
    Norsk Forlag, 1983 (report from preliminary Evian
    meeting, 1938), 108–9.
42. Koblik, Steven. *The Stones Cry Out, Swedish Response to
    the Persecution of the Jews, 1933–1945*, New York:
    Holocaust Library, 1988, 55.
43. Koblik, op. cit., 78.
44. Johansen, op. cit., Internal minute from the Ministry of
    Justice, 6.9.1939, 112.
45. Koblik, op. cit., 65, note 46.
46. The purpose of the Antikomintern treaty signed on
    25 November, 1936 between Germany, Italy and Japan,
    was an entente to prevent the advance of 'Jewish-
    Communist Soviet' in Europe. Mutually they assured

each other that none of the partners would sign an agreement with the Soviet Union without the knowledge of the others.

47. Morley, John F. *Vatican Diplomacy during the Holocaust, 1939–1943*, New York: KTAV Publishing House, 1980, 206.
48. Falconi, Carlo. *The Silence of Pius X11*, London: Faber & Faber, 1970, 52–54.
49. Documents on the Holocaust, Jerusalem, Yad Vashem, (1981), 132–35. Extract from the Speech by Hitler, 31 January, 1939.
50. Hitler's speech is commented on by Yitzhak Arad in The Holocaust of the Soviet Jewry in the Occupied Territories of the Soviet Union, *Yad Vashem Studies, XXI*, Jerusalem: Yad Vashem, 1991, 4.
51. Arad, op. cit., 5–6.
52. ibid., 8.
53. Dawidowicz, Lucy. *The War Against the Jews, 1933–1945*, New York: Holt, Rinehart & Winston, 1975, 401.
54. Robinson, Jacob. Holocaust, *Encyclopedia Judaica*, Jerusalem: Keter Publishing House, 1971, Vol. 8, 828–905.
55. Arad, op. cit., 47.
56. Wyman, op. cit., 331.
57. ibid. 335.
58. ibid. 335–38.

Chapter 3

1.   Gutman, Isaac, 'Antisemitism', *Encyclopedia of the Holocaust*, New York: McMillan, 1991, Vol. I, 55–56.
2.   It has been widely spread in the Middle East, supported by neo-Nazi propaganda, that in ancient times the Jews of Russia were not of Jewish descent, but just Russian converts. Consequently they, or the 'white Jews of Europe', have no right to return to their ancient home land of Israel.

     Historical sources prove, however, that before the Common Era, Jews had migrated across the Black Sea and settled in the Crimea and the Ukraine. In the eighth century, the prosperous kingdom of the Khazars, situated between the Christian kingdom of Kiev to the west and the Moslem rulers to the east, chose to embrace Judaism.

In ancient Russian literature, the Kingdom of the Khazars was described as 'the Land of the Jews.' At the end of the tenth century, the Byzantine Empire advanced eastwards at the cost of the Khazars, and finally around 1240, they were overrun by the Tartars. Grayzel, Solomon. *A History of the Jews*, 256–57.

Other Jewish groups migrated up through the Roman Empire to Spain, France, the Germanic territories, and settled in these countries as well as in the West Slavic areas of Eastern Europe. During the centuries of persecution in the Middle Ages, Jews moved back and forth between western and Eastern Europe, wherever they could be most at peace.

3. Ben Sasson, H.H. (ed.) *A History of the Jewish People*, Cambridge, MA: Harvard University Press, 1976, 732.
4. Ben Sasson, op. cit., 981.
5. Hertzl, Theodor. Pamphlet: *'Der Judenstaat'*, The Jewish State, 1896, 12.
6. Strauss, Herbert A. (ed.), *Hostages of Modernization, Studies on Modern Antisemitism, 1870–1933/39*, Germany–Great Britain–France, Berlin. New York: Walter de Gruyter, 1993, 1326–31.
7. Ben Sasson, op. cit., 970.
8. *Encyclopedia Britanica*, Vol. VI, cols. 826–7.
9. Nagorsky, Andrew. 'Russia, Repressed Nightmare', *Newsweek*, 19 February, 1996.
10. Roi, Yaacov. *The Struggle for Soviet Jewry Emigration, 1948–1967. Cambridge: Cambridge University Press, 1991*, 15. *States that*: Prior to the Nazi invasion the number of Soviet Jews was almost 5.2 million, but the first post-war census in 1959 showed only 2.27 million. Between 1945 and 1947, 220,000 Jews were repatriated to Poland, and assimilation through mixed marriage was high in the post-war years.
11. Grazel, op. cit., 693.
12. Wiesel, Elie. *The Jews of Silence*, New York: Holt, Rinehardt & Winston, 1967, vii–viii.

13. Franklin, Edith R. *Russia, Jews and Solzhenitsyn, Soviet Jewish Affairs* (SJA), London: Institute of Jewish affairs, 1975, Vol. 5, no. 2, 43.

14. Friedgut, T.H. *Anti-Zionism and Antisemitism, Another Cycle*, SJA, 1984, Vol. 14, no. 1, 4.

15. Gittelmann, Z. *Emigrants in the USA*, SJA, 1977, Vol. 7, no. 1, 31–46.

16. Heitman, Sidney. *Soviet Jewry Emigration in 1991*, SJA, 1992, Vol. 21, no. 2, 12–13.

17. The amazing story of Natan Sharansky needs to be completed: after his release as a Soviet dissident and exchange spy, Sharansky emigrated to Israel, where he has become an important voice to Western governments and Human rights groups as well as a spokesman for the plight of Soviet Jewry and their right to emigrate. In Israel, he was reunited with his wife, Avital. They have now two children. Sharansky later formed the emigrant party, 'Israel b'Aliya' ('Israel for Immigration'), of which he became the leader.

18. Alexander, Z. *Jewish Emigration from the USSR in 1980*, SJA, Vol. 11, 1981, 9–10.

19. Friedgut, T.H. SJA, 1984, op. cit., Vol. 14, no. 1, 8–20. Quotes from Lev Korneev, The Class Essense of Zionism, Kiev (1982).

20. *US Helsinki Watch Report, 1986*. Washington: US Helsinki Watch Committee, 88–89.

21. Gilbert, Dr Martin. *Prisoners of Hope*, London: MacMillan, 1984, 89.

22. *USSR News Brief*, (bulletin) ed. Lubarsky, C., Munich, 11 July and 17 July, 1987.

23. Women's 35 Campaign for Soviet Jewry in London, circular, 11 July, 1990.

24. *Human Rights' Report, 1992*, Washington: US Helsinki Watch Committee, 565.

25. *The Statesman's Yearbook*, London: MacMillan, 1991–92 and 1996–97.

26. Myss, Lilli. *Let My People Go* (newsletter, 3rd quarterly, September 1993).

27. Floyd, David. *Perestroika and Soviet Jews*, SJA, 1987, Vol. 17, no. 1, 3; and Feldbrugge, J.F.M. *A New Law on Emigration*, SJA, 1987, Vol. 1, no. 3, 10.
28. Freedman, R.O. *A Strategy towards Moscow*, SJA, 1987, Vol. 17, no. 3, 43.
29. *Jerusalem Post*, book review, 13 March, 1997.
30. *London Times*, 20 November, 1996.

Russia and Human Rights
31. *Forced Labour in the USSR* (A Special Report), Washington: US State Department, 1983, 1.
32. *Human Rights Report, 1986*, US Helsinki Watch Committee, USA.
33. Women's 35 Campaign for Soviet Jewry, London, circular 11, 1991.
34. US Helsinki Watch Report, Moscow Conference Report on 'Prison Reform in the Former Totalitarian Countries', November 1992.

Chapter 4

1. Twain, Mark. *Innocents abroad*, San Francisco: Library of America, 1869, 485–86.
2. Aharoni, Yohanan. *The Land of the Bible, A Historical Geography*, Philadelphia: Westminster Press, 1979, 196.
3. Edersheim, Alfred. *Bible History of the Old Testament* (1880), (reprint), Grand Rapids, Michigan: Erdman, Vol. II Ch. XV, 145–48. Edersheim, describes how he reaches this figure. It is based on Numbers 1:46, where the number of arms-bearing men was stated to be 603,550. This figure would include all mature men from the age of 20 or older. These adult men would be married and have at least one child. The number of Israelites would therefore be tripled to 1,810,650 persons. Moreover, to this figure needs to be added the number of children under that age as well as older people of both sexes. After the time in the wilderness, the number of armed men had, according to Numbers 26:51, been decreased by 1,820 persons to 601,730. Therefore, a conclusive figure for the Israelites would probably still exceed the estimated two million.

4. Marrus, M. *The Unwanted*, (1985) gives in the introduction (pp. 3–13), an overview of the refugee waves in Europe in connection with the last two world wars.

5. Comments regarding the name, 'Palestine': only for two brief periods has the 'Holy land' been named 'Palestine'. Firstly, for some years in the second century CE, during the Roman period, and then not until the British Mandate period from 1917–1948. During British rule the population were either called Palestinian Jews or Palestinian Arabs. After the UN had voted for a partition in 1947, only the Jews chose to establish their state, calling it by the ancient Jewish name, Israel.

    Had the Jews chosen to maintain the British name 'Palestine', Palestinian Arabs would never have had their propaganda tool for establishing their state.

6. Bright, John. *A History of Israel*, Philadelphia: Westminister Press, 1981, 326.

7. Peters, Joan. *From Time Immemorial*, 269–295.

8. Myss, Lilli. *Let My People Go*, April, 1990.

9. *International Herald Tribune*, 3 April, 1990.

10. *Jerusalem Post*, 19 November, 1990.

11. Myss, Lilli. *Let My People Go*, March, 1994.

12. *Jerusalem Post*, 18 September, 1990.

13. *Södertalje Tidning*, 10 November, 1994.

14. *Finmarken*, 29 August, 1997.

15. Shvili, Chaim. *Times of Salvation* (translated into Norwegian from 'Chesbonot HaGeulah'), Mjøndalen, Norge, 1969, 82; Douglas, J.D. (ed.), *New Bible Dictionary*, Grand Rapids, MI, 1962, 1152–53.

16. *New Bible Dictionary*, op. cit., 1107, col. 1–3.

17. ibid., 811, col. 1–2.

18. ibid., 481, col. 2.

19. ibid., 1285, col. 1–2.

20. Shvili, op. cit., 88.

21. Regarding Har-Magiddo and the prediction of the last battle of Armageddon in Revelation 16:16. Situated at a crossroads, strategic even around 90 AD when the Apostle John wrote Revelation, the tel or mound of the city of Megiddo was about 70 feet high as each

conqueror had built on top of the ruins of their defeated predecessors. The valley plain has witnessed not less than 20 important battles from Thutmoses III of Egypt's defeat of the Canaanite coalition in 1468 BC up to 1917 when General Allenby liberated the Holy Land from the yoke of the Turkish Ottoman Empire.

22. Shvili, op. cit., 87.

23. (a) *Zarephath*: a Phoenician town, originally belonging to Sidon, was passed on to Tyre after 722 BC.

(b) *Sepharad*: likely situated in the country of Saparda, a place to which captives from Jerusalem were deported, situated to the east and allied to the Medes. It has been mentioned in the Assyrian Annals of Sargon and Esahaddon. It is probably the same as the Persian Sparda.

Sepharad could, however, also be a location in Anatolia, as favoured by the Vulgate. (New Bible Dictionary, pp. 1353 and 1160.)

24. *Jerusalem Post*, 28 November, 1997.

Epilogue

1. Yuli Edelstein's life is in several ways parallel to that of Natan Sharansky. Edelstein was another victim of the USSR's oppressive system in the 1980s. He was accused of a trumped-up charge of 'illegal possession and use of narcotics' and sentenced to labour camp from 1984–87. He was also named a 'Prisoner of Zion'.

However, the story had a marvellous ending: ten years after Edelstein's immigration to Israel, he was elected as a Minister for Immigration and Absorption to the Likud Government in 1996.

Suggested further reading

Anatoli, A., (Kutnetzov), *Babi Yar*, New York: Farrar, Straus & Giroux Inc., WSP Pocket Book, 1971.

Arbella, Irving. *None is too many*, Toronto: Orphen Dennis Ltd, 1981.

Bentwich, Norman, *They Found Refuge, An Account of the British Jewry's work for victims of Nazi Oppression*, London: Cresset, 1956.

Bloch, Sidney, and Reddaway, Peter, *Soviet Psychiatric Abuse, The Shadow over World Psychiatry*. London: Victor Gollancz Ltd, 1984.

Dolan, David, *Israel at the Crossroads. 50 Years and Counting*. Michigan: Revell, 1998.

Gilbert, Dr Martin, *The Jews of Russia, Their History in Maps and Photographs, Jerusalem, Steimatzky*, 1979.

Gilbert, Dr Martin, *Auschwitz and the Allies, The Politics of Rescue*, Reading: Cox & Wyman Ltd, 1981.

Hess, Tom, *Let My People Go, The Struggle of American Jews to Escape to Israel*, Washington DC, 1987.

Lacquer, Walter, *A History of Zionism*, London: Weidenfeld & Nicholson, 1973.

Lightle, Steve, *Exodus II, Let My People Go*, Kingswood, Texas: Hunter Books, 1983.

Meacham, S.M., *It is still not too late, The Importance of Christian Action on behalf of Soviet Jewry*, Jerusalem: The International Christian Embassy, 1983.

Penkower, Monty, *The Jews Were Expendable, Free World Diplomacy and the Holocaust*, Urbana & Chicago Press, 1983.

Rawlings, Meridel, *Fishers and Hunters* (1982) and *Gates of Brass* (1985), Jerusalem: International Vistas Inc.

Rubinstein, W.D. *The Jews in Australia*, Melbourne: A.E. Press, 1986, and *Jews in the 6th Continent*, Sydney: Allen & Unwin, 1987.

Scheller, Gustav, *Operation Exodus, Prophecy being fulfilled*, UK: Sovereign World, 1998.

Solzhenitsyn, Aleksandr. I. *One Day in the Life of Ivan Denisovits*. New York: Bantam Books. 1970.

Solzhenitsyn, Aleksandr. I. *The Gulag Archipelago, 1918–1956. An Experiment in Literary Investigation. I–VII*, New York: Harper & Row, 1973.

Weizmann, Chaim, *Trial and Errors*, London: H. Hamilton, 1949.

White, Derek C. *Replacement Theology, Its Origin, History and Theology*, London: CFI, 1997.

White, Derek C. *The Road to the Holocaust – A Brief Survey of the History of Christian Anti-Semitism*. London: CFI, 1998.